COMPETENCE

Inquiries Into Its Meaning and Acquisition in Educational Settings

Edited by

Edmund C. Short

UNIVERSITY PRESS OF AMERICA

LANHAM • NEW YORK • LONDON

University Press of America,™ Inc.

4720 Boston Way
Lanham, MD 20706

3 Henrietta Street
London WC2E 8LU England

Printed in the United States of America

ISBN (Perfect): 0-8191-3996-3
ISBN (Cloth): 0-8191-3995-5

All University Press of America books are produced on acid-free paper which exceeds the minimum standards set by the National Historical Publications and Records Commission.

Table of Contents

Conceptions of Competence

The Acquisition of Competence

Afterword

Bibliography

Preface

This book is a contribution to sophisticated inquiry into the nature of competence and its acquisition. It is a difficult book because its topic is complex and not easily understood through ordinary experience or inquiry. The writers addressing this topic have employed a variety of advanced modes of inquiry to illuminate the problems inherent in thinking about competence. They have turned up considerable help in understanding competence in its various conceptualizations and in its implications for educational practice. They also reflect a commitment to a certain perspective on the topic which their inquiries have led them to adopt. They reject many of the notions about competence and about competency-based education that have prevailed in education over the past two decades or more. If they have any motive, other than objective inquiry, for contributing to this volume, it is in the belief that the concept of competence used in education needs to be reinterpreted and practices related to it rethought. Their hope is that these inquiries will help contribute to the adoption and use of more adequate and viable conceptions of competence throughout the educational world. They hope that in their contributing to such a goal they will stimulate other scholars and educational planners to grapple with the ideas and issues they have raised in this book and to move forward from this volume to fuller and wiser understandings of how to recognize and acquire competence.

The book is divided into two parts. The first, consisting of five papers, is concerned with the meaning of the term *competence*. The authors analyze the concept of competence using different forms of inquiry: Professor Fagan, rhetorical analysis; Professor Noddings, linguistic analysis; Professor Pearson, normative analysis; Professor Johnson, historical analysis; and Professor Aoki, critical analysis. The second part of the book is concerned with the acquisition of competence. Attention is given to the educative process necessary to attain competence from the perspectives of both student and teacher. Professor Apple deals with current practices of schooling as understood through critical social analysis. Professor Beittel gives an understanding of qualitative thinking as a basis for acquiring competence. His mode of inquiry is that of the artist. Professor Doll draws on Chomsky, Piaget, and Bruner to provide a basis for his illustration of teaching mathematical competence. And finally, Professor van Manen reflects poetically on the pedagogic relationship between child and teacher from a phenomenological perspective. A preview of each of these papers precedes the full text in each case. The book closes with a highlighting of the major ideas gleaned from the full series of papers.

With the exception of one paper, which is reprinted with permission from the Summer, 1980, issue of *Educational Studies* (Allen T. Pearson's), the papers appearing in this volume were presented in preliminary form at a conference on "Competence: Analysis, Critique, Reassessment," held at The Pennsylvania State University, May 18-20, 1980. The assistance of the University's College of Education Faculty and Administration in hosting this conference and in bringing this volume to publication is gratefully acknowledged. The cooperation of the conference speakers in preparing their remarks for publication is also acknowledged with appreciation. One paper from the conference has already been published elsewhere and is not included here. It was by Professor David S. Palermo and appears under the title, "Theoretical Issues in Semantic Development," pp. 335-364 in Stan A. Kuczaj II (Ed.), *Language Development (Volume 1): Syntax and Semantics*. Hillsdale, NJ: Lawrence Erlbaum Associates, Publishers, 1982.

Edmund C. Short
Editor

Conceptions Of Competence

1

Current usage of the term *competence* in education suggests that its precise meaning is of less importance to many people than its use for purely rhetorical purposes. The term has been used in such a variety of ways that meaningful communication on the subject of competence has been exceedingly difficult, if not impossible. Even educational practices involving the idea of competence frequently embody such different conceptions of competence that little relationship can be detected among them. Edward R. Fagan examines the several usages of the term *competence* in current educational discourse and points out certain dilemmas that the prevailing rhetoric has created. He suggests, by means of some interesting rhetorical analysis, that advocacy has tended to dominate discourse on competence to the exclusion of careful definition, objective criteria, and reasoned analysis of proposals concerning competency-based education. Fagan's paper demonstrates the need in current educational circles to unravel the existing confusions over the meaning of competence and to adopt less limited and arbitrary conceptions of competence as a basis for future educational thought and practice.

Professor Fagan is Professor of English Education in the College of Education, The Pennsylvania State University.

Competence in Educational Practice: A Rhetorical Perspective

Edward R. Fagan
The Pennsylvania State University

Background and Definitions

During the summer of 1981 the National Institute of Education (NIE) sponsored a three-day hearing on minimal competency testing (MCT). The purpose of the hearing was to inform the general public about the pros and cons of MCT, not to render a judgment about its merits within American education. Teams—for MCT headed by Popham (1981) and against MCT headed by Madaus (1981)—presented friendly and unfriendly witnesses for their cause. Popham, in advancing his cause, noted that "Critics...have leveled some strong attacks on MCT programs. By and large, these attacks rely more on *rhetoric* than reality" (italics mine). *Rhetoric* in Popham's context tends to be a pejorative, an interpretation commonly ascribed to the word. *Competence*, too, in his context tends to be defined as a function of an individual's test performance.

In many ways it was students' poor test performances on standardized tests such as the Scholastic Aptitude Test (SAT) which enkindled public interest in competence. That enkindled interest, enflamed by media hyperbole, became a hysterical criticism of all public education. Again, much of the criticism was based upon students' test performances, performances which equated high test scores with educational competence. It was the validity of the relationship between test scores and students' competence that Ralph Nader raised as an unfriendly witness during the NIE hearing. Sager (1983) described the nature of Nader's complaint as follows:

> In a Nader-published study of the Educational Testing Service (ETS)—a nonprofit publisher of more than 160 tests taken by more than 5 million people in 30 countries—it was said that the company's most widely used exam, the SAT, was no more able to predict student performance in college than would a roll of the dice. In a look at 827 ETS validity studies between 1964 and 1974, Nader found that SAT delivered an average accuracy of 11.9 percent (p. 7).

Earlier in that citation standardized tests were attacked for being "racially, sexually, and culturally biased." Heath (1980) presented strong evidence that those charges were accurate. Context of Heath's data was his reactions to Eckland's paper, "Sociodemographic Implications of Minimum Competency Testing." Heath had been working with a needs assessment of adult education in California and, prior to that, with curriculum evaluation projects (involving minority students) in Hawaii. From such foundations, Heath argues that "test performance," "schools as preparation for work and college," and "reading and computation" are not the *essential* skills of adult life (italics mine). Supporting these judgments Heath presents data which show:

> —the same employment gap between blacks and whites exists at all levels of competency.
> —if you are a high school graduate and white, your tested reading and computation competency has almost no effect on your employability.
> —being able to read and compute well...will not help you to earn more money whether you are white or black. The data in Table 4 show no relationship between test scores and "Percent Earning 100 Dollars or Less per Week" (p. 137)

These data seem to have enough substance to question Popham's description of them as just *rhetoric*. Pro MCT educators would probably regard Nader's and Heath's statements as sophistic rhetoric and dismiss it summarily. It's now time to present more objective definitions of *rhetoric* and *competence* in order to establish a common base for the perspectives which follow.

Definitions of *rhetoric* have changed. Its definition from Greece's Golden Age through the eighteenth century included traditions which made it a key discipline in all formal education. These traditions blurred as industrialization, education, and technology expanded until, as Gorrell (1967, p. 1) and Lindemann (1982, p. 56) note, "rhetoric is applied to the material, the stuff, as well as to the study of it." This dual definition, the material and the study of it, while more confusing, is paradoxically, also more accurate for the rhetorical examination of *competence* in its myriad forms. In such a context, rhetorical analysis, (the description of what happens in a piece of writing) is closely examined to discover techniques and methods whereby discourse achieves its ends. In the material which follows, it is this definition of rhetorical analysis which is used to explicate competence.

Competence, too, has a pertinent etymology which, according to *Webster's New World Dictionary of the American Language* (1980), identifies *compete* as its root with the following definitions for *compete*: "to strive together for," "contend," "contest"; *competence* picks up the striving connotation with its refined definitions such as: "a meeting, agreement," "power," "the quality of being competent."

Polarized, the rhetoric about educational competence is implicit in Gibbons' (1980) and Popham's (1980) anecdotes about it where "objective fulfilled" equals "competence." Gibbons' protagonist (a Zen master) asks his antagonist (a professor of systematic instruction) what is fulfilled when the professor has achieved an objective. The professor answers that he goes on to the next objective. The Zen master then asks, "How can the cup of one's mind receive any learning when it is so full of predictable objectives and achievements?" The Zen master's question is meant to be rhetorical and to teach a lesson, like a *koan*, a lesson about human motivation.

The *koan*, however, is nonsense for Popham's professor, an educational evaluator, who faults the Zen master for "fuzzy thinking" by noting that he had visited many of the Zen master's schools and found the instructors wanting. "Do you realize," the evaluator asked, "how many of your disciples are so fulfilled with nothing-ness that they cannot even read or write?"

The master responded, "I am not sure. I have never *measured* my disciples' mastery of such a skill."

"Well," the evaluator responded, "I did and they can't."

These anecdotes illustrate a major feature of rhetoric: its two-valued orientation—that is, phenomena are good or bad, black or white, right or wrong. It's no accident that Aristotle, with his marvelous classification system for flora, should also apply that system to logic and human communication. That binary system is a major part of Western thought, and one of its consequences is the unreconcilable differences between the Zen master and the educational evaluator. Historically, such differences mark the rise of rhetoric about competency, and one way to provide a rhetorical analysis of the topic is to examine the educational context within which it occurs. To that end, its antecedent terms such as accountability, behavioral objectives, and relevance will be described within competency structures.

Antecedents

Behavioral objectives provide one system for delivering evidence upon which competency is based—at least, according to some of the rhetoric on competency testing listed in the May 1978 edition of *Phi Delta Kappan*. According to Hawkes (1965), however, it was within the Eight-year Study (*circa*, 1938) that behavioral objectives were listed as one alternative for assessment of student learning. During the late sixties behavioral objectives were re-discovered and used as a "standard" for federal proposals by the Department of Health, Education, and Welfare. Such a standard provided educators with a saleable means for accountability.

Fusion of behavioral objectives and accountability provides a national rhetoric for competency. Sums and products of objectives could be enumerated, ranked, compared, and judged for their relevance. Behavioral objectives became sensing devices to see whether teachers, administrators, school districts, states were doing their job, were accountable. Notice the implicit polarization in the accountability movement, that is, the assumption that up until the late sixties, schools were not accountable. Such a judgment is obviously ridiculous, but gradations and continuums are not part of rhetorical conventions. The convention of polarization explains, in part, relevancy-spawned, polarized educational issues such as: basics, career education, what Brickell (1978) calls life skills and, of course, competency itself—all with negatively tunneled definitions vis-a-vis their applications to description of American education.

Imbued with such old concepts within new contexts, taxpayers' revolts, falling Scholastic Aptitude Test (SAT) scores, vandalism, teacher militancy—all catalyzed by media equally well committed to the rhetorical convention of polarization—particularly, negative polarization—it is not surprising that competence has become, in some quarters, the antimatter for educating the child of the future.

Competence: Etiology

Pipho's (1978) examination of competency testing from 1975-1978 traces the rapid growth of the concept and its impact in various of the thirty-three states which have mandated competency (in one form or another) for educational programs ranging from kindergarten through teacher preparation programs and beyond. An example of this "beyond" category is, as reported by O'Dea (1980), competency testing for recertification, as in Florida and Georgia. Pipho points out (in that same article) that taxation and public education have always been popular targets for legislative reform, and he feels that both those issues helped to leapfrog the competency movement out of local eduational channels and into state and federal legislatures where bills dealing with eduational competence were passed and mandated.

As is typically the case, *competence* has long been the concern of the Council for Basic Education (CBE) but they dealt with it under the "basics" rubric. *Basics* they defined as "reading, writing, and ciphering" and the skills which students should exhibit in those areas. The popularity of the competence ideas has won their cautious endorsement; *cautious* because, as Howard (1980) points out, they feel that *minimal* in *minimal competency* may foster mediocrity.

Mediocrity was not the catalyst for the wildfire spread of competency; instead, competency-based instruction, with what Houston and Howsam (1972, p. 4) call its "accountability principle," became the panacea for all aspects of instructional programs. Within rhetorical conventions, too, the explanatory sides of the stories—the change in college-bound populations, the standard variations in national tests scores, the outstanding teaching done in some intolerable circumstances—were left to the fine print or the afterthought newscasts because "the good that men do" makes poor press.

Media coverage of scholastic competence has long been a concern of organizations such as CBE and, since the late fifties, powerful organizations directly or indirectly provided the rhetorical planks which culminated in the competence platform. Conant (1959) and his myrmidons with their surveys of American junior and senior high schools and their subsequent recommendations for a national testing program created a climate of distrust for public education. Conant's national-testing recommendation, was initially funded by the Carnegie Foundation and later reinforced and taken over by the Department of Health, Education, and Welfare. From that beginning came the National Assessment of Educational Progress (NAEP) tests which have had subtle but powerful influences on data used to perpetuate competence. One source of that influence is the newsletter reports of test results supplied by NAEP, funded for some time by the Education Commission of the States and now by Educational Testing Service (ETS). NAEP's charge from the Congress (according to its masthead) is "to collect and report data, over time, on the performance of young Americans in various learning areas." These national "performances" were (and are) made by students aged 9, 13, 17 and "young adult"—which is defined as "up to about age 25"—on tests which dealt with areas such as reading, writing, citizenship, art, music, computation, and the like. Regional comparisons of students' performances were, and are, published in NAEP *Newsletters*, and many states adapted NAEP test formats and normative data for some of their state-wide, competency-based programs.

In spite of NAEP's indirect contribution to competency, its August, 1979, *Newsletter* addressed legal ramifications of competency ("Lawyers Look at Competency Testing") and explored alternatives to mandated competency testing (37 states) as such alternatives are being tried in the 13 remaining states. These alternatives begin with local programs which are ultimately approved by the respective states.

The rhetoric supporting competency testing generated a corollary, that is, competency-based teacher educaton. From the Flesch (1955) hysteria about reading through Koerner's (1963) calumny about teacher education to the Weaver (1979) report about teacher incompetency, the rhetorical technique is to start with a premise such as the value of reading in public education and then to develop a series of *elenchi* which fault the reading procedures and state or imply that the fault is with incompetent teachers. So widespread is the rhetorical technique and its consequential teacher blame that it took court decisions in California and New Jersey to show that education and the process of reading are functions of circumstances much wider than those of the teacher.

Court rulings about teacher responsibility for reading competency notwithstanding, the Pennsylvania Council of Teachers of English (PCTE) *Newsletter* (1979) noted an increasing trend to assess teacher competency through state tests which are "arbitrary" and "unsuitable" ("Competency Tests for Teachers"). Arkansas, Missouri, Colorado, Alabama (added to those states previously mentioned, Georgia and Florida) are all in the process of considering some form of competency testing for teachers or prospective teachers. As noted in the PCTE article, some states (Louisiana, for example) are narrowing their examinations to "knowing 58 to 66 percent of the subject matter." Performance in subject matter tests alone cannot be used to judge teachers as "competent," or "incompetent." Yet, where some Louisiana interpretations of National Teacher Examination (NTE) scores are involved, that is exactly what is implied. Moves in this direction continue elsewhere.

So the simplistic nature of competency, its binary modality, its bonds with accountability, its visible goals, its platitudes about the dollar "buying a dollar's worth of teaching"—these virtues comprising the nature of competency in a fiscally retreating economy—became a boon to legislators and to the media by providing them with an endless source of adversarial principles to be upheld with a vengeance worthy of the Old Testament. Under such popular conditions legislators could and did bypass local educational controls. Competency, its supporters felt, would be as close to a panacea for educational ills as one might find for the decade of the eighties. Or at least that is the rhetoric supporting its adoption.

Competence: Interpretation

Advocates of competence are quick to note that a given task, goal, skill has been learned, and that evidence of that learning can be verified. Questioners of competency practitioners ask, "Who establishes the task, skill, knowledge for the competence to be demonstrated?" and, "How long will the competency last?" Concerning the latter question, all of us have, at one time or another, demonstrated academic competence (that is, the ability to perform with a passing grade) in foreign languages, statistics, computer science, or the like, but an update of our test performance right now might show a loss of that competence. Had we the time, interest, and motivation to review the test materials we might re-establish that passing level competence. The lesson to be learned about losing formerly established competence is that planned reinforcement and review are crucial for its maintenance.

When we return to the first question, the identification of those who establish competence, our search for information proves even more enigmatic. The enigma is posed by engineers, computer scientists, microbiologists, technicians from a host of fields all of whom exhibit competence of one sort or another (passing examinations, licensure) but who, almost by definition, will become incompetent if they do not keep up with new information, techniques, and applications in their fields. Competence for such professionals is an emphemeral pause in the hourglass of time.

What effect does time have on competence related to the curricular contents for educational designs? One answer to that question resurrects the previously mentioned rhetorical polarity—this time, with the sciences and the humanities as the poles. New information, discoveries, inventions constantly change the contents of the sciences to the point (noted by Alvin Toffler in *Future Shock*) where a Cambridge University scientist commented that the materials students were studying today weren't even invented thirty years ago when he took his Ph.D. Opposed to the scientist's viewpoint are those of humanists who maintain that they are teaching the verities, that human nature doesn't change and that "a thing of beauty is a joy forever"; and so it is. But another aphorism or platitude (depending upon one's judgmental competence) is that "beauty is in the eye of the beholder" and when one tries to establish criteria for the recognition of beauty so that one can be declared competent in recognizing beauty, definitional conflicts occur.

Systems people, competency-makers agree that abstractions such as truth and beauty are not desirable goals for competencies—at least not in that form. By arbitrarily sequencing some of the attributes for beauty within a particular discipline (art, music, literature) one could come closer to definitional competency—characteristics of a conventionally agreed upon art form (for example) such as the golden mean. But, even here, one could differ with that definitional attribute. If, however, majority opinion or authority insist that the ability to identify the attributes of the golden mean is one of the criteria to establish competency in art or art appreciation, then conformance equals competence.

Gordon (1980) might consider the golden-mean illustration unfair to advocates of competency-based education (CBE). She reviewed a series of essays by experts and proponents of CBE. Although the CBE authors affected a neutrality about the pro's and con's of CBE, there is a pro-CBE attitude obvious from statements Gordon cites, one of which follows:

> The book inspires us, too, with the promise of an approach that—as Thomas Ewens suggested—is concerned with accomplishing what traditional approaches generally do not, namely, assuring that students "not only know the principles (of liberal education) but know how to use them effectively in practice" (p. 250).

One might find it difficult to achieve consensus about the "principles of liberal education," even among published advocates of the liberal arts. To get agreement about what comprised "effective use" of such principles"in practice" would be next to impossible. It is exactly such overstatements about CBE which make it suspect even among some of its strongest advocates.

David Riesman, according to Gordon, is such an advocate but is concerned about the need for competency-based schools to "run a tight ship." His concern was prompted, in part, by his observations of student behavior at the Antioch Law School. He noted students' desultory class attendance and apathetic attitudes toward exams and postulated that a prospective lawyer with such behaviors "...is likely to let the statute of limitations run out on a client'' (p. 248).

It is this failure of the competency theory to address tacit but contributing behavior (such as the sporadic class attendance noted by Riesman) which faults it as an evaluation system. As von Bertalanffy noted in commenting on the adequacy of General Systems Theory, the failure of a theory to account for all features of a system makes the theory suspect. Noddings (1974) provides a specific instance of an excluded category in competency theory when she points out:

> The teacher who aims for a transformation of cognitive structure is concerned with how the child thinks and not solely with the product of this thinking. The teacher, so guided, cannot enter the instructional situation with predetermined behavioral objectives for students; objectives must arise out of the situation in which, first, what is possible has been revealed (p. 364).

Noddings goes on to postulate that pattern variation is the achievement of cognitive competence, that is, that one must employ a variety of learning styles, each of which depends, in part, upon the nature of the material to be learned. One extension of that idea is that students' efficient uses of their learning styles are a major factor for determining their educational competencies.

That same aphorism from a teacher's standpoint can be found in Hogan's (1970) hunting versus fishing anecdote. Hogan points out that, as classroom teachers, we sometimes have very specific objectives and criteria for determining students' competencies for the achievement of those objectives. In teaching vocabulary, spelling, punctuation—the first cognitive level of the Bloom taxonomy—the teacher chooses a focused strategy; just as the hunter chooses rifle, shotgun, or trap with specific reference to the game hunted. Large lake or ocean fishing, on the other hand, requires experimentation and response to myriad forces—weather, baits available, season of the year—and under such conditions the fisherman has to adjust techniques to the immediate situations. While success can be achieved in both cases, the hunter who uses the deer rifle to shoot quail may not have the same degree of success as the fisherman who adjusts his technique to changing situations. Another interpretation of competence, then, is appropriate adjustment to myriad educational situations.

Misinterpretations of *competence*, however, are perennial with the press. Farr and Olshavsky (1980) cite a United Press International (UPI) editor who equates decline in SAT scores with the need to return to the basics and to establish minimal competencies. The UPI editor's rhetoric is, typically, simplistic, polarized, and can be paraphrased as follows: SAT's down—minimal competencies will correct. Farr and Olshavsky destroy the editor's simplistic notions by comparing SAT questions with questions from the NAEP tests and show that there is virtually no academic relationship between minimal competency test questions and the high-powered, sophisticated SAT questions. To propose that improved minimal competencies will improve SAT scores is deceitful, ignorant, or both.

Insofar as public schools are concerned, Tyo (1979) who surveyed the strengths and weaknesses of CBE, came to the following conclusion:

> The teacher is...a primary participant in the selection and implementation of goals, but...the ultimate responsibility for learning falls upon the student....students should not only be aware of what is expected, they should also become true partners with teachers. Learners must contribute toward *forming* and *fulfilling* expectations. Until this partnership is formed CBE remains another educational fad (p. 427) (italics mine).

The "forming" aspect of Tyo's conclusion completes the criticism of the closed ring of competency with which this section began, namely, who decides what competencies are to be achieved and what evidence (and how long a period of time) should be accepted for the judgment that the competency has been fulfilled? Unless those who are to achieve the competencies are given some part in their formation, the rhetoric about the advantages of competency are not very persuasive. And the questions about CBE in the schools can be applied to the following and concluding section, CBE in Teacher Education.

Competency-Based Teacher Education (CBTE)

From competency-based programs for students, it was a short leap to insist that teachers be held accountable for wide-ranging professional competencies. The rhetoric supporting the gap-closing used a warped syllogism to the effect that students were taught by teachers; if students were deficient in knowledge, then teachers were at fault; the solution, therefore, was to make teachers more competent. Again, the logic made sense to state legislators who, fanned on by the media and public opinion, started a whole series of bills which ultimately (as previously mentioned) culminated in recommendations for competency-based teacher education.

Ryan and Cooper (1980) identify three areas common to all CBTE programs which condense behaviors associated with teaching since at least the Charters and Waples study in 1929; these are as follows:

> (1) teacher knowledge—facts, principles, generalizations, awareness, and sensitivities that the teacher is expected to acquire and demonstrate (quite possibly measured by paper and pencil tests);
> (2) teacher performance—behaviors that the teacher is expected to demonstrate that are believed to help foster desired outcomes in children;
> (3) teacher consequences—outcomes that the teacher is expected to bring about in the pupils' emotional and intellectual growth (p. 142).

While these three areas seem simple enough, we might question in the "knowledge" areas, who determines which "facts," "principles," "generalizations," are necessary; in the performance area, we might question who sets the criteria for judgment and determines the meaning of "desired" in "desired outcomes"; in the "consequences" area questions of criteria and instruments for measuring "intellectual growth" might be raised.

In Pennsylvania, Maurer (1973) and his associates tried to get suggestions about competencies for teachers from a variety of sources. After sifting through "50,000 statements" they arrived at 66 "generic" competencies, that is, common to all levels and subjects (as opposed to specialized competencies applicable only to a specific level). These 66 were categorized under titles such as "motivational technique," "use of resources," "evaluating measurement" and consisted of competencies such as: "37. The teacher will maintain an educational environment conducive to developing positive attitudes toward learning" (p. 11).

No one would seriously question the intent behind Generic Item 37, but who is to decide whether an environment is "conducive" according to what criteria? Also, how are "positive attitudes" determined? In spite of many suggestions for the establishment of competencies from myriad professional sources, there still seems to be the aura of fiat with arbitrary criteria in the Pennsylvania Department of Education (PDE) list.

Peter (1975), although promoting a series of textbooks for the establishment of competencies in teaching, starts his Chapter 2, Conceptual Model, as follows:

> When you have completed your study of this chapter, you will be able to identify and define the components of the conceptual model: (1) elicitors, (2) behaviors, (3) reinforcers, (4) entering behavior, (5) terminal objectives, and (6) enroute objectives as well as concomitant developments occuring outside of individual instruction. You will be able to complete the practice items in Chapter Two of the *Individual Instruction Workbook* (p. 11).

As impressive as these promises are, we might wonder what would happen if we already knew what "elicitors" or "behaviors" were. Must we learn Peter's definitions? If so, we're back to conformance equals competence. There are ways around such conformance, but the rhetoric of polarity precludes Peter using them if he hopes to establish competence according to his definition.

It is these fixed definitions, criteria, hierarchies, which seem to negate the purposes of competencies, namely, more efficient and verifiable outcomes for learning experiences. Confusion between the word and the thing, between the rhetoric and its analysis threaten to become even more widespread, particularly in teacher education. Capie's (1979) description of the development and use of teacher-performance assessment instruments in Georgia is a case in point.

Over a two-year period, Georgia's Teacher Performance and Assessment Instrument (TPAI) has been thoroughly critiqued by professional educators ranging from classroom teachers through university researchers. Validity and reliability tests have been run on the TPAI instruments, and they confirm the soundness of the instruments. Although test results have been used diagnostically rather than punitively so far, if enough legislators are convinced that too many teachers are unqualified, the test will be used to eliminate teaching positions (and in fact, that has been proposed, as pointed out previously).

Again, the blandness of the TPAI statements are, like patriotism, hard to disagree with. The statement about "Plans and Materials," for example, "Plans Instruction to Achieve Selected Objectives," (p. 14) could hardly cause controversy. Nor could the five categories under it which deal with learner objectives, teaching procedures, variety of instructional levels. But for each of the five subsets of planned objectives there is a five-point scale where 1 is low and 5 is high, and where judgments from "no objectives" (Score 1) to "appropriate objectives, sequenced" (Score 5) (p. 15) imply, again, that there are givens to every lesson, and that the best way for those givens to be presented is in a sequenced pattern. Such an evaluation system implies a behavioristic style. It implies that wisdom and knowledge can be fragmented with more efficient results than a holistic, humanitarian, or random design. If there is one thing SAT tests have shown, it's that students are exceptionally poor at putting things together, synthesis. One explanation for that deficit is the deliberate use of the short-attention-span grabber. The media—from newspapers, through television, to graphic displays on interactive computers—make the message short, self-contained, and encapsulated. Students are being programmed to achieve short-term competency but long-term nihilism. The ingredient lacking in sustaining short-term competencies is the glue of incubation, which permits reflection, synergism, and opportunity for students to assemble relationships among phenomena. When competency programs can accept and apply such a holistic rhetoric, that's when educational practices can significantly imprint our children's futures.

References

Brickell, Henry M. Seven key notes on minimum competency testing. *Phi Delta Kappan*, 1978, *59*, 589-592.

Capie, William, *et al. Teacher Performance Assessment Instruments*. Athens, GA: College of Education, University of Georgia, 1979.

Competency tests for teachers: A growing controversial trend. *PCTE Newsletter*, 1979, *20*, 1-4.

Conant, James B. *The American High School Today*. New York: McGraw-Hill, 1959.

Flesch, Rudolf. *Why Johnny Can't Read*. New York: Macmillan, 1959.

Farr, Roger, & Olshavsky, Jill Edwards. Is minimum competency testing the appropriate solution to the SAT decline? *Phi Delta Kappan*, 1980, *61*, 528-530.

Gibbons, Maurice. Zen and the art of motor-behavior-cycle maintenance. *Phi Delta Kappan*, 1980, *61*, Back Cover.

Gordon, Sheila C. Review of *On Competence: A Critical Analysis of Competence-based Reforms in Higher Educaton* by Gerald Grant, *et al.* *American Journal of Education*, 1980, *88*, 245-250.

Gorrell, Robert M. (Ed.) *Rhetoric: Theories for Application*. Champaign, IL: National Council of Teachers of English, 1967.

Hawkes, Herbert E. The story of the eight-year study. In Robert O. Hahn & David B. Bidna (Eds.) *Secondary Education: Origins and Directions*. New York: Macmillan, 1965, pp. 195-199.

Heath, Robert. Reactions to Bruce Eckland's paper: Sociodemographic implications of minimum competency testing. In Richard M. Jaeger & Carol Kehr Tittle (Eds.) *Minimum Competency Achievement Testing*. Berkeley, CA: McCutchan, 1980, pp. 136-141.

Hogan, Robert F. On hunting, fishing, and behaviorism. In J. Maxwell & A. Tovatt(Eds.) *On Writing Behavioral Objectives in English*. Champaign, IL: National Council of Teachers of English, 1970, pp. 125-129.

Houston, Robert W., & Howsam, Robert B. *Competency-based Teacher Education*. Chicago: Science Research Associates, 1972.

Howard, James. Expectations of minimum competency. *Basic Education*, 1980, *24*, 9-10.

Koerner, James D. *The Miseducation of American Teachers*. New York: Houghton Mifflin, 1963.

Lawyers look as competency testing. *NAEP Newsletter*, 1979, *12*, 1.

Lindemann, Erika. *A Rhetoric for Writing Teachers*. New York: Oxford University Press, 1982.

Madaus, George. NIE clarification hearing: The negative team's case. *Phi Delta Kappan*, 1981, *63*, 92-94.

Maurer, Wallace M., *et al. Generic Teaching Competencies*. Harrisburg, PA: Pennsylvania Department of Education, 1973.

Noddings, Nel. Competence themes and the science of education. *Educational Theory*, 1974, *24*, 356-364.

O'Dea, Paul. Competency testing: A growing factor in teacher education. *Council Grams*, 1980, *42*, 14.

Peter, Lawrence J. *Competencies for Teaching*. Belmont, CA: Wadsworth Publishing Company, 1975.

Pipho, Chris. Minimum competency testing in 1978: A look at state standards. *Phi Delta Kappan*, 1978, *58*, 585-588.

Popham, James W. A mountaintop mentality. *Phi Delta Kappan*, 1980, *61*, Back Cover and 662.

Popham, James W. The case for minimum competency testing. *Phi Delta Kappan*, 1981, *63*, 89-91.

Ryan, Kevin, & Cooper, James. *Those Who Can Teach* (3rd ed.). Boston: Houghton Mifflin, 1980.

Sager, M. Testing anxiety. *Washington Post Magazine*, January 16, 1983, p. 7.

Tyo, John. Competency-based education. *The Clearing House*, 1979, *52*, 424-427.

von Bertalanffy, Ludwig. *Problems of Life*. New York: Harper Brothers, 1960.

Weaver, Timothy W. In search of quality: The need for talent in teaching. *Phi Delta Kappan*, 1979, *61*, 29-32. 46.

2

Nel Noddings continues this series of analyses of competence by the application of the tools of linguistic analysis to the concept of teacher competence. She, first of all, raises the issue of the relationship of specific competencies or specific performances to the assertion of competence, as identified in teachers judged to be competent. Next, she contrasts this empirically-derived reductionist notion of competence with theoretically-derived conceptions of competence. This latter form of deriving descriptions of competence aims at conceptualizing a system of definitions, ideas, and rules for relating them that accounts for instances of competence—yielding a theory of competence. Noddings concludes that this sort of competence theory in the domain of teaching actions is likely to be elusive, if not impossible, to construct. She next turns to a theory of competence as motivation. In discussing teacher education, she contrasts a motivation theory of competence (which allows the novice to explore, appropriate, and organize) with the competency-based model (which focuses intensely upon particular performances). Additional objections to CBTE are argued. On logical grounds, she concludes that a motivational theory of teacher competence can give guidance to connecting ends and means in teacher education, though this approach has not yet been attempted in practice.

Professor Noddings is Associate Professor of Teacher Education and Curriculum in the School of Education, Stanford University.

Competence in Teaching: A Linguistic Analysis

Nel Noddings
Stanford University

Linguistic analysis has obvious limitations. It is neither neutral, as we once believed, nor is it capable of producing recommendations for practice. If we begin, however, with a confessed predilection, linguistic analysis may help us to make our complaints or approbations explicit. We may finish up, then, with a more well-considered argument and, perhaps, even a mild appreciation for the view we oppose. Further, since we recognize the limitations of linguistic analysis, we may deliberately move beyond it in an attempt to add construction to criticism.

Many of us are opposed to CBTE: Competency Based Teacher Education. Assuming that the "competency" in CBTE reflects an intention to produce *teacher competence* and not simply a new form of teacher education that may or may not induce competence, we feel the need to explore two large questions: What is teaching competence? How might we prepare competent teachers? These two questions will provide the focus for my exploration. First, I shall explore views that may shed some light on the problem of defining competence. Second, I shall inquire into the relation between competence and human action in an attempt to discover how competence is developed. Finally, I shall ask how CBTE is related to education and whether its goal of providing competent teachers is likely to be realized.

I

Before attempting to analyze "teacher competence," we might reasonably ask about the meaning of "competence." The definitions that I have been able to find associate "competence" with "capacity," "ability," "having the necessary prerequisites." In all of these definitions, *competence* is differentiated from *performance*. Over many trials in a broad range of related activity, competence is *necessary* for adequate performance, but it is not sufficient. In any particular instance, as we shall see, competence is neither necessary nor sufficient for adequate performance.

In a dispositional analysis of capacity (or competence) terms, Gilbert Ryle notes several uses of the capacity word, "can":

(1) John Doe *can swim* if he has learned how and has not forgotten.
(2) Richard Doe *can swim* (learn to swim) if he is competent to follow and apply instructions and demonstrations.
(3) You *can swim* if you try.
(4) I *can swim* if I want to.[1]

Clearly, there are several interpretations we may attach to "X can swim," but none of these by itself allows us to assume a particular performance. I *can swim*, if I want to, but I may not want to. Competence, ability, or capacity words are, under Ryle's analysis, dispositional terms.

> Dispositional statements are neither reports of observed or observable states of affairs, nor yet reports of unobserved or unobservable states of affairs. They narrate no incidents. But their jobs are intimately connected with narratives, for, if they are true, they are satisfied by narrated incidents.[2]

According to Ryle, then, when we speak of X as competent in Z, we may have in mind incidents that have led us to judge X as competent or we may expect to see certain kinds of incidents under an appropriate set of conditions. "Competence" does not refer to some unobservable system lying beneath the world of action; rather, it is a linguistic device we use to evaluate a constellation of observable performances.

There are major difficulties in this position. It is, I think, true that if I believe X is competent in Z, I expect X to perform well in tasks associated with Z. At the same time, however, I realize that X and Y, both competent in Z, may differ substantially. Suppose X and Y are competent philosophers. X lectures easily and spontaneously on the stoics; Y can say almost nothing about the stoics or their philosophy. Y, on the other hand, easily answers questions about modal logic; X has forgotten whatever he/she once knew in this field. We might argue, of course, that there are some things both can do that, say, engineers cannot do, and these are precisely the things that constitute their competence as philosophers. But this seems wrong. X's ability to lecture and do research on the stoics is part of his/her competence in philosophy. Y's ability to handle modal logic is an important reason for Mathematical U. to prefer Y over X in its search for a new philosopher. So it is not clear to me that the statement "X is competent in Z" raises *specific* expectations for X's performance. I need to know more about Z as a domain of analysis, and I also need to know more about the strengths of X's performance in Z-related activities. One great strength may outweigh a number of small weaknesses.

There is even greater difficulty moving in the opposite direction. Under what conditions will I label someone competent? In Ryle's analysis certain narrated occurrences "satisfy"dispositional claims. He says, for example:

> 'John Doe has just been telephoning in French' satisfies what is asserted by 'John Doe knows French.'[3]

It is not clear to me that Ryle is right on this. Certainly, the first statement is compatible with the second, but it does not "satisfy" it in any strong sense. Doe may have been reading a prepared script that he has rehearsed. Indeed, he may even perform satisfactorily without knowing what he is saying. So if competence, as capacity, is to be retained as groundwork for performance, then the problem of identifying reliable indicators of competence arises and this, it seems to me, is a tough problem demanding sophisticated methods and extensive investigation.

CBTE describes observable performances. It transforms competence (capacity, ability) into *competencies*—a list of expected performances. As Peter Goldstone has pointed out, these *competencies* can be individuated and counted, whereas *competence* cannot be so neatly separated.[4] What, then, is the relation between competence and the listed competencies? In what way is the set of competencies derived from a prior description of competence? My first specific complaint against CBTE is that its *competencies* are not convincingly related to *competence*. Advocates of CBTE may now respond that they do not wish to quibble endlessly over language; they may, indeed, concede my first point and call their program *PBTE*. The new title refers honestly to observable behaviors, performances. But I shall still want to know how these performance demands are derived.

One answer is that the competencies are derived empirically. We somehow capture competence, and then we analyze it for component competencies. Is it possible that we might indentify definite components in competence? As Gerald Reagan suggests, in his response to Goldstone, we can and do talk about things such as "particulates of smoke."[5] But we have first to capture the smoke and, while there may be certain common constituents of all smokes, the noxiousness or innocuousness of a particular smoke is not decided wholly on the volumes of the common constituents. The absence of chlorine in Smoke 1 does not make Smoke 1 tolerable; its presence in Smoke 2, however, makes Smoke 2 intolerable.

It is not a definition of smoke that makes our analysis possible but the fact that it exists materially and can be studied physically. When we have analyzed Smoke 1, we may be in a better position to analyze Smoke 2, but we do not expect to find the same constituents in Smoke 2. Similarly, if we study Competent Teacher 1, we may be in a better position to study Competent Teacher 2, but we should not expect to find exactly the same constituents in 2 that we found in 1. I am not sure, however, that advocates of CBTE make a serious attempt to capture the competence-in-action of competent teachers. Those lists that I have seen distributed by state departments of education have been compiled and distilled from *statements* made by practicing educators. This procedure is compatible with Ryle-style behaviorism, but I have already commented on the problem of validity of indicators that emerges in that paradigm.

It seems to me, then, that a description of competence that is to be empirically based must rely on comprehensive, naturalistic study of actual teachers indisputably held to be competent.

The next question to ask is whether we can capture "competence in Z" without reference to some X who is active in Z-ing; that is, we shall ask whether a description non-empirically derived might be useful.

II

There are those who contend that, in order to construct a coherent theory of performance, we must begin not with raw performances or behaviors but with a description of competence. On this view, we begin with a body of knowledge or characteristic set of behaviors, but we do not attempt to sort our way piece-wise through the set nor do we formulate and test hypotheses *ad hoc* as we observe behaviors. Rather, we ask: What *competence* must be attributed to an idealized subject in order to account for this body of knowledge? By "competence" here we mean some system of basic elements, definitions, and rules of combination and transformation that is capable of producing the existing body of data.

Systems thus constructed are sometimes called "competence theories." Norm Chomsky's generative/transformational grammer is a competence theory.[6] As a system of constructive rules, it is designed to produce all and only the well-formed expressions of the language under study. Further, it purports to describe a possible scheme of mental organization that might account for the observable production and comprehension of language. It does *not* claim to describe conscious operations by which an actual speaker produces or comprehends language, but it attempts to describe the underlying organization, or competence, of an abstract entity that handles the language flawlessly.

Similarly, Jean Piaget's mathematical description of the stages of human intelligence represents a competence theory.[7] A system so organized should be capable of producing all and only the responses characteristically observed at the given stage. Piaget contends that systems of this sort must be judged by two criteria:

(1) those schemata should be logically valid.

(2) they should have an adequate application to the findings of experimental psychology.[8]

Clearly such theories are not susceptible to obvious or direct verification or falsification, but they are enormously powerful in the orderly production of hypotheses. Ultimately, the weight of empirical evidence may allow us to judge the plausibility or implausibility of the theory.

There are two clear advantages in starting a study of Z with an abstract, logically systematic description of competence in Z. One is that we have an orderly procedure for generating hypotheses about performance in Z. A second is that we have a ready-made scheme of interpretation for what we find empirically. The bits and pieces of empirical study can be examined and evaluated with respect to their possible positions in a pre-cut frame. Without such an explicit frame, we either remain at the bits-and-pieces stage or we introduce implicit assumptions that change over time to suit our purposes and conditions. We thus induce a problem of consistency, but we do not always *realize* that we have done so, because we have not made explicit the various assumptions under which we have been working.

The problem of consistency arises dramatically in the construction of teaching competencies. Consider the following competency:

> The teacher will select, evaluate, and implement the most appropriate principles of learning currently available to education.[9]

Surely, the selection of an appropriate learning principle depends upon one's philosophical beliefs. I am not likely to use prestated objectives and systematic reinforcement of prescribed responses even if I am well aware of *how* to use them, if I am Deweyan or Rogerian in my philosophical orientation. Further, it seems likely that erratic behavior on my part—choosing a principle from one learning theory here, from another there—might be confusing to my students. Indeed, such rattle-brained eclecticism might well be considered one mark of *in*competence. My point in all this is that we do not avoid the problem of consistency by refusing to provide a basic, systematic description. On the contrary, we aggravate it to the point of absurdity.[10]

Is it possible to construct a competence theory for teaching? I suspect it is not. For one thing, we do not have an organized body of knowledge comparable to language with which to begin. The intuitions against which we should have to check our constructions are ambiguous. Consider the following word-strings: (1) He don't want any. (2) Any want he don't. There are native English speakers who would assent to (1), even though many of us would declare it "ungrammatical," but none would accept (2). We *do* have language intuitions to guide us. But there is nothing comparable to the word-strings of language on which we might operate in constructing a theory of teaching. Second, mental organization does not seem to be as central to teaching as it is to language or to reasoning. Dynamic characteristics—personality and motivational factors, beliefs—seem to be far more significant in describing teaching. Finally, a complaint leveled against all competence theories can be brought with special force against any such theory proposed for teaching: It ignores cultural and individual influences on the phenomena being described.

While I believe it is not possible to construct a theory of teaching that is a competence theory as described here, I do believe it is possible to construct theories that have some degree of the desired systematization. They will not be capable of producing particular strings or responses, but they should be capable of producing categories that will aid us in describing competence and in evaluating it.[11] Further, I think that competence theorizing may be possible in the area of *learning*, and these theories might be useful instruments in teaching.[12]

Let's turn next to a view that may be more useful for teaching.

III

Suppose that, for purposes of our present discussion, we regard competence as mastery over a set of environmental conditions—as the ability to produce effective responses to or changes in the environment. If we restrict the environment to a domain of activity Z, we should expect one who is competent in Z to be active in it and to exhibit some control over it. The requirement that one be active in a domain in order to be adjudged competent is clear. We might say of someone who has recently given up medical practice, "X is a competent physician, but he is no longer practicing." If, however, X has not practiced in years, we would be more likely to say, "X was a competent physician, but he has not practiced for so long that I am no longer sure of his competence." In this section, I want to inquire into the connection between competence and action.

Just as we can use emotion-words to describe either an inner feeling ("I was boiling mad") or our reason for doing something ("I hit him because I was angry"), so we can use "competence" to describe either a prepared state or a motive for engaging in certain activities. In one case, X is already competent, and he displays his competence in action. In the second, X engages in certain activities in order *to become* competent. Competence as desired end-state is his reason for acting.

A theory of competence as motivation has been elaborated by Robert W. White.[13] According to this theory, the desire for competence—for mastery over a particular set of conditions deemed important to the individual—is significant in human motivation. The small child goes up and down, up and down, a small flight of stairs. He is exploring and practicing in order to achieve mastery over his environment. But his activity is not purely instrumental, and it may not be consciously connected to a particular goal. The activity is engaged in for itself; it produces a "feeling of efficacy." White says:

> ...it is maintained that competence cannot be fully acquired simply through behavior instigated by drives. It receives substantial contributions from activities which, though playful and exploratory in character, at the same time show direction, selectivity, and persistence in interacting with the environment. Such activities in the ultimate service of competence must therefore be conceived to be motivated in their own right.[14]

What I want to consider now is how a notion of competence as motivation might guide us in training teachers. A person motivated by the desire for competence engages in a domain of activity Z both to enjoy it and to master it. He or she identifies and practices those component activities that are clearly part of Z. Some features of the environment (such as stairs for the young child) must be mastered in order to function even minimally. One would suppose that acquaintance with apparatus and fundamental terms might play a fundamental role in medicine and that familiarity with legal terms and basic procedures might provide a foundation for lawyer-like behavior. It seems likely that exploratory and even playful manipulation of these basic components is involved in mastering the domain. Indeed when one is pretending to be a physician or lawyer, skillful pretense at manipulating the basic tools makes the performance convincing. In a naive state, one might suppose that reading textbooks and other materials and providing interpretations suitable for given client groups might be fundamental for teaching. We might suppose, that is, that teachers should be able to read and write effectively and that they should be able to discuss interpretively the subject matter they expect to teach. One might suppose that a desire to master certain fundamental subject matters and to explain them to others might motivate the prospective teacher.

Let us maintain our naive state for a bit. What sort of experience might we provide for prospective teachers? We would, I think, allow them to immerse themselves in the subjects they would teach, provide opportunitiess for them to engage in a variety of teaching situations, and keep an eye on their performance. We might expect that persons planning to teach would be immersed, from the time they made their decision, in studying their subjects, teaching in some controlled situations, and discussing problems of teaching in a clinical setting. The environment would be so constructed that teachers-in-training would be continually faced with problems to solve, information to be gathered, skills to be mastered. Further, this environment would, ideally, be stimulating but not intensely so. There would be time for extensive exploration and reflection—for breadth in learning.[15] White points out that intense motivation tends to hamper acquisition of breadth:

> (It) "has the effect of speeding up learning at the cost of narrowing it." Attention is concentrated upon the task at hand and little that is extraneous to this task is learned for future use.[16]

One wonders whether the concentration artificially induced by the statement of behavioral objectives or competencies might have a similar deleterious effect. Might it not be the case that the definite, rather precise requirements of credentialing might displace the natural urge toward competence? This is not to say, of course, that we should cease to look for evidence of competence in performance. Rather it is to suggest that we may err when we *intensify the focus* in our teacher education programs. When one knows exactly what one must do, the urge to explore, to appropriate, and to organize may be diminished.

An obvious and related difficulty with discrete competencies measured individually at specified times is that they disappear.[17] Teachers working in school districts that have adopted competency testing at the K-12 level are becoming increasingly aware of this problem. Students pass, say, a test on computation with fractions and then move on to other topics. Predictably, a few weeks later, they can no longer compute adequately with fractions. There might be no harm in stating what we would like students to be able to do at various end-points in instruction (old-fashioned tests did this fairly well), but to suppose curriculum can be fashioned sequentially to go at these objectives directly is a great mistake. Students must be immersed in situations that continually call forth the desire for competence; that is, educational situations must be so designed that students acquire knowledge and skills self-organized into systems of increasing power. What has been learned must be repeatedly called forth in situations of greater and more intricate complexity.

There was a time in which teachers answered routinely the perennial student question, "What do we have to know for the test? with a resounding, "Everything!" This attitude implied that the task of organization and integration was the student's special task. Is is the student who must struggle with components that he has not mastered; it is the student who will, if we provide appropriate opportunities, work his or her way toward competence. This does not mean that we let students decide when they are competent. It means, rather, that the locus of control for competence lies in the student, not in a set of external criteria. We properly make judgments about competence in close association over extended intervals of time. We *do* judge on performance but not on *a* performance. We do this best when we serve both as supportive evaluators and as models of competence.

IV

So far I have argued that CBTE exhibits two important weaknesses: (1) The connection between *competence* and the so-called *competencies* is unclear; and (2) the establishment of discrete competencies implies an external locus of control that ignores the urge toward competence as a basic, natural motivation. Along the way, I have made explicit several other objections that might be subsumed under these two.

Now I want to ask: Is CBTE a form of *education*? There is more than one definition of education, of course, but most views suppose that when we *educate* we pay some attention to the development of critical thought; to the inculcation, construction, or clarification of values; to the acquisition of a system of coherent and consistent knowledge and beliefs. Even those who *oppose* educating assume these goals are part of educating.

Further, a plan for educating implies more than the establishment of objectives that describe desired end-state behaviors. There is *method* to consider. One is tempted to say that there is *curriculum* to consider. But *is* there? Let's start with that question and then move on to consider the problem of method.

Some advocates of CBTE hold that the competencies are guides to curriculum construction, that once we know how we want people to behave as a result of our instruction we can better decide what topics to include in our courses of study.[18] Other influential advocates of behavioral objectives (and the competencies are obviously such objectives less specifically written) insist that the objectives properly stated *are* the curriculum.[19] Now suppose I am philosophically opposed to the use of pre-specified objectives. Suppose I want to describe my subject matter globally at the outset and locate specific objectives in interaction with my students. Or suppose I want my students to read Pestalozzi, Herbert, Montessori, and A. S. Neill, but I do not care to prescribe how they will behave as a result of their readings. Suppose I want my students to understand learning theory (in the technical "learning theoretic" sense) so that they will see how empty it is for education and reject the techniques that come out of it. It seems to me that all of these things are hard to include in the CBTE framework. CBTE places enormous constraints on curriculum construction, but it does not itself provide what most of us would call a curriculum. It is built on a behaviorist foundation that effectively precludes the free exercise of other respectable philosophical views.

Advocates of CBTE sometimes respond to this objection with the assurance that things are not all that bad. After all, most competency lists include items suchas the following:

(a) The teacher will formulate a personal philosophy of education.
(b) The teacher will demonstrate knowledge of philosophical implications in the establishment of educational program directions.

Therefore, philosophy of education and other foundational subjects can still be taught, and all we have to do is bring about some observable change in our students' behavior.

But suppose that my student is persuaded by the arguments of, say, Carl Rogers? Suppose he or she is dedicated to freedom, significant learning, non-directive teaching, and all the rest? What does he/she do with the other competencies in the list? How will he or she manage the following?

(c) The teacher will prepare comprehensive learning sequences and long range instruction for accomplishing specific educational objectives.
(d) The teacher will select, identify, and implement classroom procedures which are consistent with instructional objectives.

CBTE is *not* philosophically neutral. It is loaded with specific behavioral language that prejudices our efforts from the start. It encourages us to turn out teachers who are crazy-quilts of impotent beliefs, inconsistent values, and doubtful techniques. Its advocates generously invite me to rewrite their objectives so that the set includes what I take to be important. The invitation assumes the very point I refuse to concede.

Finally, in the matter of curriculum, recall an earlier objection. If we teach people directly and discretely a set of items, it is entirely possible that they will produce adequate performance in X on Day 11 and total failure in the same X on Day 57. If this fear is a well-founded one, even the respectable desire to be accountable is likely to be frustrated under CBTE. We risk inducing temporary performances that are not reliable indicators of competence.

Now, what of method? How are we to accomplish the ends set forth in CBTE? Here we are left completely free. Or are we? The ends are prescribed, but we may invent or select the means. But what if I believe that ends and means are inextricably intertwined? Suppose, for example, that I want *my* students to treat *their* students with respect and appreciation. Can I *teach* this behavior? In what sense of "teach"? How do I bring my student-teacher to the point where he/she

(e) communicates personal enthusiasm
(f) demonstrates warmth and friendliness
(g) shows sensitivity to needs and feelings?[20]

These qualities are important, I agree. They are part of what was missing in our earlier naive view which required some mastery of subject matter and an ability to interpret it. But are they *competencies*? Do I want to stress them as *performances*, or do I really want teachers who *are* enthusiastic, warm, friendly, and sensitive? If we want the latter, we might tell our prospective teachers that we shall look for certain personality traits before awarding a teaching credential. We might provide initial psychological screening (as many medical schools do) and advise some students that they should undergo a program of therapy if they want to prepare for the profession. I am not yet advocating such practices but merely pointing to them as possibilities. To list *qualities* such as these along with requirements that describe mastery of routine "learning the ropes" techniques seems irresponsible. The initial neglect of method has led us to put things together that are significantly different.

Another specific complaint, then, is that the categories into which many competencies are organized give no guidance for *education* in the competencies. CBTE is purportedly an approach to teacher education but, like its counterparts in the lower schools, it says nothing about the methods teacher educators might use, nothing about how we should treat our teachers-in-training, nothing about how our beliefs and personalities affect the methods we choose and find compatible. In short, it does not seem to be a mode of education at all.

V

I have examined several views of competence and their possible relation to CBTE. "Competence" may be thought of as a linguistic device that expresses either our judgment of past performance or our expectations for future performance. Under this view, the problems for advocates of CBTE include the following: to find reliable indicators in performance; to establish criteria for the evaluation of the indicators (which are strong, perhaps even *constitutive*? which are age- or subject-bound?); to avoid inconsistent expectations for performance; to allow educators of incompatible philosophical persuasions to function in teacher education.

A second view of competence concentrates on the mental organization of idealized subjects with respect to the field under consideration. The value of this view for educational theory lies in its emphasis on systematic description. I see a logical relation between this view and programs of teacher education that refer to competence, but no program of CBTE that I know of takes this view seriously.

A third view, that of competence as the ability to control environmental conditions and the motivating urge to achieve increasing capacity for control, seems to hold great promise for teacher education. It yields some guidance for the connection of means and ends. Again, I know of no program in CBTE that takes this view seriously.

It was my task to examine the logical foundations of CBTE. As CBTE is conceived and represented in existing programs, its logical foundations seem to be missing. We shall have to look toward social and political explanations to find out what in the world is supporting it.

Footnotes

[1] Gilbert Ryle, *The Concept of Mind*. New York: Barnes & Noble, Inc., 1949, pp. 129-130.

[2] Ibid., p. 125.

[3] Ibid., p. 125.

[4] Peter Goldstone, A plea for incompetence, *Proceedings of the Philosophy of Education Society*. Champaign, IL: Philosophy of Education Society, 1978, pp. 44-61.

[5] Gerald Reagan, C/PBTE, academic freedom, and Goldstone's plea, *Prodeedings of the Philosophy of Education Society*. Champaign, IL: Philosophy of Education Society, 1978, pp. 62-69.

[6] See Norm Chomsky, *Aspects of the Theory of Syntax*. Cambridge, MA: The M.I.T. Press, 1965, pp. 3-62; *Language and Mind*. New York: Harcourt Brace Jovanovich, Inc., 1972.

[7] See Jean Piaget, *Logic and Psychology*. Manchester, England: Manchester University Press, 1953.

[8] Ibid., p. 26.

[9] *Generic Teaching Competencies*, An Interim Report. Harrisburg: Pennsylvania Department of Education, 1973, p. 7.

[10] This point is elaborated in Nel Noddings, Some comments on competency based teacher education, Paper presented at the Pennsylvania ASCD, November, 1973.

[11] One such promising attempt is described in Donna H. Kerr and Jonas F. Soltis, Locating teacher competence: An action description of teaching, *Educational Theory*, 1974, *24*, 1, 3-16. See also Nel Noddings, Teacher competency: An extension of the Kerr-Soltis Model, *Educational Theory*, 1974, *24*, 3, 284-290.

[12] See Nel Noddings, Competence theories and the science of education, *Educational Theory*, 1974, *24*, 356-364.

[13] Robert W. White, Motivation reconsidered: The concept of competence, *Psychological Review*, 1959, *66*, 297-333.

[14] Ibid., p. 329.

[15] See White's comments on the work of Bruner, *et al.*, ibid., p. 327.
[16] Ibid., p. 327.
[17] For an elaboration of the point, see Nel Noddings, The logic of performance tests for teacher effectiveness, *Proceedings of the Far Western Philosophy of Education Society*. Tempe,AZ: Arizona State University, 1974, pp. 95-104.
[18] See, for example, Robert W. Houston (Ed.), *Competency Assessment, Research, and Evaluation*, A Report of a National Conference. Washington, D.C.: American Association of Colleges for Teacher Education, 1974; Robert W. Houston (Ed.), *Exploring Competency Based Education*. Berkeley,CA: McCutchan Publishing Corporation, 1974.
[19] Robert Gagne equates objectives and "content" in "Curriculum Research and the Promotion of Learning," in Ralph Tyler, Robert Gagne, & Michael Scriven, *Perspectives of Curriculum Evaluation*, AERA Monograph 1. Chicago: Rand McNally, 1967, pp. 21-22.
[20] The limited competencies (a-g) are found in the Beginning Teacher Assessment Instrument. See C.E. Johnson,*et al.*, *A Summary of the Competency Verification Survey Study with Selected Findings*. Athens, GA: University of Georgia, 1976.

3

Using judgmental or normative analysis, Allen T. Pearson further explores the meaning of competence. He shows that being competent is more than being merely knowledgeable but less than being an outstanding authority. Some necessary criteria for being considered competent are implied by the term, some level of performance that is judged commendable. These value judgments, says Pearson, are of the essence of the concept of competence. In identifying or preparing a competent teacher, three judgments are made: (1) a standard to be met to be declared satisfactory (neither just minimally nor maximally), (2) the skills to be required to perform at this level, and (3) the decision as to whether a person has these requisite skills. The first of these judgments is most commonly left unspecified, unless it is resolved by indicating some arbitrary expectation. Pearson thinks, however, that standards cannot be derived from examining actual teacher actions, only by positing certain conceptions of what good, proper, or correct teaching is. There are obviously many possible candidates for such a conception. Each, of course, represents a value judgment. Each implies a different standard, different skills, and ultimately a different assessment as to the competence of a particular teacher or student teacher. Most CBTE programs mask the conception of teaching that is embedded in them, according to Pearson, obscuring the fact that alternative conceptions are possible, while presuming to be value-free on this issue. He makes one final distinction between ''habitual'' skill knowledge (fostered by CBTE) and ''intelligent'' skill knowledge, in which judgment is required. Pearson's own view of teaching is the latter. ''Teaching is nothing,'' he says, ''if not a set of activities that require understanding, clear thinking, and good sense.''

Professor Pearson is Professor of Educational Foundations in the Faculty of Education, University of Alberta.

Competence: A Normative Analysis

Allen T. Pearson
University of Alberta

Educational thought is often dominated by slogans. At various times certain slogans take pre-eminence. The progressive era was marked by a great deal of talk about teaching children, not subjects—a claim which, if taken literally, is nonsense. The curriculum reform movement made a great deal of reference to the structures of the disciplines with the concept of structure used in a very metaphorical way. Present discussions of education use the concepts of performance and competence in a similar manner. Current educational discussions are punctuated frequently by references to competencies and performances. These words have moved beyond demarcating certain descriptive attributes; they now operate as passwords which reveal whole sets of values and commitments. This sort of language was first heard in discussions of teacher education. Given its appeal there, it is not surprising that this language has spread to other areas of education. In this paper I want to investigate some of the logical features of the use of the concept of competency. In doing so, I will not, of course, specify what competencies a teacher needs. Instead I hope to make more clear what is involved, logically, in those attempts to specify the competencies of teachers. I hope that as a result of such a discussion our thinking about the competencies of a teacher will be clarified.

Let us look first at a simple, non-educational judgment of competency. This should give us some insight into the logic of the concept without prejudging any educational issues. We might say of a person that he is a competent car driver or that he drives a car competently. What information has been alleged about the person when this judgment is made? At a very minimum the person is not ignorant of how to drive a car. To say that a person drives a car competently implies that he knows how to drive a car. Competency, then, implies knowledge. In other words knowledge is necessary for competency, but it would not seem to be sufficient. That is, it is possible in logic to say that a person might know how to drive a car but not be a competent driver. A person might know all the routine of getting a car started, moving, stopped, etc. The person might know how to maneuver in traffic, how to navigate freeway and city streets, how to park and all the rest of the things a person needs to know in order to drive. But the person might create havoc everytime he ventures forth on the highways. He might cut people off, change lanes without looking, drive through intersections without looking at traffic lights, and knock pedestrians down. I think we would not hesitate to call such a driver incompetent. This, then, is an example of an incompetent who knows how to drive. So competency is more than knowing how to do something. But at the other extreme, to say that a person is a competent driver is not to credit the person with being a superior or outstanding driver. Awards and certificates are given to outstanding drivers. Competent drivers merit no such commendation. Indeed we expect every driver to be competent, we are glad that some are outstanding, and we hope that the police and courts will clear the streets of those people who know how to drive but are yet incompetent.

Competence is, then, distinct from authority. A person is regarded as an authority on a topic, if he, by virtue of his training, experience or position, is likely to have relatively thorough knowledge of the topic. We turn to authorities for expert opinion. When one needs technical information or more complete information, an authority is one source from which it can be obtained. Such knowledge is not generally sought from a person described as competent in the field. The competent person is regarded as a source of basic information, but not advanced, highly abstract or highly technical information. Such knowledge is the domain of experts or authorities. The criteria for being authoritative in a subject are more rigorous than those for being competent. Competency suggests the mastery of basic knowledge in the field. Authority suggests the mastery of the higher reaches of the field. There are, however, some twists to note. A person who is competent in a field may be regarded by some as an authority. A person ignorant in a field may judge someone competent in the field to be an authority. One ignorant of medicine, say, will regard a competent physician as a reliable source of knowledge on disease. But other competent physicians would not regard each other as authorities; they would look to someone with special training for expert advice. That is, judgments of who is an authority can in part be comparative. Compared to someone who is ignorant of a field a competent person may speak authoritatively. But for people within a field the standard of competence is lower than the standard of authority.

So competency implies more than mere knowledge but does not imply outstanding knowledge on the part of a particular person. If we can think of a continuum ranging from just knowing how to do something at the one end to knowing how to do something very well at the other, knowing how to do something competently would fall somewhere along this continuum. The question now becomes how one tells which levels of performance fall above the competency mark from those which fall below. In other words, the question becomes a request for the criteria for a competent something or other.

Another point to notice that will help us make clear the nature of these sets of criteria is that to attribute competency to a person or thing is to commend the person in some way. We can often describe a competent driver or teacher as being a satisfactory driver or teacher or even as a good driver or teacher. Competency does not then describe a level of performance somewhere between just knowing and knowing very well how to do something. Rather it indicates the level at which a person's performance becomes commendable. Judgments of competency then are value judgments. So the criteria that are used to pick competent performances will have to include value premises. This is not at all to suggest that judgments of competency are less objective or less rational than judgments that do not include values. It does suggest though that judgments of competency will be more difficult and controversial than those judgments which are purely factual in nature.

To pursue further this point that judgments of competency are a kind of value judgment, we can notice that competence is always directed toward some end or purpose. That is, we can always ask for what end is a person competent. In my earlier example of the competent driver the standard that was implicit was one of safety and consideration. The competent driver is one who is able to drive in such a manner that he does not present dangerous situations to others or is not inconsiderate of others. This is not an exceptionless standard; competent drivers may have the occasional accident. Competency claims are claims of generality; the competent driver is for the most part safe and considerate. The standards of safety and consideration can be used for judgments of who is to count as a competent driver because these are worthwhile characteristics for automobile drivers to have. One can easily see how a justification of these standards would go. Because of the obvious dangers involved in driving and because of the numbers of people using the roadways, it is clear that one must drive safely and considerately in order to avoid injuring and possibly killing other people. The rightness of avoiding injury is obvious, so there is little dispute about the standards expected of a competent driver. This is obviously not so for a task such as teaching where the desirable outcomes are much less clear.

The next step in a competency judgment is to identify the characteristics by which one tells whether a person meets the standard which is held to be desirable. That is, one must decide what is required for a person to drive competently which we have seen means that the person drives safely and considerately. In this case we would porbably give a fairly lengthy list which would include items such as the following: the driver obeys the laws and regulations, keeps to the right, adjusts speed in accordance with weather and traffic conditions, does not change lanes without signaling, and so on. We would then use the list of characteritics in our judgment of whether a person is a competent driver.

To generalize this discussion to the field of education, to identify a person as a competent teacher means that three judgments have to be made. The first is the judgment of what standard a teacher ought to meet in order to teach satisfactorily, rather than just minimally. Second is the judgment of what skills are required in general for a person to perform at this level. And third is the judgment that the person in question has these requisite skills. Of these three judgments I think the first is the most controversial in that behind this question there lurks a systematic ambiguity.

The questions, "What standard ought a teacher meet in order to work satisfactorily?" and "What standards are teachers obliged to meet in order to work satisfactorily?" are similar in form but are very different. Because of the similarity they are easily confused and because of differences this confusion is damaging. The first question, the "ought to" question, is a value question. In this question one is asking for the principles, criteria, standards, etc., that are to guide one's actions. There is no suggestion in this question that the answer will necessarly involve a description of what people in fact do. Rather it asks for a proposal of what they should do. On the other hand, the second question, the "obliged to" question, is a factual question. It asks for those standards that teachers are as a matter fact expected to live up to regardless of whether those standards are indeed worthwhile. That is, this question makes no suggestion as to the desirablity or value of the standards that will be given in response. So, the possible answers offered to these quesions are very different. For the "ought to" question the response will be the statement of a value position. For the "obliged to" question the response will be a description of what people are in fact expected to do. And clearly, an account of what people do in fact sheds little, if any, light on the question of what they should do. Indeed, it is not inconsistent for people to be obliged to do what they ought not to do. One needs only to think of any form of civil disobedience.

Given, then, that the "ought to" question is very different from the "obliged to" question, it is clear that an account of what teachers do in fact do, or what they are in fact obliged to do, is irrelevant to the answering of the first question in the competency judgment which was what standard ought a teacher meet in order to work satisfactorily. An account of what teachers do is never by itself enough to answer this value question. At this point in the judgment of what competencies a teacher must have one must introduce a value premise. This value premise involves a conception of what a good teacher should be doing. The competency judgment assumes this sort of premise, and until the value premise is made the competency claim cannot get off the ground.

The decision, then, of what the standards of a competent teacher are cannot be made on the basis of analysis of what teachers do in fact do. On the basis of observing teachers one can at best determine what teachers are obliged to do. Of course, the actions of teachers will include more than what they are obliged to do, and it can be difficult to distinguish those actions that they are obliged to do as teachers from those that they are not obliged to do. But even if this distinction can be made, the description of their actions reveals nothing that might answer the question of what they ought to be doing. The judgment of what a teacher ought to do presupposes a conception of what good, proper, or even correct teaching is. A statement that teachers ought to teach in a certain way implies that certain ways of teaching are more desirable or more appropriate than others. The judgment of desirable or appropriate ways of teaching is, of course, a value judgment. It is based in part on one's commitments and beliefs about how teachers and students should interact with one another. Such beliefs, while not unrelated to facts on how people interact, do go beyond the facts. Of all the ways in which people can interact, a person may believe that some modes of interaction are better than others. These judgments may include educational or social considerations. But in any case, they are based on more than a behavioral description of teachers' actions. So a judgment of what a teacher's competencies are is in part a value judgment.

The remaining two issues in the competency judgment, the judgments of what skills are required for a person to meet the standard and the judgments whether a particular person has those skills, are both factual questions. To judge what skills are required to meet the standard of a satisfactoy teacher is a purely empirical matter but by no means an easy matter. The tests that have to be performed at this point are not what are the skills such that if a person has the skills then he will be a satisfactory teacher, but rather what are the skills such that if the person does not have them then he cannot be a satisfactory teacher. Because one is seeking required or necessary skills, the focus must be on those skills such that if they are lacking they would prevent the person from reaching the goal. By dealing with skills that are lacking rather than skills that are present the situation is vastly complicated.

Another complication stems from the possibility that a skill might be necessary for a teacher *qua* person, rather than *qua* teacher. That is, one must ask for what end a particular skill is necessary. For example, a necessary condition, at least at present, for being a teacher is to be a human being. In order to operate at a satisfactory level as a human being it is necessary that one be able to breathe. So a competency of being human is being able to breathe. Since teachers are human, it would seem to follow that a competency for the teacher is the ability to breathe. But it is odd to include this as a competency for teachers. The problem here stems from the fact that teachers can in general be described under many different headings: human beings, parents, hard workers, lazy people, leaders, followers, etc. One needs, I think, to be clear about what the required skills are for.

There are other skills about which it is more difficult to determine the end for which they are required. Some might want to include the ability to work with other people as a competency for teachers because teachers do belong to staffs, and it may be that the education of children is helped when teachers communicate and cooperate in the planning of programs. But it may be that the ability to work with others is required for adequate functioning in social groups, that is, that it is a competency for being a member of society. The ability to work with others may not be, then, a competency for teaching *per se* but a competency for people living and working in social groups which of course includes teachers.

The final step is the judgment of the skills of a particular person. Once one has judged what the general goals of teaching should be and what skills are required to meet those goals, one must ask whether a particular person has those skills. If so, he will be judged as a competent teacher. This is probably the most straight-forward part of the general competency judgment.

To this point I have focused on the general logic of competency claims. What I have said is, I hope, applicable to any use of the concept of competency. But in the field of education the concept of competency has been introduced in certain contexts. I now want to consider some of the overtones or connotations the concept has from its particular uses in edcucational contexts. The concept of competency arose in discussions of teacher education in conjunction with the rise of something called performance-based teacher education. This all arose out of discussions of accountability in education which is itself an offshoot of behavioral objectives.[1] So, competency is used in discussions of education that arise out of the behaviorist ideology. (I use "ideology" to suggest that I am talking about a particular view of man, rather than the methodological principles of behaviorist psychology.) Under the behaviorist ideology, a person is what his environment shapes him to be. A person brings nothing to the learning situation except a capacity for being changed.[2] This view of man has a long, and honorable, history. Perhaps its clearest exponent was Locke who introduced the metaphor of the mind as a *tabula rasa*, a blank tablet. Experience, and only experience, makes marks on this tablet and determines what a person will be.

The competency concept fits into this picture in the following way. By identifying the competencies of a teacher, or whatever, in behavioral terms, one is providing the basis for training a person to work satisfactorily in a given field. It makes no matter what the person to be trained brings to the situation. The assumption is that the person is completely malleable. Anyone, if given the appropriate training, can be made into a competent teacher. And because the skills are put in behavioral terms one can tell by the simple observation of another person whether he is a competent teacher. It must be noted that these points assume a connection between behaviorism and competency which I have suggested is a contingent relation. As can easily be seen from my earlier discussion, there is nothing in the concept of competency that logically assumes the behaviorist ideology. But it remains true, I believe, that in educational contexts proponents of competency-based programs for teachers belong to the behaviorist school of thought and critics of competency-based programs are generally critics of behaviorism and are often labeled humanists.

Another overtone of the use of competency concept in education would seem to be a conservative, *status quo* view. By giving at the outset a characterization of the skills required for satisfactory teaching, and then using that list of skills as the basis for preparing teachers, one is training teachers in a set mold. Since the definition of a competent teacher is done prior to the training and since the definition of a competent teacher is probably based to some extent on the then current practices in schools, the mold or object of training is likely to reflect the way things were well before training. And this makes the use of the concept of competency one which is likely to maintain the *status quo*.

The role definition given to students of teaching under competency-based programs is cut-and-dried and one determined prior to training. Since the role definition is not vague or questionable by the student, the student is not likely to think of the role definition as fluid or changing. Hence competency-based programs are likely to maintain the *status quo*. This is of course not to evaluate the program. There is nothing desirable or undesirable in maintaining the *status quo*. It would all depend on what the *status quo* is. My point here is simply to point out an apparent assumption behind the use of this concept in educational contexts.

One final point remains that I wish to discuss. Earlier in discussing the concept of competency I claimed that a person who is competent at something knows how to do something at more than a minimal level. My final point stems from the sort of knowledge implicit in this claim. This sort of knowledge can be labeled "skill knowledge." Skill knowledge can be divided into two general classes. On one side we have those skills that a person can perform routinely without reflection. Examples would be knowing how to tie one's shoes, knowing how to open a jar of pickles, knowing how to determine if one's car needs oil, and knowing how to thread a sixteen-millimeter projector. On the other side we have those skills whose performance requires insight, understanding, and intelligence. Examples here would be knowing how to conduct survey research, knowing how to solve historical problems, knowing how to implement a curriculum so that the developer's intentions are preserved, and knowing how to teach. For the sake of convenience I shall call the former sort of knowledge "habitual skill knowledge" and the latter sort "intelligent skill knowledge."

One theme running behind the behaviorist ideology is that intelligent skill knowledge can be reduced without loss of meaning to habitual skill knowledge. That is to say, for any particular intelligent skill knowledge, such as knowing how to construct a curriculum or how to teach, there is a set of habitual skill knowledges—the specific competencies expressed in behavioral terms—such that the set of habitual skill knowledge is equivalent to the original intelligent skill knowledge. Or, in other words, for any general skill there is a set of specific behaviors which captures entirely the meaning of the general skill. I want to suggest that this view is false. I shall do this by suggesting that there is not a unique set of habitual skills that comprise the intelligent skill. When we say that a person is a competent teacher we are saying many things about him. But the exact range of things we are saying is left undetermined. That is, of such a person we would say that he understands the subject being taught, he displays organizational attributes and enthusiasm, he understands how to sequence materials in view of the child's psychological development, etc., etc. That is, we want to leave open the exact range of things that he can do well, because teaching itself is such a broad activity that one cannot specify in advance all that the teacher will be called upon to do. But we expect him, as a competent teacher, to do a satisfactory job of whatever, related to teaching, he is called upon to do. Hence we cannot provide a set of habitual skills that is equivalent to the intelligent skill, because we cannot tell in advance everything which can possibly fall under the intelligent skill.

Let me close with a few sketchy comments about professionalism. I apologize for bringing up again this hoary subject, but I have come to think that the mark of a professional is his ability to do intelligent skills well. That is, he can teach, heal, design, whatever, with intelligence, good sense, understanding, or considered opinion. The distinguishing characteristic of the professional is that he does what he does intelligently, not routinely. It seems to me that to accept competency-based programs and the concomitant behaviorist ideology is to see teaching as a routine, non-professional activity. And this seems to me to be wrong. Teaching is nothing if not a set of activities that require understanding, clear thinking, and good sense.

FOOTNOTES

[1] N. L. Gage & P. H. Winne, Performance-based teacher education. In Kevin Ryan (Ed.), *Teacher Education*, Seventy-fourth Yearbook of the National Society for the Study of Education, Part II. Chicago: University of Chicago Press, 1975, pp. 146-172.

[2] J. Langer, *Theories of Development*. New York: Holt, Rinehart & Winston, 1969.

4

The history of teacher competence—or more rightly, the history of the quest for the competent teacher—is the subject of this paper by Henry C. Johnson, Jr. The competency movement, both in its recent social and educational context and in its remoter, more unfamiliar forms, is reviewed and interpreted critically in light of a definition of the educational problem it was intended to address. Johnson points out that the problem was defined as a technical one rather than as a normative one, as it truly was and is.

With wry humor, born of the advantage of historical perspective, he traces the history of where that tangent took us in our educational thinking and practice. He first covers the post-World War II era, documenting the ups and downs of the competency movement in order to demonstrate the pervasiveness of the doctrines that gave rise to and perpetuated it. Then, he turns to the literature between 1894 and 1950 to illustrate similar efforts in earlier times. An enormous number of studies are cited, which dealt with attempts at defining and measuring teacher competence.

Analysis of the issues this research raised is followed by interpretive, historical analysis, in which Johnson links the technical solutions extant in business and industry with the needs in education to bring human factors under rational control, under one interpretation of the new Darwinian thought. Johnson ends by reminding us that answers, now as before, tend to resemble the questions and methods of inquiry we employ to obtain them. The problem put in managerial terms—how to distinguish the competent teacher from the incompetent one—was answered in terms of actions and productivity rather than in terms of factors inherent in teaching and the educative situation where determinate actions and standard conditions are less relevant to competence than in enterprises seeking efficiency and control. Embedded in this tracing of historical antecedents of the competency movement are many clues to the selection of more fitting alternative approaches to meeting the cry for competence.

Professor Johnson is Professor of Educational Theory and Policy in the College of Education, The Pennsylvania State University.

Teacher Competence: An Historical Analysis

The Quest for the "Competent" Teacher: An Historical Exploration of the Managerial Matrix and the Bahaviorist Connection

Henry C. Johnson, Jr.
The Pennsylvania State University

"I am a great believer in the sanctions and sanctities of history."
John Dewey

When Dewey uttered these words as he opened an address to the Parents Association of his laboratory school at the University of Chicago on Thursday, January 28, 1904, a Spectre was already beginning to haunt American school people: the myth that some particular technique had been (or at least could be) found to guarantee the success of virtually every teacher. His address raised the question: "What light does history throw on the significance of the School of Education?"[1] He answered it by an examination in general historical terms of the social and cultural developments that he believed had to be kept continuously in view if educational theory and practice were to be soundly guided. That this theme was no mere rhetorical convenience is evident from the fact that his own curriculum for preparing practitioners included a massive component of the history of educational thought and practice in their cultural and social context.[2] It was so constructed because Dewey's aim for neophyte practitioners was the development of intelligence in relation to practice as a pattern of action, not the inculcation of a doctrine, let alone a particular technique.

In the ivory-tower world of our day-to-day school practice, the myth still persists that some such technique is at least in principle available and, provided we only stop fooling around and pay attention to the managers and researchers, will be found. The latest term for this all-powerful technique is "competence." But this concept is hardly new. And, if the history of "competence" is a long and on the whole an unsuccessful one—and I shall strongly urge that it is—it seems to me that we ought to pause in our continuing pursuit of it and ask whether there are not more radical difficulties associated with the quest itself than just the "state of the art" or the recalcitrance of local professionals.

To this end I will review the immediate historical context of the competency movement. I will then take the movement backward to what I take to be its primary source, examining not only its varying content but its crucial fundamental logic. Finally, I will attempt to set out the issues it continues to raise—issues which drive to the very heart not only of professional preparation and practice but of the whole educational enterprise.

From Positive Thinking to Pedagogical Pessimism

Cast your mind back to the later 1940s and the early 1950s. For the second time in less than thirty years we had just concluded a war which made the world safe once again, if not for democracy at least for international industrial capitalism. Under the unpretentious leadership of Harry Truman (except for a brief but bloody excursus in Korea) we turned our attention to manufacturing the good life. ("Better things for better living, through chemistry," the DuPont people told us. And we believed them.) Those who witnessed those days will recall the enormous energy that was unlashed, and the mood of hopefulness that was unstopped, as hundreds of thousands of men and women poured out of foxholes and "war plants" into factories and classrooms, out of barracks and walk-ups into tract-housing and suburbs, out of tanks and "6 x 6s" into Chrysler convertibles and unutilitarian "personal cars."

With the advent of Mr. Eisenhower, the sense of progress reached its apogee. Dwight was in the White House and all *was* right with the world. There were, of course, many ways in which the long years of war had changed and otherwise influenced us, but there is one in particular to which I wish to draw attention: World War II had been unquestionably the most complete and brutal war in history—and the most "mechanized," as we were fond of putting it. It had been won, as had every war since our Civil War, by "industrial might." But, because we had been caught unprepared, we had first to get organized; and organize we did. North Africa, and Anzio, and Iwo Jima, and "D-Day." Aircraft plants and aluminum works and shipyards. And, above all, "*The* Bomb." What were these? Miracles of organization; miracles of management. In comparison, all previous attempts at engineering performance were as crude as horse-cars.

Now, of course, all was *not* right with the world, even the momentarily comfortable world of the United States. By the Fifties, disturbing spots began to appear on our socio-economic x-rays. Even Mr. Eisenhower, whose theme had been "let it grow, let it grow, let it grow," had reason to pause and warn of a new "military-industrial complex" as he accepted a gracious retirement (complete with farm and Angus herd) from a grateful people. The cities were beginning not to work. Mr. Galbraith and Mr. Whyte and Mr. Mills saw a variety of rather substantial goblins in the night.[3] The relation between our private lives and the public interest became an issue again. And there was racism and a cruelly intransigent poverty in the midst of plenty. The list grew; it need not be catalogued. And, as had been customary for at least a hundred years, the nation looked to its schools, now larger, more elaborate, more pervasive, and very much more costly than ever before in history. We had, it appeared, fallen asleep, only to be rudely awakened by Sputnik and the Supreme Court's prohibition of prayer and white supremacy.

Suddenly, we saw a very differnt picture indeed. Critics now became very fashionable, displacing even Norman Vincent Peale as the apothesis of the American spirit, particularly in respect of our schools. Mr. Conant sallied forth from arcadian Cambridge to look, first hand, at cities and at schools and their teachers.[4] Mr. Bestor proved to our satisfaction that our teachers had lost their minds—if, indeed, they had ever had any—and he and Mr. Koerner demonstrated that the teacher educators had done it.[5] And then there was Silberman, and...well, again, one need not go on with what is mere multiplication of details.[6] Where decades before we had fretted about "laggards" and "truants," we now anguished over "drop-outs" and "gangs" and vandalism. We lengthened the period of compulsory attendance and demanded that teachers and administrators keep order and teach them anyway. Our schools were "blackboard jungles," but the talk on the patio and at the PTA was of achieving a "zero failure rate" and making "every kid a winner."

When the illogic of these demands proved incommunicable, the teachers moved more decisively than ever before to protect themselves by unions *nee* professional associations. Their moves brought to completion a process of balkanization in the enterprise that had begun decades before in the pursuit of professional autonomy and specialization, enhanced by an overpowering thrust toward the division of labor. Education and schooling, which had ended the last century in an already strained and tenuous unity, by the sixties and seventies had become thoroughly polarized and politicized: Well organized school boards, administrators, teacher educators, researchers and other specialists, were now universally wary of each other and protective of themselves. And, by now, a powerful segment of state and federal bureaucrats, and an incredibly more unified and powerfully organized "edubiz," were ready to provide "bold new programs" and hardware and software on demand.

But there were further complexities, and we must not get ahead of the story. The sixties were crucial. Mr. Kennedy was elected because he promised to get us going again, and Mr. Johnson saw to it that the machine got a quantum leap in energy, capped by the most dazzling of all displays of the power of technology and efficacious management: we sat in our living rooms and watched ourselves walk on the moon. The answer to our school problems also appeared to be massive, carefully channeled, federal intervention. The logic of rational social engineering was extended to every problem—health, employment, social and personal services, housing. The school was included and everywhere built into the scheme. The whole thrust was perhaps the last uncritical vote of confidence in social engineering we shall see, particularly in the use of schooling as the omnicompetent and universal medium not only for deliberate social policy but for every personal difficulty as well. Ostensibly—though it had been naive to believe it—the revolutionary aid was to be mostly technical: just a few goods and services, a bit of advice and some benign guidelines. Policy was still to be a local and/or professional prerogative. Assuredly, the revolution was merely managerial. It was the American way.

Even as the salvific programs were being mounted, however, in the context of an ever deepening conflict over an unpopular Asian war and an ever more threatening world, there were other revolutions and a whole new genre of critics. The new romantics proved we were abusing our children in schools—indeed, if we were over twenty-five we were abusing them just by being around! The folk squirmed while reading Holt and Kohl and Kozol (and a dozen others) in still cheap paperbacks and Sunday supplements. (We brought their books into our college classrooms to prove we were "with it," and one of the teachers' unions in Pennsylvania bought large bill-boards to advertise that "to teach" was "to love.") We wanted local control and autonomy and massive federal "initiatives" with appropriate directions attached. We wanted more hard stuff in the schools *and* more freedom in classes. We wanted less "oppressive" buildings and classroom management *and* a guaranteed realization of the right to be able to read, write, count, get a job, be healthy, and emptied of our "hang-ups." (It was what Daniel Bell called the "revolution of rising entitlements," juxtaposed with the open classroom and doing one's own, very, very personal thing.[7]) A society, and hence a school, was good if, and only if, it met every individual's expectations, *when* they were expected. And all this without those most horrible of punishments: irrelevance and boredom. That is to say, we wanted it the way they did it on "Ding-dong School," "Sesame Street," and "The Electric Company."

Now, of course, we didn't do it. The problem is, we school people said we would. By the late sixties and into the seventies, the romantic critics were answered by the romantic educational utopias. Who can forget those Robinson Crusoes and Thoreaus, those Buck Rogers and Star Treks of the pedagogical world? They were, as my analogues suggest, of two forms, the romantic retreats to simplicity and the equally romantic advance to super-technology.[8] Neither worked then; neither is working now. But that is not important; what is important is, first, the radical novelty of the criticism of the sixties and the seventies and second, *how* we thought the schools could be made to work to accomplish *all* these things.

What is Good for General Motors is Good for the School

Although we were loath to notice it, the really radical criticism of the previous decade and a half was both novel and frightening—which may explain our reluctance to notice it. Horace Mann told us that schools would save us, and when the problems increased, Joseph Mayer Rice told us only *better* schools would save us—by which he meant, of course, more efficient schools.[9] What Illich (and others, in varying degrees, including now many of the folk themselves) have been telling us is that schools and schooling may not only be no solution but perhaps even the problem![10] Or, at least, any *system* of schools. The motives and reasons alleged for coming to such a conclusion are mixed, of course, but who can hear such a thing? Think of what it would entail!

It can come as no surpise, then, that just as both the programs and the protests were reaching their crescendo, in 1970 or there-abouts, school people suddenly found the answer. It is not surprising that the answer resembled the definition of the problem. The problem, we would discover, was technical and managerial—a definition that had the unexaggeratable advantage of being cast in the categories most familiar and most acceptable to Americans; categories (let me suggest) that countered hopelessness and assuaged guilt; categories that required us only to change our ways, not our selves.

A look at the then current literature in and about schooling is instructive. But, first, some qualifications are necessary. My concern with the technical (here and later) is not focused on teaching machines or computers. Its purpose is to point to the "technical" as a way of looking at things and doing them—a strategy quite as legitimate, say the advocates of this technical revolution themselves, as seeing it in merely mechanical terms. Similarly, my concern with the "managerial" will be not simply with organizational charts but with the definition of resources and the specification of results, because it is here that our present problem begins. Finally, I have surveyed this literature as cited by its own advocates as bearing upon the competency movement.[11] I lay it out as providing their own sense of the movement's "history," not merely mine.

The context to be kept in mind, as I have said, is on the one hand the enormous expansion of the education "industry" following the war and the simultaneously mounting and increasingly radical criticisms of the schools on the other. By the late Fifties *Fortune* was challenging the "Low Productivity of the 'Educational Industry'."[12] By the Sixties, educational leaders were talking in the same terms: Gardner and Howe were asking, "What Are Americans Receiving in Return for Their Heavy Investment in Education?"[13] The "heavy investment" was pre-eminently in the NDEA and ESEA appropriations, which had finally been steered through Congress by Edith Green.[14] As it entered its most dramatic expansion in history, the business world had been placing a heavy emphasis on highly sophisticated planning and monitoring, on what they were calling "executive accountability," and on "scientific" personnel management with a heavy dose of psychological control thrown in. The models and the metaphors, and the resultant management techniques, were everywhere eagerly and consciously accepted. Those in peculiarly vulnerable positions, at the intersection of publically financed expansion and rising criticism—e.g., school boards and administrators—were particularly receptive.[15]

As we traverse the sixties, the controversy deepens. There is, as has been suggested, an enormous criticism of the schools—witness the virtually numberless books and articles by and about the critics. B.F. Skinner is, from the technical side, a paramount example: he explains "Why Teachers Fail."[16] Among the most popular gadflies is Hyman Rickover, a literate admiral celebrated for managing a complicated job![17] There is much talk of going to a "free market," of treating parents and students as consumers and seeing the schools' responsibility as the provision of a commodity or service.[18] It is a familiar and attractive notion, perhaps because it evades the conflict between centralized efficiency and local control, and perhaps because it casts the educand in an entirely passive role: The student should be free to purchase any services that do for her precisely what is wanted. From their side, school board members, administrators, and the dramatically expanding army of bureaucrats, specialists, and managers, are casting about for something to resolve what the *Saturday Review* now calls "the Crisis of Confidence."[19] By the end of the decade, the "revolution" is beginning. The term (that is to say, the managerial technique) is "auditing" at first. But, very quickly a rather less abrasive term is found: "accountability," at first in its most dramatic form—performance contracting.

The effect is electric, and indisputably measurable. In 1969 there are a handful of articles dealing with accountabiltiy and specifically with performance contracting—then being put into effect most notably in Texarkana and Gary.[20] In 1970, some seventy articles appear focusing on accountability, nearly twenty describing and advocating performance contracting.[21] *School Management* had proclaimed, in 1969, "Educational Auditing: Here to Stay."[22] By the next year, the *American School Board Journal* recorded the comforting fact that "Two out of Three Boardmen Buy Performance Contracting."[23]

It would be tedious (and unnecessary) to examine this literature in minute detail, though I recommend you do so when you have time. (Pay particular attention to the organs in which it is published, because they represent the particular concerns and interests involved.) One or two themes, however, must be given more substantial grounding. The "accountability octopus" (as the *Times* of London called it) had some bafflingly complex tentacles.[24] Education and schooling involved a tangled mass of intertwined and overlapping federal programs; a vast array of new state agencies and programs; a host of new quasi-public, quasi-private programs and centers for "R and D," often closely tied to industry; a confusing web of "funds" and "foundations." These were frequently extra-professional and usually extra-campus. The new specialist was the grantsman; the life blood was money; the heart was Washington. If you had dropped a bomb on Washington's Dupont Circle on any given day, half the "leaders" of American education from the preschool to the post-doctoral level would have been removed at a stroke. The project was direct influence on Congress to keep the blood flowing; the goal was a single, unified federal cabinet post (which could be controlled by one of the contending parties). The problem was how to keep track of it all.

Even an octopus must have a central nervous system. In the new commercial-industrial organism that means a management system. And a nervous system must have clear, logical pathways and processes. It must also have discrete, irreducible message units. For the system, "auditing" was too vague a notion, "performance contracting" so absurd and unworkable as to be quickly forgotten. "Accountability" struck just the right systemic note. In 1969, Leon Lessinger asked in the *Nation's Schools* "After Texarkana, What?" and answered his own question a year later in *Phi Delta Kappa*: "Engineering Accountability for Results in Public Education." Thereafter he frequently explained what it meant, often in the pages of *The Nation's Business*.[25] Roger A. Kaufman, writing in *Educational Technology*, helped put it all together: "Accountability, a System Approach and the Quantitative Improvement of Education—An Attempted Integration."[26] The message unit? *Competencies.* Most of the full-scale treatments of CBTE, by its advocates, indulge in little historical reflection. But almost all—indeed, I know of no exceptions—point to something called "federally-funded initiatives" of the mid- and late sixties as the day of creation. Most precisely, they refer to the ten "model" elementary teacher-education projects sponsored by the USOE in 1968, with frequent reference to the Teacher Corps and the TTT projects as well. All included a planning and monitoring system largely borrowed from the government-industry projects of then recent years. All focused on competencies.

Houston and Howsam, perhaps the supreme pontifs of the revolutionary movement, make all this unequivocally clear in what is the primary source for understanding these matters, their (1972) *Competency Based Teacher Education: Progress, Problems, and Prospects.*[27] The "real thrust" of the movement, say the authors, had been "generated" in the USOE. By then seventeen states had already made some sort of commitment.[28] Why? In times of change, the authors insist, education must change; but not in the old fashion, now "in systemic terms." Of the five formative elements that have combined to produce this promising phenomenon, the key is: "The application to education of new technologies and management systems." In fact, say Houston and Howsam, accountability, as applied to all aspects of the instructional program, simply means competency based instruction "coupled with an appropriate management and delivery system."[29]

Further on in these scriptures, Richard Burns informs us that "the *production* of competent teachers can be approached as a management problem, using many of the techniques developed for industrial management."[30] William Smith likewise credits the USOE (under Sidney

P. Marland) as aiming at better management by using the equivalent of competency evaluation.[31] (There is a pervasive sense of destiny and difficulty. The chapter on "Implementation" has at its head a quotation from Machiavelli on the difficulty of bringing about change!)

Hall and Jones, in another important work, *Competency-based [teacher] Education: A Process for the Improvement of Education*, echo a similar view: Why is the movement so sweeping?[32] A teacher surplus looms; there is a demand for accountability; taxation is approaching the breaking point, as failing bond issues showed. The house must be gotten in order, it must be rationalized. "Responsibility is Relevant," the PTA had said.[33] How? Systems theory, born, say Hall and Jones, out of the "aero-space industry."[34] They quote Stanley Elam's widely disseminated manifesto for the AACTE on the crucial role of "the emergence of private industry as a force influencing school decisions, and development of new concepts of management." We did it before and we can do it again, so to speak—this time with the schools. And all this possible, thanks to a sort of Leibnizian pre-established harmony revealed in "the conincidental timing of research and development efforts related to instruction and learning."[35]

The state and federal folk, with generous (and generously sponsored) advice from the new industry-based specialists, met together lengthily and frequently.[36] The *Journal of Secondary Education* noted the conjunction: "Accountability and the Emerging Leadership Role of State Education Agencies."[37] Mostly they met to establish the message unit. The process and its logic were, it was widely asserted, already inevitable. (One either climbs on, or is crushed by, a Juggernut.) The secondary education people hastened to learn about "Planning for Accountability via Management by Objectives."[38] *Educational Technology* explained about "Specifying Objectives for Performance Contracts."[39] As might be expected, the Rand Corporation got a piece of this action, issuing a lengthy report, with only a brief word of criticism in the appendix.[40] Perhaps most revealing of all, *College and Univeristy Business* insisted that "Accountability Method Makes Failure the Teacher's Fault."[41] The logic is clear. The decisive issue is management; and we can now specify and measure in precise technical terms just what is to be expected. With such a lever, what world cannot be moved, what educational goal cannot be accomplished?

The crucial element in the system, as I have suggested, was the unit. For this the conventional *global* notion of competence was refined to *a* competence, a non-collective, non-abstract noun, plural: "competencies."Competence, said Houston and Howsam, was "ordinarily defined as 'adequacy for a *task*' or as 'possession of required knowledge, skills, and abilities'." But even that sort of generalized notion has been all too vague and suspiciously intellectualist, they believe, and a new term is required: Competency must come to mean ' "the ability to do,' *in contrast to* the more traditional emphasis on the 'ability to demonstrate knowledge'." "Competency-based" is the newly coined term that is to stand for unit-and-system. They tell us that it is a "word of recent origin."[42]

The particular term "competency-based" may have been of recent origin, but the enterprise was not. The previous two decades (the Fifties and Sixties) had been busily laying the groundwork. The thrust toward developing applied, behaviorally specified, descriptions of human activity in a variety of fields and contexts was already there for educators to carry forward. The prestigious American Educational Research Association had mounted a large scale research project and issued its "Report of the Committee on the Criteria of Teacher Effectiveness" in 1952, followed by a second report in 1953.[43] Chroniclers of the CBTE movements often cite E.L. Thorndike's *Personnel Selection* and R. R. Sear's article on "A Theoretical Framework for Personality and Social Behavior" as furnishing an earlier impetus.[44] A. S. Barr and the "Wisconsin" group and H. H. Remmers and his students and colleagues at Purdue had authored an enormous number of articles and experimental studies.[45] (We shall examine Barr's important conclusions later on.) There were also W. Rabinowitz and R. M. Travers, "Problems of Defining and Assessing Teacher Effectiveness," and a number of major reviews of prior thought and work—e.g., D. D. Castetter (*et al.*)"Teacher Effectiveness: An Annotated Bibliographly."[46]

Amongst the most widely circulated and cited work was that of D. G. Ryans, especially his "Teacher Behavior Theory and Research: Implications for Teacher Education."[47] And, virtually in a class by itself, and demonstrating the close tie between government and education there was J. E. Morsh and E. W. Wilder's enormously influential *Identifying the Effective Instructor: A Review of the Quantitative Studies, 1900-1952*, published by the Air Force Personnel and Training Research Center in 1954.[48] In fact, by 1968 the Bureau of Research of the USOE had already issued H. D. Schalock's *A Competency Based Approach* and the pieces were "in place," as they are fond of saying.[49] And the pieces included the new machines—from Skinner's first crude teaching machines to the sophisticated CAI devices—the technology in the mechanical sense which Houston and Howsam would soon proclaim as absolutely necessary for *freeing* the student *from* the teacher! We were ready, then, for the lyrical celebrations of the "new education" coming to be.

The Pursuit of Productivity

Before examining the remote history of this post-war revolution, a few reflections will help to tie the two periods together and suggest what is to come. Our seeing the problems of education and schooling exclusively in managerial and technical terms was not, of course, necessary. It was merely a plausible outcome of restricting our thinking to such terms for some time previously. The question, I repeat, which now for the first time appeared settled, was the unit by means of which efficiency *could* be guaged.The notion that efficiency *should* be guaged had already been argued for some eighty years. And it had always been defined as an essentially managerial-technical problem, as we shall see. But, was this unit some mental attribute of the student or the teacher? Was it a personality trait or charcteristic, or some more professionally defined pedagogical method? All these approaches (and others) had their day. The answer, "generated" most transparently in the 50s and 60s and "implemented" in the 70s, was to reject these alternatives. The unit would be a "productive" classroom "teaching behavior." It would be isolated by absolute and specific determination of the ends to be achieved; it would be defined, made possible, and warranted by "research." Details might (and, of course, did) differ, but the logic would be the logic of behaviorism—whether in the hard, soft, or middle-of-the-road eclectic sense made little real difference. That is to say, it would be defined by the concepts and research paradigms that had on the whole governed education and schooling ever since Edward Lee Thorndike forsook William James to consort with the likes of Cattell and Boas and Galton.[50] The triumph of this (usually) mild-mannered behaviorism was in fact celebrated in the 1941 edition of the *Encyclopedia of Educational Research*, which offered only a slim article on the subject of behaviorism on the grounds that it was now so widely accepted that nothing more was needed.[51] And it was this behaviorism that would make a narrow, *atomistic* task possible and the new mechanical technology appropriate, just as the managerial imperative would guarantee that the "revolution" was to be centered in an atomistic *task* analysis.

I will approach this more remote history first through the professional literature. There are over a thousand "major discussions" of "competence" between 1894 and 1950. Entry to that enormous body of literature may be had through a considerable number of "reviews" pulled together from time to time throughout the period.[52] The first thing that strikes one is an interesting quantitative pattern. T. M. Balliet's "What Can Be Done to Increase the Efficiency of Teachers in Active Service?" (1894) was perhaps the first "modern" response—that is to say, an analysis from the perspective of productivity rather than a traditional definition of the "ideal teacher" in largely philosophical terms.[53] There are a handful of discussions over the next ten years. They are, however, the work of what were then called "premier superintendents," and the issue to be debated is clear already: Aaron Gove insisted in 1895 that no "test" is possible, since teaching is an art and not the product of an "artisan."[54] And, when H. E. Kratz, in 1896, asks 2411 pupils to characterize the best teacher, he is crudely initiating what was to be a major thrust for several decades.[55]

By 1905, the National Society for the Study of Education is ready to devote its fourth yearbook to the question of teaching competence.[56] The same problem ushers in the new and influential Teachers College

"Contributions to Education" series with a volume on *Normal School Education and Efficiency in Teaching* by Junius Meriam, including an attempt to correlate student grades and the performance of 805 elementary teachers rated by their principals.[57] The National Education Association also begins to pay attention, inaugurating another long-lived controversy: merit systems and their connection with promotion and salary—the long standing inadequacy of the teachers' wages having at last become a crucial professional issue.[58]

The quantity of literature begins rapidly to increase, as the following rough table shows:

1894-1900:	6
1901-1905:	4
1906-1910:	11
1911-1915:	41
1916-1920:	58
1921-1925:	69
1926-1930:	202
1931-1935:	192
1936-1940:	143
1941-1945:	132
1946-1949:	139

From 1910 onward, a number of leading figures in the movement are identifiable: E. C. Elliott publishes his "Outline of a Tentative Scheme for the Measurement of Teaching" and explains its use in the NSSE Yearbook on *The Supervision of City Schools* (1913).[59] His "How Shall the Merit of Teachers be Tested and Recorded" also found a place in the first issue of the newly born journal, *Edcuational Administration and Supervision*.[60] Another important figure is A. C. Boyce. Boyce, like Ellott, pays a great deal of attention to city schools. He also offers what he takes to be evidence that "results" and "techniques" are the teacher's most important qualities, his or her academic and professional preparaton being the least associated with general merit.[61] "Rating cards" begin to be a standard feature of the teacher's life. But, there are a few critics: Bruce Smith insists that "industrial standards" are inappropriate, since the teacher is more than a "craftsman."[62]

The U. S. Bureau of Education begins to disseminate information on the matter in 1913.[63] David Snedden, writing in *Educational Review*, insists that before efficiency can be achieved we must define in more precise terms our educational objectives.[64] Soon the examination of teacher *failure* attracts major interest and by 1914 the measurement of student achievement begins to be offered as the ultimate criterion. In a 1915 study, 4856 teachers are examined through reports by 116 supervisors, and the 270 "failures" are singled out for special analysis.[65] Some protest and call for an end to the practice of rating, but the answer, says Elliott to the administrators, is more, and especially more fundamental, research.[66] A continuing "efficiency record" for teachers is proposed and A. D. Yocum writes for his *School and Society* readers on the interesting theme of "Compelling of Efficiency through Teacher Training."[67]

In the next ten years, especially during the Twenties, there is an increasing emphasis on technique and sophistication of measurement. L. J. Brueckner introduces "time activity analysis" and "job analysis," and students are being measured by "Achievement Quotients."[68] By 1925, the NEA "Committee on Teacher Rating" can report that 75% of all cities over 25,000 had a systematic rating program—though the report also points out that there just aren't enough data on the relative importance of the particular factors leading to teacher "success."[69] Finally, perhaps the high point of quantitative research was reached with the publication of the *Commonwealth Teacher-Training Study* in 1929 by W. W. Charters and Douglas Waples (University of Chicago Press). Working from some 235,000 "activity statements" submitted by teachers, Charters and Waples distilled 1001 teacher activities, in seven categories, for checking by administrators. They also found 83 "basic" traits, which could be observed through 798 "trait actions," and reduced further to some 25 on a "Master-List of Teachers' Traits." Amongst these traits and actions were "conventionality" (item: "does not comb hair in an odd way") and "personal advancement" (item: "investing in securities").

At this point, we shall shift our viewpoint and look at the movement for teaching efficiency through the career of A. S. Barr. No figure better represents the main stream of effort. Barr began as a methodological protege of E. L. Thorndike, and devoted himself with Thorndikean energy and single-mindedness to the solution of the problem of measuring teacher performance. He began as an advocate of rating procedures, analyzing them for evidence on the nature and role of specific teaching techniques and teacher "behavior patterns." His early research culminated in a 1931 study of 209 available scales, which produced 6939 separate items![70] In 1935 Barr surveyed the entire field again in "The Measurement of Teaching Ability" and did an intensive study of the relationships between four particular criteria of "teaching success."[71] The correlations between these four criteria and 19 "predictor variables" ranged from zero to .35, he reported to the AERA. Understandably, such ambiguous results led him to call for a "more functional test measuring the teachers in action"—something he thought "sound recording" could help provide. But in 1939 he still had to confess that there was little agreement among "workers in the field" about the qualities that led to success, their definition, or the amount needed.[72] The answer, in the best tradition of techno-science, was not to examine the whole quest but to mount yet another continuing 10-year study of 2500 pupils in the social studies under 260 teachers in the rural schools of Wisconsin. Still, in 1940, he could only report that interest was flagging. He appealed editorially for rededication to research on pupil change, direct evaluation, and the measurement of ever more specific qualities.[73]

Eight years later, reviewing matters again, Barr looked at 153 studies, comparing them with the results of his own 1931 study. Though insisting that we must learn how to predict teacher success, because it is crucial for management decisions and shaping the "training program," Barr could again report only very disappointing results. "The product sought," he said, "is not too well defined in most instances." More information is needed about how "traits, competencies, and behaviors control function to make a good teacher."[74]

Now, if that is a curious result for nearly sixty years of effort, it is clearly not because we had not tried. If we look at Domas and Tiedeman's 1006 "discussions," covering the entire period, some further interesting themes emerge: The attempt had been made to link the competence of in-service teachers to students performance in some seventy cases; to administrative judgment 88 times, to pupil judgment 45 times, to lay person's judgments twice. It was thought to be assessable by testing procedures 23 times. Attempts to define a good teacher had been based on judgments of professional faculty twice, lay persons 3 times, fellow teachers 22 times, administrators or bureau personnel 29 times, and to judgments of pupils 41 times. Actual lists of acceptable characteristics of practicing teachers had been furnished by supervisory personnel in 63 cases; the teachers themselves provided lists of characteristics in only 27 cases.

The nature and purpose of this vast literature and the efforts it manifests falls readily into certain categories. (1) To a very large extent it is discussion by and for administrators and it is usually published in their journals. (2) The principal issue is what we shall take as the object of our attention: Shall we look at pupil change? Teacher traits or behaviors (personal or professional)? Successes or failures? What, in short, *is* "teaching" anyway?[75] (3) Whom shall we ask? Administrators? Teachers themselves? Students? The nadir of naive empiricism was perhaps reached when, in 1947, the NEA *Journal* summarized the contents of some 12,000 letters solicited from school children—from grades 2 to 12—on "the teacher who has helped me most."[76] (Or, was it when the AERA asked the Quiz Kids to tell them what had made them so successful?)[77] (4) There is a continuing and crucial dispute, based on contradictory bodies of evidence, over the relationship of the teacher's general and professional knowledge and "intelligence" to the teacher's professional success. (5) There is a clearly discernable movement from a general notion of competence to a highly particular one. This movement is also clearly parallel both to tendencies toward the division of labor in business and industry and to the increasingly narrow scope of "educational" research.

Measurement Scales and Ability Atoms

Providing an historical analysis of this professional movement and its unmistakable characteristics does not seem difficult. The discernable flurry of activity at the turn of the century, out of which grew the logic governing the quest for competence over the intervening years, was the consequence of a complex historical phenomenon. The period following the Civil War had been marked by dramatic changes in the life of the American people, with enormous implications for schooling. Industrialization was proceeding at a furious pace, producing on the one hand a seemingly endless supply of palpable "miracles" and on the other hand engendering social, economic, and political problems of a scale and seriousness never before encountered, including a revolution in "work" of incalculable significance. Urbanization was becoming a difficulty in its own right—cities, it turned out, were not towns and villages writ large—and the closely allied phenomenon of immigration, on a scale never before encountered in recorded history, posed novel problems.

By the late Eighties onward, disorder and conflict (involving class, region, and increasingly race and ethnic heritage) had reached such proportions that many doubted the "noble experiment" could survive. The reformist temper, never wholly absent from the American scene, became demonstrably more effective, manifesting itself in institutional reform. Reform of government and an unprecedented increase in its scope and role and a similar expansion of the role and scope of schooling, likewise coupled with reform, were movements of crucial importance. Moreover, in respect of schooling, the criticism and reform were of a new sort. The paradigmatic new critic-reformer was Joseph Mayer Rice. Rice's criticisms, which aroused the populace and angered the profession, began to be issued in 1893.[78] Rice is very clear: Schooling is still the answer, but we are not (as in the past) simply to enlarge the enterprise. We are to test it empirically. Henceforth our strategy will be grounded in what gets results and the judgment about results will not be rendered by woolly-minded philosophers or self-interested school personnel but by businessmen. Good schooling, he makes abundantly clear in everything he writes, is a problem in scientific management, first and foremost.

The demands of the social and educational situation were genuine and inescapable, as a few salient statistics will suggest. In 1870, there were about 7,500,000 pupils at the elementary level, and 80,000 in high school. By 1900, 15,000,000 and 519,000. By 1910, almost 17 million and 915,000 respectively. The teaching force had stood at about 200,000 in 1870; by 1900 it reached 423,000. From 1870 to 1890, immigrants numbered some over 8,000,000. From 1890-1910, more than 12,000,000. (There were 1,285,349 in the year 1907 alone.) By 1909, 67.5% of all students in Chicago schools, and 71.5% of those in New York City were either foreign born or the children of immigrants.[79]

Changes in scale and scope, and problems within the "profession" itself, lent plausibility to the rapidly rising demand for a new concept of education and schooling. Illinois educator John Williston Cook, who had witnessed the decades of change, laid the facts before the NEA Convention in 1914. Education and schooling had become a big business, he noted. Last year the public schools (alone) had enrolled more than eight million students and employed some 550,000 teachers. They had an aggregate budget of a half-billion dollars, and a plant worth three times that amount. However, only half the school population (5-18) was enrolled and a quarter of the students were absent every day. The "average" child, in fact, attended only ninety days a year.[80]

And what about the profession? A "generous estimate," as he put it, of the professional life of a teacher was six years. What that meant in practical terms was that more than 80,000 *new* teachers were needed (including meeting the demands of expansion we have already noted) every year at the elementary level alone. Since the normal school system could furnish only 20,000 each year, some 60,000 completely untrained teachers were beginning work each year. Another 60,000 hadonly one year's experience and still another 60,000 had only two. Thus, something like a third of the "force" or "corps" was either completely unprepared or had had no more than two years on-the-job experience. The answer, according to Cook? Teaching has been an art, but it must become a science.

Science of what sort? And who was to be the scientist? Surely not the ill-trained, under-paid, and incrediby transient, rank and file of the "profession"—nothwithstanding some twenty years of idle rhetoric urging Miss Jones and Mr. Smith to view their classrooms as laboratories. The pivotal figure in all this was the administrator (the superintendent, the principal, and the new "supervisor"), the hero and the goat in the constant round of success stories and exposes which mark the schools especially from the Nineties onward. The administrator was changing rapidly, and separating himself (or herself) from the teaching force in more than an organizational sense. Gone was the dusty mentor and counsellor, the master teacher, making his humble rounds of the district and neighborhood schools. Like the board or committee to which he was primarily responsible, and as befit a new multi-billion dollar enterprise, he was a leader and a manager of a commercial-industrial sort.

The model chosen was fraught with significance for the future of the schools—a future which includes us—and a manifestation of the ambivalence of the moment. As I have suggested, messianic industrialism was simultaneously the source of many of the problems which were tearing the country apart and also the source of the dazzling wonders that filled the pages of the books and periodicals and transformed the day-to-day lives of ordinary folk—railways, bridges, canals, ships, autos, flying machines, devices for communication. Similarly, the captain of industry was simultaneously the rapacious capitalist entrepreneur *and* the fearless leader who got things done. Pre-eminently, the entrepreneur was the nexus between knowledge and action, science and success. In his image, and quite outspokenly, the school administrator became the executive scientist, the scientific executive. He (or she) *could* be a professional; in fact, *the* professional; the teacher would be the worker—just a bit more than a carpenter, remarked E. L. Thorndike.[81] The manager determines ends, directs efforts, mediates standardized procedures (the gift of the promising new techno-scientific enterprise), and evaluates performance—the last in terms not analogous to, but *precisely the same as*, those used in any other production process.

Ordering confusion, inefficiency, chaos means managing it. Managing it means asking managerial questions, those questions which are naturally derived from one's function and responsibility. Thus, it is not surprising that our brief glimpse at the hundreds and hundreds of proposals and studies demonstrates that the operative question is three-fold: how do I, as an administrator, select and reward (or eliminate) fit (v. unfit) instruments? Important, but in a significant sense subsidiary, are two second order problems: how does the profession train and improve the worker? My point must be clear: although there is interest in training and improvement, training and improvement are not abstract questions in a disinterested context; they are to be thought and developed in terms which are ultimately managerial. Hence they will necessarily rest on standardized managerial techniques capable of objective measurement.[82]

There was a brief hiatus between the first articulations of this managerial revolution—e.g., those of Rice— and its full scale implementation. The problem was the state of the art—or, perhaps better, the state of the "science." It was one thing to standardize the manufacture and application of steel or locomotives or talking machines, quite another to convert an educational enterprise that at least pretended to be moral, personal, and holistic into a bureaucratized and routinized production process. In a classic case, the solitary shoemaker of the 1880s had been disintegrated into some sixty-five factory-located task, from binders, blockers, boot-liners, and beaters-out to taggers and tip-makers, turners, and vampers.[83] That process had taken a fairly extensive period of time. All things considered, the schools responded with remarkable rapidity to accomplish similar ends. In teaching, we kept, at least as the central figure, the solitary worker; the worker's task, however, was itself atomized, standardized and made neatly linear in a curious resemblance to the soon-to-be-born assembly line.

Such a radical transformation could hardly be the work of one person, and it was not, One figure, however, so embodied the revolution that we may read its lessons from him. That figure was Edward Lee Thorndike. Thorndike was not, of course, the sole contributor to the movement we have been examining nor was his doctrine the only one available. There were many others—e.g., Pillsbury, Starch, Watson, Hall, Terman. Their doctrines differed in details, but their logic was essentially similar, stemming from figures such as Galton and Boas and articulated with both rigor and persuasiveness by Karl Pearson.[84] Nonetheless, Thorndike had mastered the principles of scientific social reform, traced them to what he thought their evolutionary roots, and translated them into a practical regimen for the schools just as the criticisms reached their crescendo. For fifty years, in countless classes and lectureships and through the medium of nearly five hundred published works (including seventy-eight books), Thorndike served as midwife to the new techno-pedagogy.

Thorndike had a clear sense of purpose and an incredible consistency of focus in his thought and research. The principal element was the reform of man and his institutions through the agency of science, and particularly by a science of education, which he now thought finally possible. Education he defined as the deliberate "production" of human change, even "the possible development of a super-man from an infra-animal."[85] Thanks to Darwin, we had discovered what Thorndike liked to call man's "original bodily nature" and the laws which governed both its structure and , in psychology, its behavior and change. Of the psychologists, however, Thorndike preferred the new sort who were, he pointed out, more frequently "first trained in physics or engineering." Since, "in the long run, the only cure for national ills and the only foundation for progress is science, sure and verifiable knowledge, directing a good will toward men," the crucial activity is the quantitative analysis of psychological data, not speculations about any "human nature" spouted by philosophers or philosophical pschologists.[86]

For Thorndike, the task, then, is to bring human beings under control, and that control is precisely the kind of "rational" control characteristic of Messianic Industrialism in the midst of which he and other educators dwelt.[87] The new science of the classroom can, so to speak, offer exact guidance for practice in education, just as physics can determine directly what constitutes good procedure in engineering, because we have discovered the true nature of the learning *process* and hence the principle of manipulation and control of any being that learns, from the invertabrates through the primates. This learning is the consequence of an associative mechanism and is definable in terms of stimulus and response. The laws governing this process, are the Law of Effect and the Law of Exercise. According to the Law of Effect, any response that satisfies the organism will become connected with the situation and repeated in similar situations. According to the Law of Exercise (later the Law of Readiness), the more frequently a response occurs the more strongly it will be connected. The so-called higher human faculties, upon which educators have wasted their efforts for some twenty-five hundred years, are nothing but extensions of these primitive characteristics.[88]

Because the new science, as Thorndike understands it, provides us with access to the tightly woven causal web of "Nature," and because we now have its laws in respect of behavior change (i.e., learning), we can fashion whatever "human" product we like. Education and schooling can thus become directly *productive* processes. Correspondingly, "the first law of behavior, one fraction of the general law of the uniformity of nature, is that with life and mind, as with mass and motion, the same cause will produce the same effect—*that the same situation will, in the same animal, produce the same response*." Given the educator's goal as "the production and prevention of changes in human beings," however, we must measure them. We must find the requisite "component ability atoms" and construct a scale with a zero point and rigorously defined intervals. There is in principle no limit to what can be accomplished by this method, until we reach "a perfect and complete knowledge of human nature."[89] Such knowledge will

> tell the effect of every possible stimulus and the cause of every possible response in every possible human being. A teacher could then know just what the result of any act of his would be, could prophecy just what the effect of such and such a page read, or punishment given, or dress worn, would be—just how to get any particular response, or attention to this object, memory of this fact, or comprehension of that principle.[90]

Darwin's discoveries provided the justification for the whole Thorndikean apparatus. They had shown that human behavior is "as natural as the behavior of an atom of hydrogen."[91] And the upshot of Darwin's work was that we could no longer "suffer the caprice of persons to be considered a cause of mental events, of human psychology, of the history of men and nations." We arrive here at the crucial juncture, I believe, the origin of the dream that made the quest possible. Darwin had brought about perhaps the most sweeping change in anthropological viewpoint in history. Contrary to much conventional wisdom, Darwin's thought and "evolution" were eagerly and quickly accepted, especially by educators. But the meaning and potential effect of Darwin's thought were neither clear nor simple—even to him. The consequence was, it is fair to say, as many Darwinisms as there were Darwinists. But it is possible to make a rough division of importance for our purposes. On the one hand, there were those who realized that Darwin had posed new questions, the meaning of which (let alone the answers to which) would require a long period of patient thought. I number here people such as Peirce and James and Baldwin and Dewey, to name only those most germane to our subject. On the other hand, there were those for whom Darwin had answered once and for all a long-standing question: How can we account for the actions of human beings in the same way we account for the behavior of any other "natural"—and that is to say *physical*—phenomenon? Such people even hailed Darwin as the "Second Newton." What they did was to assimilate the very difficult and problematic ideas of Darwin, ideas having much to say about a logic of *bios*, to the much more comfortable logic of mechanism of the classical Newtonian sort. What Darwin had done, they thought, was to bring man under the old logic of Nature as machine. He had not (so far as they appeared to notice at any rate) brought to light another, quite different, one which at least potentially might demand the re-examination of all logics, including that of Newton as well as that of Aristotle. It was to this second party,I believe it is easy to demonstrate, that Thorndike and most of his professional education colleagues belonged. It was also the position of most other "scientific" reformers, in an age of triumphant reform, for it offered a ready basis for the social engineering and an accompanying techno-pedagogy that was demanded by the times and conditions, both in society in general and in the schools in particular.[92]

Education and the Problem of the Two Balloons

I will close with what must be a very brief restatement of the problem presented to us by the ideas and developments we have been studying. It is, I believe, the chief educational problem that has been ours since the turn of the century and still is ours today, differing only verbally from the form in which it was posed at least seventy-five years ago. Returning to the inspiration from which I began my remarks, the analysis will be developed in "Deweyan" terms, so to speak.

If you want to know what an idea, a theory, or a concept means, inquire about the real or intended action from which it takes its rise and to which it points. Actions—at least if they are human actions—are impenetrable apart from consideration of the actor. If you want to understand the actor, look carefully at the social and cultural context which both prompts and qualifies the action. To say this is simply to say, with William James, that thought is a "teleogical instrument," indissolubly linked to our human strivings and purposings. It is also the case that answers resemble the questions which generate them and the methods of inquiry employed to resolve them. Hence, to understand the "competency" movement historically is to ask who had to act, in what circumstances, and (most of all) for what purposes. Thus, to understand the answers the movement has left us is to examine the questions out of which it arose, the means selected to conclude them, and the career they have subsequently enjoyed.

It is, I believe, abundantly clear that the three closely related questions that gave rise to the "competency"answer were: (1) How do I select and hire better teachers than I presently have? (2) How do I reward those who produce what I want? and (3) How do I "eliminate" those who do not? The actor, the agent in this case, was the administrator, who was the sole "professional" of the time, and the person then (as now) possessing both a duty and an authority in the premises. It was also assumed (then, as it is now) that any answer to these questions would have "implications" for both the preparation and the continued professional development of teachers. What was not noticed, I think, was that the primary questions—primary in the sense of being linked to the primary action and intent of the agent—would so restrict the potential range of answers that any answer chosen would be ill-fitted to bring about progress in resolving the secondary question at issue. The secondary question was how to improve the educational process. Although primary for us, the question was secondary for the administrator at the time. The first question was good management, from which good education would ostensibly follow. It was, in short, a classic and pernicious means-ends dualism of the sort Dewey so trenchently criticized.

The "competency" answer, I have argued, arose out of the concurrence of a number of factors, the chief being a particular notion of technically oriented science and a particular brand of Darwinism which had fallen victim to an illicit assimilation to the mechanicalism it in fact contradicted. The competency answer was selected, furthermore, in a crudely behaviorist form—that is to say, in an atomistic, reductivist, linear-causal form—not because definition in terms of such a psychology was truer but because in that form it satisfied almost effortlessly the demands of the situation and the agent. Subsequently, both the notion of competence and its psychological definition were refined in a variey of ways. Softer, less pretentious forms of behaviorism were utilized on occasion. Other psychological doctrines have also been tried. But the logic of the problem and its solution has remained essentially the same. It is a managerial logic and assuch it has precluded the very educational development it was presumed to guarantee. It has coerced us, for example, into paying attention almost exclusively to something called "learning theory" and "method," usually in highly individualistic—if not, indeed, anti-social—terms. We have been preoccupied, to put it another way, with the production of "learning" to the virtually total neglect of educational theory.

The question is not whether the practical management of the enterprise of schooling is somehow too crass and mundane for the educator to think about. The question is whether the educator (either theorist or practitioner) can ask and answer *educational* questions while captive to exclusively managerial intents in his or her schoolkeeping—however necesssary they may be on occasion. The appropriate task is to find a mode of "management" which flows from our educational goals rather than to adapt to our uses techniques which corrupt or destroy them.

The second and final difficulty I want to raise is really an extension and illustration of the first in more particular terms. I take it that education is about persons, and that the education of teachers assumes the education of teachers as persons. The theories, concepts, and methods for looking at teaching we have developed as a consequence of the practical logic and form of our questions have too often been—to use an old-fashioned term—"physicalist." They essentially deal with persons as objects, indeed as substances. Objects, substances, have no "insides"—or at least none that come into view through our theories. Their differences are only numerical and contextual. We expect one atom of hydrogen to resemble another, to differ only in number and location. We anticipate that hydrochloric acid will "act" in a determinate fashion. Indeed, to be hydrochloric acid *is* to act in a determinate fashion. (If a substance acts differently it is not an unusual example of that substance, it is not that substance at all.) But we do not anticipate that Jones or Smith will act in a determinate fashion. We do not wish them to do so, because the *human* action we are trying to bring about is interactive in a much more profound sense than we are permitted to envision when we look at merely physical interaction. Furthermore, suppose, if you will, that we have tested a "teaching substance," (a "teaching instrument,"if you prefer) and have observed it to have demonstrated the activity, the competence, we desire. What will our observation prove? That something *has* occurred, not that it *will* occur in the future. Even in the physicalist view, it will continue to occur if and only if standard conditons continue to prevail. If we are thinking and talking in human social terms, we not only do not expect but do not want standard conditions to prevail. If we are thinking and talking in educational terms, the notion of standard conditions and determinate actions are equally—no, even more outrageously—foreign.

Dewey draws, in *Human Nature and Conduct*, a vital distinction between "narrow" and "broad" intelligence.[93] Narrow intelligence focuses on particular considerations and conditions in order better to accomplish a *given* intent. Broad intelligence seeks to enlarge considerations to form better intents. "Competency" thinking is a supreme example of narrow intelligence, and its career (and present mischief) amply demonstrates its inadequacy for educational thinking and acting. What it comes down to is that it is simply incapable of serving as a method for thinking about persons and it is incapable of thinking *life*. (Forgive that last, unruly—seemingly sloppy—word. The categories in which education must be thought are never as neat as we would like them to be. That has always been the problem.)

I said that the whole techno-managerial psychology was vigorously resisted. One example of that resistance was Hugo Munsterberg, who set out the problem for all to see in an 1898 article in *Educational Review*.[94] The laboratory psychologist must, for his peculiar purposes, "decompose" things, Munsterberg insisted. But that is precisely what the teacher must not do. The "atomizing attitude" of the researcher has its uses, of course, but it is "directly antagonistic to the attitude of the true practical life, and thus opposite to the natural instincts of the teacher toward his pupils." Although such a "naturalistic decomposition" may be necessitated in strict psychological inquiry (or so Munsterberg thought), the difficulty is that "the purposes of life and friendship and love and *education* are others." If, he says, you offer to the teacher, as the object of his or her activity, a child, whose singular, concrete emotion is "composed of circulatory and muscular elements" or whose particular will is "made up from muscle and joint and slim sensations," you are doing something akin to offering a thirsty man "one balloon filled with hydrogen and one filled with oxygen instead of a good swallow of water." "The chemist," Munsterberg points out, "is quite right: that *is* water; the fainting man insists that it is not, and life [and, I would suggest, education] speaks always the language of the thirsty."

FOOTNOTES

[1] John Dewey, "The Significance of the School of Education," *The Elementary School Teacher*, 2(1904), 441. George Herbert Meade was the President of the Association.

[2] John Dewey, *Lectures on the Philosophy of Education*, edited by Reginald D. Archambault (New York, 1966). See esp. pp. 354-360.

[3] John Kenneth Galbraith, *The Affluent Society* (Boston, 1958); William H. Whyte, Jr., *The Organization Man* (New York, 1956); C. Wright Mills, *The Power Elite* (New York, 1956) and *The Causes of World War III* (New York,1958). It could be argued, of course, that this chapter in fundamental social criticism had already begun with Gunnar Myrdal's *An American Dilemma: The Negro Problem and Modern Democracy* (New York, 1942).

[4] James B. Conant, *THe American High School Today* (New York, 1959) and *The Education of American Teachers* (New York, 1964). The literature of both the critics and those who propose solutions respecting teachers and teaching is almost overwhelming. In this brief essay, I can only cite representative and useful works. Many important references have to be omitted and such omissions are not meant to suggest that any particular contribution is unimportant.

[5] Arthur Bestor, *Educational Wastelands* (Urbana, IL, 1953) and *The Restoration of Learning* (New York, 1955); James D. Koerner, *The Miseducation of American Teachers* (Baltimore, 1964) and *Who Controls American Education?* (Boston, 1968). See also the various publications of the Council for Basic Education.

[6] Charles E. Silberman, *Crisis in the Classroom* (New York, 1970). For an important scholarly analysis of this whole issue, see Merle L. Borrowman, *The Liberal and the Technical in Teacher Educaton* (New York, 1956) and *Teacher Education in American* (New York, 1965).

[7] Daniel Bell, "The Revolution of Rising Entitlements," *Fortune*, 91(April, 1975), 98-103, 182, 185.

[8] I have in mind the movement for small-scale, alternative schools on the one hand and the movement toward "high-tech" super schools on the other. An interesting example of the inherent romanticism of the "high-tech" approach can be seen in George Leonard, *Education and Ecstacy* (New York, 1968), which was also given popular circulation in *Look*. The movement was also heavily psychological, subjective, and individualistic—the sort of thing criticized so trenchantly by Philip Rieff and explored by David Riesman. The roots lay, as some candidly admitted, in Rousseau. It is, I believe, a curious fact that the really substantial critics, such as Edgar Z. Friedenberg—*Coming of Age in America* (New York,1963) and *The Vanishing Adolescent* (Boston, 1959)—and Paul Goodman—*Growing Up Absurd* (New York, 1960) and *Compulsory Miseducation* (New York, 1964)—were given less attention than they deserved.

[9] Joseph Mayer Rice, *Scientific Management in Education* (New York, 1912). Rice will receive more adequate treatment later in this essay.

[10] Ivan Illich, *Deschooling Society* (New York, 1970). The literature of the new radical revisionist critique is also vast, but the important work of Clarence

Karier, Michael Katz, Martin Carnoy, and Joel Spring will provide rapid access to it.

[11] Among the several bibliographies and reviews of research that most clearly show the genealogy of the competency movement, one of the most useful is Leon M. Lessinger and Ralph W. Tyler, eds., *Accountability in Education* (Worthington, OH, 1971), pp. 80-85. I have given considerable weight to their judgment as to the work that provided primary influence. See also Henry C. Johnson, Jr., "Not One 'Unnecessary Wriggle:' Some Questions about the Presuppositions of C/PBTE," *Educational Theory*, 25(1975), 156-167.

[12] Daniel Seligman, "The Low Productivity of the 'Educational Industry'," *Fortune*, 48(October, 1958), 135-138, 195-196. Seligman asks, "What should 4.76 billion buy?" Pointing out that per-pupil expenditures have risen from $184.07 in 1929 to $423.55 in 1956, he insists that both productivity and quality must rise with expenditures and the key is "*scientific managers*" (italics are Seligman's).

[13] James Gardner and Harold Howe, "What Are Americans Receiving in Return for their Heavy Investment in Education?" *American Education*, 2(1966), 24-26.

[14] Naomi Ross, "Congresswoman Edith Green on Federal Aid to Schools and Colleges." Unpublished Ph.D. Thesis, The Pennsylvanis State University, 1980. Ms. Green insisted on much tighter accountability as essential to increased federal aid.

[15] Note that much of the literature on accountability and associated matters is found in journals for administrators and schoolboards or is frequently addressed to the business-minded public.

[16] B. F. Skinner, "Why Teachers Fail," *Saturday Review*, 48(October 16, 1965), 80.

[17] Hyman G. Rickover, *American Education: A National Failure* (New York, 1963), and *Education and Freedom* (New York, 1959).

[18] See, for example, Russell Kirk, "Free Choice: A Voucher Plan: Giving All Students the Choice of Attending Either a Public or a Private School," *National Review*, 21(1969), 598; Christopher Jencks, "Education Vouchers," *New Republic*, 163(1970), 19-21. There is, of course, a large literature on the voucher plan in particular, an idea popular partly because it promises to unlock the private-public, church-state dilemma. The important theme for our purposes, however, is the "consumer" approach.

[19] J. Cass, "Crisis of Confidence and Beyond," *Saturday Review*, September 19, 1970, pp. 61-62.

[20] My figures are drawn from articles listed in *Education Index* for 1969. Leon Lessinger's own writings were numerous and influential. A new journal quickly arose to keep up with developments in the performance contracting movement, *Education Turnkey News* (Washington, DC). Useful additional sources are John W. Adams and Karen H. Kitchak, *A Guide to Performance Contracting* (Madison, WI: The Wisconsin Department of Public Instruction,1971) and Leslie H. Browder, Jr., ed., *Emerging Patterns of Administrative Accountability* (Berkeley, CA, 1971). Teachers were to be specially prepared for the new movement by, e.g., Dwight W. Allen and Eli Seifman, eds., *The Teachers Handbook* (Glenview, IL, 1971).

[21] See *Education Index* for 1970.

[22] Jerome Bahr, "Educational Auditing: Here to Stay," *School Management*, 3(1969), 53-54.

[23] "Two Out of Three Boardmen Buy Performance Contracting," *American School Board Journal*, 158(1970), 35-36.
[24] K. Bevans, "Accountability Octupus Gains New Territory," *The Times Educational Supplement* (London), May 11, 1970.
[25] Leon Lessinger, "After Texarkana, What?" *Nations Schools*, 84(1969), 37-40; "Engineering Accountability for Results in Public Education," *Phi Delta Kappan*, 52(1970), 217-225.
[26] *Educational Technology*, 2(1971), 21-26.
[27] W. Robert Houston and Robert B. Howsam, eds., *Competency-Based Teacher Education: Progress, Problems, and Prospects* (Chicago, 1972).
[28] Ibid., p. viii.
[29] Ibid., pp. 1-3.
[30] Ibid., p. 19 (italics added).
[31] Ibid., p. 177.
[32] Gene E. Hall and Howard L. Jones, *Competency Based Education: A Process for the Improvement of Education* (Englewood Cliffs, NJ, 1976), p. 2.
[33] D. Harris, "Responsibility is Relevant," *PTA Magazine*, 64(1970), 24-26.
[34] Hall and Jones, *op. cit.*, p. 5.
[35] Ibid., p. 5. See Stanley Elam, *Performance-Based Teacher Education: What is the State of the Art?* (Washington, DC: AACTE, 1971).
[36] For example, *Education Change through State Leadership* [papers from three meetings for ESEA Title III personnel of state departments of education] (Albany, NY: The New York State Department of Education, 1970).
[37] Harry L. Phillips,"Accountability and the Emerging Leadership Role of State Education Agencies," *Journal of Secondary Education*, 45(1970), 377-380. James E. Allen, "Education and the Renaissance of State Government," *School and Society*, 97(1979), 148-151.
[38] John D. Kennedy, "Planning for Accountability via Management by Objectives,"*Journal of Secondary Education*, 45(1970), 348-354.
[39] H. M. Harmes, "Specifying Objectives for Performance Contracts." *Educational Technology*, 2(1971), 52-56.
[40] J. P. Stucker and G. R. Hall, "The Performance Contracting Concept in Education," *Rand Memoranda* #699.1 and #699.2 (critique), May, 1971.
[41] "Accountability Method Makes Failure the Teacher's Fault," *College and University Business*, 49(1970), 45.
[42] Houston and Howsam, *op. cit.*, p. 3 (italics supplied).
[43] H. H. Remmers [Chairman], *et al.*, "Report of the Committee on the Criteria of Teacher Effectiveness," *Review of Educational Research*, 22(1952), 238-253. H. H. Remmers [Chairman], *et al.*, "Second Report of the Committee on Criteria of Teacher Effectiveness," *Journal of Educational Research*, 46(1953), 641-658. The committee included A. S. Barr, N. L. Gage, C. R. Pace, and D. G. Ryans.
[44] E. L. Thorndike, *Personnel Selection* (New York, 1949). R. R. Sears, "A Theoretical Framework for Personality and Social Behavior," *American Psychologist*, 6(1951), 476-483.
[45] I have already cited some of Remmer's work, *vide supra*, footnote 43. To get some idea of the scope and quantity of work by both Remmers and Barr, and many other contributors prior to 1950, the indispensible aid is S. J. Domas and D. V. Tiedeman, "Teacher Competence: An Annotated Bibliography," *Journal of Experimental Education*, 19(1950), 101-218. Domas and Tiedeman show 27

major works by A. S. Barr. Remmers has fewer, but both, through their students as well as their own work, were enormously influential.

[46] William Rabinowitz and R. M. Travers, "Problems of Defining and Assessing Teacher Effectiveness," *Educational Theory*, 3(1950), 212-219; D. D. Castetter, *et al.*, "Teacher Effectiveness: An Annotated Bibliography," (Bulletin of the Institute of Educational Research I, No. 1; Bloomington, IN: Indiana University School of Education, 1954).

[47] D. G. Ryans, "Teacher Behavior Theory and Research: Implications for Teacher Education," *Journal of Teacher Education*, 14(1963), 274-293. See also Ryans' earlier "Theory of Development and the Study of Teacher Behavior," *Journal of Educational Psychology*, 47(1956), 462-475.

[48] J. E. Morsh and E. W. Wilder, *Identifying the Effective Instructor: A Review of the Quantitative Studies 1900-1952* (San Antonio, TX: Air Force Training Research Center, 1954) and also J. E. Morsh, *Systemic Observation of Instructor Behavior*. USAF Personnel Training Research Center Development Report No. AFPTRC-TN-65-52 (1956).

[49] H. O. Shalock, *A Compentency-Based Approach* (Washington, DC: Bureau of Educational Research, USOE, Bulletin FS5.258:58020, 1968). A new and useful tool for examining the competency movement in its modern form is Marjorie Powell and Joseph W. Beard, *Teacher Effectiveness—An Annotated Bibliography and Guide* (New York, 1983). Their work covers 3041 citations from 1965-1980. Even the Rorschachs of teachers, and other personality tests, were examined as providing a possible basis for identifying the competent. See, for example, Percival M. Symonds and Stephanie Dudek, "Use of the Rorschach in the Diagnosis of Teacher Effectiveness," *Journal of Projective Techniques*, 20(1956), 227-234, and John C. Gowan and May S. Gowan, "Teacher Prognosis Scale for the MMPI," *Journal of Educational Research*, 49(1955), 1-12.

[50] E. L. Thorndike, autobiography in Carl Murchison, ed., *A History of Psychology in Autobiography* (Vol. III; Worcester, MA, 1936), pp. 263, 270. See also his "Darwin's Contribution to Psychology" in *University of California Chronicle*, 12(1910), 65-80, and his *Introduction to the Theory of Mental and Social Measurements* (New York,1904), which brings out very plainly his debt to Galton and Pearson through Boas. The crucial relation between Thorndike and this particular notion of science (largely fashioned by Pearson) will be more fully explored further on.

[51] W. S. Monroe, ed., *Encyclopedia of Educational Research* (New York, 1941), s.v. "Behaviorism."

[52] As previously noted, for the period prior to 1950, Domas and Tiedeman (see note 45) is the most useful source. But see also A. S. Barr's review of 209 rating scales (comprising 6,939 items!) in his *An Introduction to the Scientific Study of Classroom Supervision* (New York, 1931), pp. 295-365 and his later examination of 153 schemes in "The Measurement and Prediction of Teaching Efficiency: A Summary of Investigations" in *Journal of Experimental Education*, 16(1948), 203-283.

[53] T. M. Balliet, "What Can Be Done to Increase the Efficiency of Teachers in Active Service," *Addresses and Proceedings of the National Education Association* (Washington, DC, 1894), pp. 377-332. Henceforth, this invaluable series for studying educational thought and practice will be briefly titled by initials and year of the *Proceedings*—e.g., NEA, 1894. (Titles vary slightly, as do place of publication.)

[54] W. C. Warfield and Aaron Gove, "How to Test the Quality of a Teacher's

Work, with Discussion," NEA, 1895, pp. 218-231. Warfield saw character formation in the child as the best indicator of teacher effectivenss, not mere academic proficiency.

[55] H. E. Kratz, "Characteristics of the Best Teacher as Recognized by Children," *Pedagogical Seminary*, 3(1896), 413-418.

[56] *Education and Training of Secondary Teachers* (Fourth Yearbook of the National Society for the Study of Education, Part I; Bloomington, Illinois, 1905). This important series will be identified with NSSE and year of issue.

[57] Junius L. Meriam, *Normal School Education and Efficiency in Teaching* (New York, 1905).

[58] "Merit System of Appointing and Promoting Teachers: Symposium," NEA, 1905, pp. 241-253.

[59] E. C. Elliott, *Outline of a Tentative Scheme for the Measurement of Teaching Efficiency* (Madison, Wisconsin, 1910) and "A Tentative Scale for Measuring Teacher Efficiency," *The Supervision of City Schools* (NSSE, 1913, Part I.)

[60] Edward C. Elliott, "How Shall the Merit of Teachers be Tested and Recorded?" *Educational Administration and Supervision*, 1(1915), 291-299.

[61] A. C. Boyce, "Methods of Measuring Teachers' Efficiency," NSSE, 1915, Part II. Boyce analyzed the replies of 242 large-city superintendents as to methods of evaluation in use and also examined the ratings of 424 teachers by 39 supervisors on the "Boyce Teaching Efficiency Record." "Qualities of Merit in Secondary Teachers," *Journal of Educational Psychology*, 3(1912), 144-157. See also A. C. Boyce, "A Method for Guiding and Controlling the Judging of Teaching Efficiency," *School Review Monographs* (No. 6; Chicago, 1915), pp. 71-82.

[62] Ben Blewett and Bruce Smith, "Tests of Teaching Efficiency," *Educational Review*, 45(1913), 99-102. See also Ben Blewett, "How to Measure the Efficiency of Teachers." NEA, 1913, pp. 290-292.

[63] *Promotion of Teachers on Qualifications and Efficiency* (Bulletin No. 31, U.S. Bureau of Education, Washington, DC, 1913, pp. 31-33.

[64] David Snedden, "Tests of Teaching Efficiency," *Educational Review*, 45(1913), 515-517.

[65] Sherman Littler, "Causes of Failure Among Elementary Teachers," *School and Home Education*, 33(1914), 255-256. Henry Buellsesfield, "Causes of Failure Among Teachers," *Educational Administration and Supervision*, 1(1915), 439-452. On achievement, see P. Klapper, "Efficiency in Class Instruction—Its Causes and Test," *Educational Review*, 48(1914), 498-513.

[66] A. L. Parrott, "Abolishing the Rating of Teachers," NEA, 1915, pp. 1168-1173. Edward C. Elliott, "How Shall the Efficiency of Teachers be Tested and Recorded?" NEA, 1915, pp. 469-473.

[67] For the "efficiency record" see C. C. Green, "Promotion of Teachers on the Basis of Merit and Efficiency," *School and Society*, 1(1915), 705-709. A. D. Yocum, "Compelling of Efficiency Through Teacher Training," *School and Society*, 1(1915), 469-477.

[68] L. J. Brueckner, "The Value of a Time Analysis of Classroom Activity as a Supervisory Technique," *Elementary School Journal*, 25(1925), 518-521; and "Diagnostic Analysis of Classroom Procedures," *Elementary School Journal*, 27(1926), 25-40.

[69] Anna M. Thompson, "Report of the Committee on Teacher Rating," NEA, 1925, pp. 375-377. See also pp. 200-215. The 103 rating plans actually in use were

examined. It is worth noting that the term "success" is now common.

[70] A. S. Barr, *An Introduction to the Scientific Study of Classroom Supervision* (New York, 1931), pp. 295-365. Barr began his major publications in 1924 and produced some 37 major works individually and with students and colleagues.

[71] A. S. Barr, "The Measurement of Teaching Abiltiy," *Journal of Educational Research*, 28(1935), 561-569. For his recommendation see "Measurement of Teaching Ability: Excerpts," *The Application of Research Findings to Current Educational Practices* (Washington, DC, 1935), pp. 173-176.

[72] A. S. Barr, "Systematic Study of Learning and Teaching Efficiency," *Journal of Educational Research*, 32(1939), 641-648.

[73] A. S. Barr, "Measurement of Teaching Ability," *Review of Educational Research*, 10(1940), 182-184, 267-268; "Some Problems in the Measurement of Teaching Ability," *Journal of Educational Research*, 33(1940), 363-365.

[74] A. S. Barr, "The Measurement and Prediction of Teaching Efficiency: A Summary of Investigations," *Journal of Experimental Education*, 16(1948), 203-283. The quotation is at p. 225, in the midst of Barr's telling observations. He cautions, it is important to note, against facile correlations and suggests that this practice may account for the tendency of research to indicate that "intelligence is not a factor in teaching success" (p.225). Indeed, he says, statistical procedures designed for "physical phenomena" simply "may not apply in many important respects to human behavior." Yet, Barr still thinks "the overall picture and future for the measurement and prediction of teaching efficiency and its prerequisities seems promising" (Ibid.) Barr also provided other continuing reviews of the state of the art in a series, "The Measurement of Teaching Efficiency," in the *Review of Educational Research* in 1940, 1943, 1946, 1949, and 1955.

[75] The problem, in my opinion, is that the definition of teaching cannot be reduced to crudely empirical terms, but this runs counter to the cannons of investigation that have exercised the controlling influence since the turn of the century. For an extended discussion of this question and an alternative view, see Henry C. Johnson, Jr., Dent Rhodes, and Robert E. Rumery, "The Assessment of Teaching in Higher Education: A Critical Retrospect and a Proposal," *Higher Education* (Great Britain), 4(1975), 173-199, 273-303.

[76] Paul A. Witty, "Analysis of the Personality Traits of the Effective Teacher," *Journal of Educational Research*, 90(1947), 662-671; "Teacher Who Has Helped Me Most: Summary Ratings by Children All Over the Nation," *NEA Journal*, 36(1947), 386.

[77] Paul A. Witty, "Evaluation of Studies of the Effective Teacher," *Improving Educational Research* (Washington,DC, 1948), pp. 198-204. (Here Witty also analyzes 13,000 pupil letters describing the *poor* teacher.) Still useful to explore this issue and the general questions it raises is Bruce J. Biddle and William J. Ellena, eds., *Contemporary Researchon Teacher Effectiveness* (New York, 1964). See esp. the essays by Bruce Biddle and Hazel Davis.

[78] J. M. Rice conducted the first extensive empirical investigations of pupil performance beginning in the early 1890s. His results were published in *The Forum* magazine and in two books: *The Public School System of the United States* (New York, 1893) and *Scientific Management in Education* (New York, 1912). For his impact on the educational scene, see Leonard P. Ayers, "History and Present Status of Eduational Measurement," NSSE, 1918, Part II, p. 11. It is to events and figures such as these that we owe the adoption of the questionable

logic of deducing teacher effectiveness directly from student performance, a research paradigm that surfaces periodically despite its theoretical untenability. It is also worth noting that Rice's demands for efficiency coincided with the nation's worst depression to date, and that parallel between the economy and school efficiency continues.

[79] On immigration, see Mark Krug, *The Meeting of the Ethnics: Education of the Immigrants, 1880-1914* (Bloomington, Indiana, 1975), *passim*. E. G. Hartmann, *The Movement to Americanize the Immigrant* (New York, 1948) is the best source. Statistics on school growth may be found in *Historical Statistics of the United States from Colonial Times to 1957* (Washington, DC: U. S. Department of Commerce, 1960).

[80] John W. Cook, "Professionally Prepared Teachers," NEA, 1914, pp. 113-115. Cook likens teachers to factory workers and their apprenticeship.

[81] E. L. Thorndike, *The Principles of Teaching* (New York, 1906), p. 2. "Production" analogies and figures of speech are constant in Thorndike. An important source for understanding Thorndike is, of course, Geraldine Joncich, *The Sane Positivist: A Biography of Edward Lee Thorndike* (Middletown, CT, 1968).

[82] John W. Cook put the matter succinctly: "How can the Superintendent Improve the Efficiency of the Teachers Under His Charge?" NEA, 1900, pp. 276-287. Dewey strongly criticized this shift toward "autocractic" administration and pointed out its serious implications for the quality of teachers in "Democracy in Education," *Elementary School Journal*, 4(1903), 193-204. It is interesting to note that the literature of teaching evaluation contains virtually no reference to Dewey whatsoever.

[83] William Miller, *A New History of the United States* (New York, 1958), p. 273.

[84] *Vida supra*, note 50. One principal aim of the new logic was to make it possible to reduce educational questions to mathematical problems. As Pearson explained: "The distinction between the physical and the biological sciences is really only quantitative." See *The Grammar of Science* (3rd edition, New York, 1957), p. xii. If we carefully classify, observe, correlated, and sequence our "facts," the "resulting *absolute*" will be real knowledge, "as opposed to the individual judgment" or mere "bias" (p. 28, italic supplied). This pattern will wipe out our false distinction between various kinds of knowledge (which arise because "imagination" supplants "reason" in ordinary life) and rigorously unify the real truth about the world. Pearson (1857-1936), scholar and fellow of King's College, Cambridge, was appointed Professor of Applied Mathematics and Mechanics at London in 1884 and in 1911 became the first "Galton Professor of National Eugenics."

[85] E. L. Thorndike, *Animal Intelligence* (New York, 1911), p. 274 (italics supplied).

[86] Thorndike uses the phrase "original bodily nature" (or some variant of it) very frequently, but see *Animal Learning*, p. 251, *The Original Nature of Man* (Vol. I of *Educational Psychology*, New York, 1913), *passim*, and his latest views (largely unchanged) in Chapter 1, "The Original Nature of Man: The Genes of the Mind," in *Man and His Works* (Cambridge, MA, 1943). For the quotation on "progress," see "The Contribution of Darwin to Psychology" in *University of California Chronicle*, 12(1909), 80. For Thorndike's antipathy toward philosophy and philosphers, see his autobiography in Murchison, esp. pp. 263, 264, 270.

[87] In psychological science, Thorndike says, we can see "the influence of Darwinism beginning to spread to statesmanship and social control." "The Influence of Darwin on Psychology," p. 80. The persistence of this focus on "control" is clearly evident in Daniel Starch: Every "Part" and 31 of the chapters and subdivisions of his popular *Controlling Human Behavior* (New York, 1936) use the word "control" in their titles!

[88] The "laws of learning" are frequently discussed, of course, but see esp. *Animal Learning*, p. 244; and E. L. Thorndike and Arthur I. Gates, *Elementary Principles of Education* (New York, 1929), pp. 89-97. *Animal Learning*, p. 243.

[89] *Principles of Teaching*, pp. 1-10. For the causal connection see *Animal Learning*, p. 241 (italics are Thorndike's!). For measurement and "ability atoms," see "The Measurement of Educational Products," *School Review*, 20(1912), 290. The entire issue of this journal is highly significant.

[90] *Principles of Teaching*, p. 9 (under subtitle "The Value of Psychology").

[91] "The Contribution of Darwin to Psychology," pp. 78, 79, for all quotations. He also adds that human history is "as natural as the history of the stars."

[92] It should be carefully noted that there was much resistance to these grandiose claims in educational psychology, in particular to the notion of psychology as the "flip side" of pedagogical theory. I have already noted Dewey's opposition, which is also clearly evident in (just two of many possible examples) *Human Nature and Conduct* (New York: Modern Library, 1957) and *Liberalism and Social Action* (New York, 1963). William James did not share this inflated view, nor James Mark Baldwin, nor (probably) Edward Bradford Titchener. Nor (at least later in his life) did Chicago's Charles H. Judd, who, in his autobiography in the Murchison volumes, quotes (approvingly) William James as telling him, respecting the place of educational psychology: "I think there are about six weeks of it." Although space precludes my documenting their opposition, one of the clearest cases is Hugo Munsterburg, who will be discussed in my conclusion.

[93] *Human Nature and Conduct*, p. 200.

[94] Munsterburg engaged in an extensive exchange over the issue, beginning with "The Danger from Experimental Psychology" in *Atlantic Monthly*, (February, 1898), followed by a further defense of his views in the June issue. He was sharply attacked in the pages of *Educational Review* and *The Forum*. The furor continued, in part of course because Munsterburg enjoyed enormous authority as James's hand-picked successor at Harvard, culminating in Munsterburg's lengthy exposition of his position, "Psychology and Education" in *Educational Review*, 16(1898), 105-132 (the lead article, incidentally), from which my account is taken. The "balloon" quotation is at p. 124 (italics are Munstrerberg's).

5

Finally, in this section on identifying and assessing various conceptions of competence, Ted T. Aoki treats the topic from the perspective of critical social analysis. He finds it fruitful to think of competence as a metaphor. He distinguishes two perspectives embedded in this metaphor—competence as instrumental action and competence as practical action. As Johnson and Noddings would say, each conception rests on an entirely different *theory* of action. A major contribution of Aoki's paper is his careful analysis of the differing interests, assumptions, role of the teacher, teaching approaches, and ultimate evaluative criterion associated with each of these two perspectives. The pro's and con's of each perspective are argued forcefully, but there is no denying that Aoki finds the analysis of competence as practical action (as praxis—acting and reflecting) more fitting to the realities of education. Examining one's intentions and assumptions, as a teacher, frees one from doing those unconsciously repressive or dehumanizing acts which can sometimes be associated with mere instrumental actions. Thus, this theory of competence provides a logic for relating means and ends that is neither arbitrary nor determinate. As a kind of foreshadowing of what is addressed more fully by writers in the second half of this book—the analysis of the acquisition of competence—Aoki describes a concrete teacher education program in which the issues between competence as instrumental action and competence as critical praxis converge and are confronted.

Professor Aoki is Professor and Chairman of Secondary Education in the Faculty of Education, University of Alberta.

Competence in Teaching as Instrumental and Practical Action: A Critical Analysis

Ted T. Aoki
University of Alberta

Competent, adj. 1. Having sufficient ability or authority. 2. Possessing the requisite natural or legal qualifications; qualified. 3. Sufficient; adequate. [MF competent competens, -entis, ppr. of *comptere*. Be fit, be proper. *com-* together *petere* go, seek.]
—Britannica World Language Dictionary

Introduction

In discussing "competence" from the perspective of critical social theory, I have felt tension, doubly. First, because I experienced this tension as an alien to a strange country might experience it. Trained as a teacher and teacher educator mainly in the tradition of, broadly speaking, positivistic science, I have been finding the world of critical social theory somewhat foreign to me, and my initial coming to an understanding had been as that of a North American visiting Continental Europe for the first time. I become increasingly aware that I am North American. Schooled as I have been in psycho-social theories applied to education in the tradition of North American scholarship, I have been dwelling in a world somewhat distanced from the domain of critical social theory. Hence, as many monopolarized strangers are wont to be, I know I am suspect in my occasional and maybe frequent tendency to reduce what to me is new by interpreting it within the framework of what has been familiar to me. Knowing this, you will appreciate my uneasiness.

Second, I also experienced tension because of my initial inclination to give meaning to the term "competence" within a framework wherein I have been making-sense of activities such as "*competency*-based curriculum development," "*competency*-based testing," "*competency*-based teacher education," "management by *competency*-based objectives," and the like. My first inclination has been to make sense of "competence" by reducing it to the instrumental sense of techniques and skills. Thus, having lived in and where I find myself now living within a world in which positivistic science and its derivative technological world view is dominant, I find myself struggling against my own initial enculturated tendency to totalize *a* way of interpreting "competence" into *the* way, the instrumental way.

Thus, I find myself caught within my own self-constituted limit-situation, and in attempting to understand "competence" differently, I am experiencing a struggle to attempt to break through my self-imposed walls. Fundamental to this struggle are the contradictory meanings of competence that dwell within me. What follows is a portrayal of this contradiction.

Competence as Instrumental Action

In discussing teaching competence within a concrete program, allow me to ground my discussion in two segments of the undergraduate teacher education program in our own Faculty of Education at the University of Alberta, Canada, from which I hail. For the past few years, our Faculty has been engaged in the revision of the teacher education program guided by the content of a Faculty approved report entitled, *A Report on the Revision of the B. Ed. Program.*[1] In it are two contradictory interpretations of competence in teaching. My interest is to illuminate this contradiction.

SEGMENT 1

Segment 1 describes briefly a compulsory core course in curriculum and instruction. It prescribes a repertoire of "basic skills and strategies of teaching" thought to be key to the classroom teaching situation. These basic teaching skills and strategies read as follows:

1. *Classroom management and discipline*

This would include such topics as organizing and managing routine tasks and physical arrangements, individualizing and grouping for instruction, behavior management and/or modification, and pupil reinforcement.

2. *Curriculum planning*

Included in this area would be the development of skills in relation to goal setting, writing lesson objectives, lesson and unit planning, motivation of students, and selection of appropriate materials and aids.

3. *Instructional strategies or methods*

Students should be provided examples of and opportunities to practice different skills related to the presentation and discussion of information. Included would be such items as questioning, explaining, and demonstrating, along with methods of achieving lesson closure and giving directions.

4. *Assessing and evaluating student behavior*

This would include observation and listening skills, other diagnostic techniques and record keeping.[2]

The notion of "competence" exhibited in the foregoing as management skills, planning skills, instructional skills, assessing skills is legion and is of the same order as many typified expressions we find in current educational literature—"competency-based teacher education," "competency-based curriculum development," "competency-based testing," "management by competency-based objectives," and their many derivatives. As such, "competence" reflects what might be seen as the current mainstream metaphor of teaching, schooling, and curriculum thought.

This metaphor sees "competence" as means to given ends, skills and techniques oriented towards interest in efficient control. Such a knowing-how-to-do view of competence is embedded in scientific and technological thought and action within the framework of which curricular competencies such as "teaching competence," "curriculum development competence," or "curriculum evaluation competence," are seen strictly within a technical ends-means framework, reducing competence to instrumental reason and instrumental action. As such, the teacher, the curriculum developer, or the curriculum evaluator are seen as rule-oriented, rule-governed beings cast within a manipulative ethos, an ethos in which even the future is conceived in terms of rules.

It is to this kind of phenomenon dominant in North America that men such as Edmund Husserl, Jurgen Habermas, Trent Schroyer, Michael Apple, and others have been referring as a crisis of Western reason. (Henry Johnson, in questioning "What's good for General Motors is good for the school," was also pointing to this crisis.)

Trent Schroyer in *The Critique of Domination* speaks of this crisis as reflected in two symbolic events of the sixties, man's landing on the moon and the founding of the Woodstock nation. According to Schroyer, the first, the moon-landing feat, represents the zenith of technical progress; the latter, popular or not, the affirmation of a communal sentiment. These, according to Schroyer, mark a fundamental contradiction between an orientation committed to technological progress and that committed to the improvement of personal and communal life.[3]

Of the two, the paramount mainstream reality seems to be the technological, devoted to the belief that problems and conflicts can be managed through purposive rational action based on precise quantification and systemic decision-making. What is here reductive and damaging is the fact that emphasis upon technical strategy as a means for efficient decision-making effectively submerges the ideology of socio-cultural values, and leaves the "neutral" standards of purposive rational action, what could be called "competence as instrumental reason."

This same crisis manifested as a reflection of the contemporary image of advanced industrial society shows as an internal crisis in the curriculum world indicated by, though still few, an increasing number of curriculum scholars.[4] Central to this crisis, writ large or small, is the issue of the adequacy of the social theory or social theories undergirding it. By social theory I mean the philosophical presuppositions and root metaphors which inform curriculum and pedagogy.

To date in the field of education the dominant social theory has been guided by an instrumental notion of reason which, I believe, impoverishes us by submerging or even denying the meaning of cultural reality. By adopting technocratic strategies and allied decision-making social theories, we are asked to admit the rational necessity of extending centralized management theories to more and more areas of the life of teachers, students, and administrators in the classroom and the school. This assumption has been so reinforced by positivistic thought and action by our intoxication with the technical power of science and technology, and by the unreflective adoption of business management techniques, that it has become a mainstream doctrine of educational thought. To question this position requires a radical re-examination of the foundations of social theory and an exploration of alternative modes of inquiry and socio-cultural organization.

Those of us in the realm of curriculum who are wedded to an instrumental concept of competence—that is, competence viewed as naive scientism of our technocractic guidance system—should become vitally sensitive to the limit-situation that blocks our capacity to recognize the socio-cultural significance of the living acts of teachers and students. It is a new metaphor of teachers and students we need—one that will avoid reduction of teachers and students from beings-as-humans to being-as-things.

Competence as Practical Action (Praxis)

I now wish to turn to another segment in our Faculty Report previously mentioned for undergraduate teacher education program revision in an attempt to secure a more vital sense of competence.

SEGMENT 2

Segment 2 in the Report is entitled "The Senior Elective." It reflects a desire to provide undergraduate students in their final year of their four year program opportunities to bring together the diverse program elements in which they have been immersed in a course "committed to integration and synthesis."

Here is an extract from that document:

> 1. A suitable SENIOR ELECTIVE experience is one in which a student combines personal action and...reflection on action;
> 2. A suitable SENIOR ELECTIVE experience should expand the student's awareness of the teacher's role by...analysis of assumptions and values; by reconceiving the role of the teacher as a skilled leader and by being aware of the dynamics of organizations and of human relationships therein;
> 3. A suitable SENIOR ELECTIVE should seek to link the universal with the particular, the concrete, day-to-day world of personal action with the world of ideas, values, symbols, or more generally, with systems of meaning.[2]

What is the notion of teaching competence to which this textpoints? What is the underlying perspective of this text on "competence"?

Even from this sketchy text from Segment 2, we can begin to trace the contours of the underlying view of competence in teaching and the teacher situated in the everyday commonplace of the classroom and the school. To view the "teacher"as "actor/reflector upon action" or "teaching" as "action and reflection with others in a social context" is sharply in contrast with the view of "teacher" as "behavior-modifier" or "teaching" as "instrumental skills" so paramount in Segment 1. Teaching as reflected in Segment 2 no longer espouses the instrumental and technical view of competence as was reflected in Segment 1. No longer is teaching viewed merely in terms of technical skills of classroom management, questioning, "behavior modification," and the like.

To help explore this view of competence, let us uncover the root etymology of "competence." The disclosure of the Latin root reveals a fresh view. The Latin root is "com-petere": "com" meaning "together," and "petere" meaning "to seek."[5] In a root sense, then, to be competent means to be able to seek together or to be able to venture forth together. This root meaning of "competence" as "communal venturing" holds promise for a fresh view of what it means to be a competent teacher. (This, I feel, is embedded in the question Henry Johnson posed: "What does it mean to be human?")

I now seek support from a phenomenological scholar whose works I have recently come to know. He is a Polish scholar, by name, Karol Wojtyla, who speaks in a context broader than that of education. Yet, his denouncement of competence as instrumental action has meaningful relevance for us. I understand that Wojtyla became skeptical of the reductive tendencies of instrumental reason embedded in materialistic and positivistic thought inherited from the 19th century and spreading into all domains of thought in Poland. He had recognized that since Descartes, knowledge of man and his world has been identified with cognition, the ensuing post-Cartesian attitude extending it as reflections in behaviorism, utilitarianism, and determinism. His efforts to transcend objectivism appear in his book *The Acting Person* dealing with the *communal venturing of man* as experienced through acting and reflecting throughout one's life. Unravelling the network of man's constitutive tendencies and strivings, Wojtyla in his book, attempted to reveal man's status in the world, the meaning of emancipation, and of human fulfillment. He probed by means of ontological hermeneutics the constitutive dynamism integrated by the acting person. Believing that man is no mere creature of circumstances conditioned and encapsulated by his social milieu, he proposed man's worthy life venture as self-disclosure and self-governance as he fashions a personal and social life worth living. By emphasizing both the communal conditon of man and the irreducible transcendence of the human person with respect to the current of social life, he counteracts the deviant, reductionist tendencies so prevalent in contemporary philosophy and culture. Furthermore, he sees man as a *historical being*, man as a maker of his own history, who together with others are seen as co-makers of history.

It is to this framework of acting and reflecting that we must turn to make sense afresh of competence in teaching. Within such a framework, competence in teaching is anchored in a situation of inter-actions among teachers and students mediated by everyday language, oriented towards practical interest in establishing open inter-subjectivity and non-violent recognition on which communicative action depends. But these inter-actions are rooted in a network of meanings actors within that situation give. Hence, understanding the day-to-day life of teachers and students in the classroom requires at least understanding in terms of the meaning structures actors in the classroom give. However, to be able to venture forth together in the meaningful way Wojtyla speaks of, requires not only an understanding of this meaning structure but also action rooted in critical reflection on these meaning structures.

I would like to interpret what I can now refer to as critical venturing together more concretely, within this critical framework. The teacher in becoming involved with his students, enters into their world as he allows them to enter his and engages himself with students mutually in action-reflection oriented activities. He questions his students as well as himself as he urges students to question him and themselves. Mutual reflection allows new questions to emerge which, in turn, leads to more reflection. In the ongoing process which is dialectical and transformative of social reality, both teacher and students become participants in open dialogue.

However, it is important for the teacher to remember that a critical perspective is a two-bladed knife, cutting both ways.Werner states:

> We must be reflective of the very perspective we use for critical sense-making. Any clarifying of perspective of others...is itself perspective guided. In arguing for point-of-viewism one cannot presume himself free of a viewpoint. One way to deal with this dilemma is to make explicit and reflect upon the theoretical and methodological beliefs within which our own thinking and acting are situated.[7]

Reflection in the sense used here is not the kind of activity that teachers and students as actors engage in their typical daily life. For in their day-to-day existence, acting persons deal with their concerns in routine ways often without probing beyond the immediate exigencies. Often, actions are without thought. Missing is a conscious effort to examine the intentions and assumptions underlying their acts. However, in critical reflection the everyday type of attitude is placed in "brackets," as it were, and examined in an attempt to go beyond the immediate level of interpretation. In this sense, critical reflection is thoughtful action, i.e., action full of thought. Critical reflection thus leads to an understanding of what is beyond; it is oriented towards making the unconscious conscious. Such reflective activity allows liberation from the unconsciously held assumptions and intentions that lie hidden. These may be repressive and dehumanizing aspects of everyday life which man needs to face in his personal and social life. For example, at the personal level the content of reflection may be the "rationalizations" an actor uses to hide underlying motives for his action. Or at the societal level, the content of reflection may be the "ideology" used to speak for social policies and practices, rendering obscure society's coercive interests that lie beneath. In this sense critical reflection demonstrates interest in discovering the hidden "true" interests embedded in some given personal or social condition.

Reflection, however, is not only oriented towards making conscious the unconscious by dis-covering underlying assumptions and intentions, but it is also oriented towards the implications for action guided by the newly gained consciousness and critical knowing. It is interested in bringing about a re-orientation through transformation of the assumptions and intentions upon which thought and action rest. There may be preconceived norms, values, images ofman and the world, assumptions about knowledge, root metaphors, and perspectives. Competence as critical venturing together, then, with its interests in liberating man from hidden assumptions and techniques, promotes a theory of man and society that is grounded in the moral attitude of liberation.[8]

Conclusion

What I have attempted to do is to portray competence employing the categorical distinction between "technique" and "praxis," i.e., instrumental action and practical action, between beings-as-things and beings-as-no-things, signifying two frames of reference in which reality is constituted. (See chart which contrasts these two "Perspectives on Competence.")

In the framework of "technique" (instrumental action), reality is objectified, that is, it is constituted as the being of things according to nomological laws. Competence within this framework assumes actions of beings-as-things oriented towards interest in control, efficiency, and certainty. In contrast, in the framework of "praxis" (practical action), reality is constituted by the inter-subjective actions of beings-as-humans, oriented towards cognitive interest in mutual understanding, and also, the practical interest in securing authentically the always precarious inter-subjectivity. In this framework of competence as communicative action and reflection, reality is constituted as a community of actors and speakers.

Within the framework of "praxis" and emancipatory actions, these actors and speakers are oriented towards "de-naturalizing" that which commonsense declares to be human nature; they explore and condemn the commonsensical dismissal of alternative realities, and they attempt to restore the legitimacy of those existential issues which commonsense, following human historical predicament, pulverizes into a multitude of mini-problems as can be articulated in purely instrumental terms.

Ultimately, critical competence or competence as praxis as I have outlined it is for people for whom the way competence is known by mainstream America is not reason enough for the way competence is known by mainstream America. In essence, critical competence is the way we choose to act to oppose inhumanity in songs and acts of joy, be they in the everyday idiom of music, art, play, poetry, pottery, or everyday language.

FOOTNOTES

[1] *A Report on the Revision of the B. Ed. Degree*, Committee on Basic Skills and Knowledge of the Faculty of Education, University of Alberta, Edmonton, Canada. 1978.

[2] Ibid. Appendix III, pp. 1 & 2.

[3] Trent Schroyer. *The Critique of Dominance*. New York: George Braziller, 1973.

[4] For the work of critical scholars, see William Pinar (Ed.) *Curriculum Theorizing: The Reconceptualists*. Berkeley, CA: McCutchan Publishing Corporation, 1975.

[5] See extract from *Britannica World Language Dictionary* at the beginning of this paper.

[6] Karol Wojtyla, *The Acting Person*. Boston: D. Reidel Publishing Co., 1979. (*Analecta Husserliana, The Yearbook of Phenomenological Research*, Vol. X)

[7] Walter Werner, Evaluation: Sense-making of school programs, *In* T. Aoki (Ed.), *Curriculum Evaluation in a New Key*, (a monograph). University of British Columbia, Centre for the Study of Curriculum and Instruction, 1978, p. 20.

[8] Ted Aoki, Toward curriculum inquiry in a new key, *in* J. Victoria & E. Sacca (Eds.), *Phenomenological Description: Potential for Research in Art Education*, in University of Concordia, Montreal, Series *Presentations on Art Education Research*, 1978, pp. 47-75. Also published as Occasional Paper No. 2, Department of Secondary Education, Faculty of Education, The University of Alberta, Edmonton, Canada.

PERSPECTIVES ON COMPETENCE

Perspective A

COMPETENCE AS INSTRUMENTAL ACTION

(Theory and Practice in Linear Relationship)

INTEREST IN

- Interest in *controlling* teaching situation through psycho-social theory(ies).
- Instrumental interest in applying reason to teaching practice (thought to action) effectively, efficiently.
- Interest in applying theoretical understandings in curriculum and instruction into classroom practice.

ASSUMPTIONS ABOUT TEACHER AND CLASSROOM WORLD

- The classroom is a world which can be changed with certainty by the application of theory.
- Thought and action (theory and practice) are separate realms linearly connected.
- "Practice" is actualization of theory.
- The theoretical world is paramount reality (therefore, theoretical knowledge is more important than applied knowledge).
- Instrumental knowledge is "applied" knowledge.
- Teacher is instrument of theoretical knowledge.

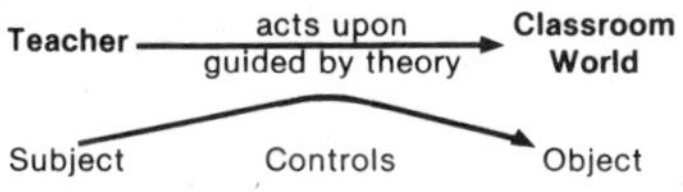

APPROACH

- Teacher applies theoretical rules to practical situations; therefore, instrumental in approach.
- Planning lessons, managing class, and teaching guided by "theoretical rules."

EVALUATION QUESTION

TYPE: How efficiently was "theory" implemented in "practice"?

Perspective B

COMPETENCE AS PRACTICAL ACTION (PRAXIS)

(Theory and Practice in Dialectical Relationship)

INTEREST IN

- Interest in "venturing forth" together with students.
- Interest in self-improvement by reflecting upon and freeing self from self- or socially imposed constraints.
- Interest in the teacher interpreting the classroom world, acting with and upon that world, and reflecting and acting upon both self and world.

ASSUMPTIONS ABOUT TEACHER AND CLASSROOM WORLD

- The teacher as acting person is in dialectical relationship with the classroom world.
- Assumes reality is not given directly in appearance, hence requires critical reflection to enable the teacher to discover deep structure not given in *appearance*.
- Theory and practice are in integrated unity (praxis). (Praxis is thoughtful action; action full of thought.)
- The teacher has unlimited possibilities for growth.
- The teacher is engaged in the writing of his own history.
- Praxical knowledge is "critically reflected" knowledge.

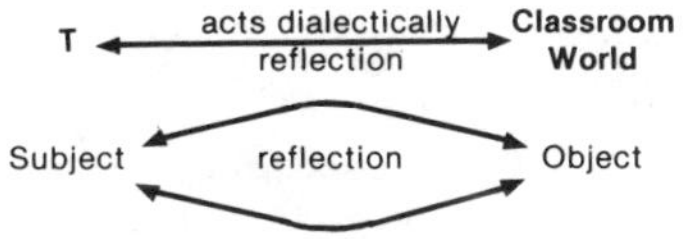

APPROACH

- Acting and reflecting upon the world the teacher helps students to construct and transform reality.
- Becoming aware of own teaching acts as possible object-in-view.
- Reflection as going beyond the framework of everyday instrumental action.
- Seeks moment for conscious connecting of teacher's awareness and the teacher's intentional world.
- Becoming aware of the writing of history in which he is engaged—the history that is the activity through which the teacher creates himself. (Teacher is maker of own history.)
- Becoming aware that personal praxis involves social praxis.
- Becoming aware of the personal, social, cultural, and political context in which praxical activity is conducted.

EVALUATION QUESTION

TYPE: What is the quality of the underlying perspective of my action? What makes it possible for me as a human being to act the way I do in my pedagogical activities? Is it adequate?

The Acquisition Of Competence

6

The way one acquires competence inevitably depends in part upon the conception of competence held. It also depends upon many other factors related to the actual educational practices and processes used to facilitate the acquisition of competence. Knowing which educative forms contribute most appropriately to the achieving of competence has always been difficult to pin down. There are psychological processes within the student that must be taken into account, and there are other contributing factors, many of which will be examined in the second half of this book. Among these are social-cultural factors, a number of which permeate the very form of schooling itself, the curriculum, and teaching. These forms, and their influences upon acquisition of competence, even upon the notion of competence that becomes accepted within the social-cultrual context of schooling, are analyzed by Michael W. Apple in this opening paper of the second half of this book.

He observes some current practices which have come into use without much deliberate intent on the part of educators, but which carry powerful vestiges of hidden influence on the ways competence is acquired in schools and the dominant meaning given the notion of competence. The ideology of technical control is what Apple describes at work here in the everyday tasks of teachers and students. He shows how this ideology resides in the technical and the social-cultural dimensions of many educational practices. In his analysis of these ordinary events of curriculum and teaching, Apple reveals a prevailing conception of teacher competence which has little place for pedagogical decision-making that demands great knowledge, skill, and judgment. The teacher, instead, is "deskilled" and "reskilled" to provide management and control of an externally designed process created to produce an outcome in the learner via pre-packaged content and procedures. Not only is teacher competence down-graded in this process; a similar down-grading of pupil competence under this form of technical control is also revealed in Apple's analysis.

Profound implications, both for the use of certain forms of educational practice and for the interpretation of competence embedded in them, follow from Apple's critical social analysis. The intellectual tools and language Apple uses to reveal these previously veiled realities may be unfamiliar to many readers, and perhaps not those preferred by some, but his revelations are difficult to deny.

A later version of Apple's paper appeared in Michael W. Apple (Ed.), Education and Power (Boston: Routledge & Kegan Paul, 1982), pp. 135-164. The paper appears here in its original form through the kind permission of its author and Routledge & Kegan Paul.

Professor Apple is Professor of Curriculum and Instruction, and Educational Policy Studies in the School of Education, University of Wisconsin-Madison.

Curricular Form and the Logic of Technical Control

Michael W. Apple
University of Wisconsin-Madison

Current attempts by the state and industry to bring schools more closely into line with "economic needs" are evident on both sides of the Atlantic. In the United Kingdom, The Great Debate and the Green Paper stand as remarkable statements to the ability of capital in times of economic crisis to marshall its forces (Donald, 1979). In the United States, where governmental policies are more highly mediated by a different articulation between the state, the economy, and schools, this same kind of powerful pressure exists as well. Often the workings of industry are even more visible. Chairs of Free Enterprise devoted to economic education are springing up at universities throughout the country. Teaching the message of industry has become a real force. The Ryerson Plan, for example, is a corporate plan to have teachers spend their summers working mainly with management in industry so that they can teach their students "real knowledge" about corporate needs and benefits (Ryerson, no date).[1] Though there has been serious resistance to this kind of approach by progressive forces in the United States, the movement to "teach for the needs of industry" is growing rapidly enough so that a clearinghouse, appropriately named The Institute for Constructive Capitalism, has been established at the University of Texas to make the material more available (Downing, 1979).

Now I do not want to minimize the importance of such overt attempts at influencing teachers and students. To do so would be the height of folly. However, by keeping our focus only on these overt attempts at bringing school policy and curriculum into closer correspondence with industrial needs, we may neglect what is happening that maybe just as powerful at the level of day to day school practice. One could fight the battles against capital's overt encroachments (and perhaps win some of them) and still lose within the school itself. For as I shall argue here, some of the ideological and material influences of our kind of social formation on teachers and students are not most importantly found at the level of these kind of documents or plans, but at the level of social practice *within* the routine activities in schools.[2]

In essence, I want to argue that ideologies are not only global sets of interests, things imposed by one group on another. They are embodied by our commonsense meanings and practices (Williams, 1977). Thus, if you want to understand ideology at work in schools, look as much at the concreta of day to day curricular and pedagogic life as you would at the statements made by spokespersons of the state or industry. To quote from Finn, Grant, and Johnson, we need to look not only at ideologies "about" education but ideologies "in" it as well (Finn, Grant, Johnson, and the C.C.C.S. Education Group, 1978, pp. 3-4).

I am not implying that the level of practice in schools is fundamentally controlled in some mechanistic way by private enterprise. As an aspect of the state, the school mediates and transforms an array of economic, political, and cultural pressures from competing classes and class segments. Yet we tend to forget that this does not mean that the logics, discourses, or modes of control of capital will not have an increasing impact on everyday life in our educational institutions, especially in times of what has been called "the fiscal crisis of the state" (O'Connor, 1973). This impact, clearly visible in the United States (though I would hazard a guess it will become more prevalent in Canada, Europe, and Latin America as well), is especially evident in curriculum, in essence in some very important aspects of the actual stuff that students and teachers interact with.

In this essay, I shall be particularly interested in curricular *form*, not curricular content. That is, my focus will not be on what is actually taught, but on the manner in which it is organized. As a number of Marxist cultural analysts have argued, the workings of ideology can be seen most impressively at the level of form as well as what the form has in it (Jameson, 1971; Williams, 1977; Apple, 1978). As I shall argue here, this is a key to uncovering the role of ideology "in" education.

In order to understand part of what is occurring in the school and the ideological and economic pressures being placed upon and which work their way through it, we need to situate it within certain long term trends in the capital accumulation process. Recently these trends have intensified and have had a rather major impact on a variety of areas of social life. Among these trends we can identify certain tendencies such as:

> the concentration and centralization of capitals; the expansion of labor processes that are based on production-line technologies and forms of control; the continuing decline of "heavy industry" and the movement of capital into modern "lighter" forms of production, most notably the production of consumer durables; and major shifts in the composition of labor power—the secular tendency to "de-skilling," the separation of "conception" from "execution" and the creation of new technical and control skills, the shift of labor out of direct production and into circulation and distribution, and the expansion of labor within the state (Clarke, 1979, p. 239).[3]

As we shall see, the development of new forms of control, the process of deskilling, the separation of conception from execution, are not limited to factories and offices. These tendencies intrude more and more into institutions like the school. In order to unpack this, we shall have to examine the very nature of the logic of corporate deskilling and control.

Deskilling and Reskilling

At first, let me speak very generally about the nature of this kind of control. In corporate production, firms purchase labor power. That is, they buy the capacity one has to do work and, obviously, will often seek to expand the use of that labor to make it more productive. There is an opposite side to this. With the purchase of labor power goes the "right" to stipulate (within certain limits) how it is to be used, without too much interference or participation by workers in the conception and planning of the work (Edwards, 1979, p. 17). How this has been accomplished has not stayed the same, of course. Empirically, there has been a changing logic of control that has sought to accomplish these ends.

Given this history, it is helpful to differentiate the kinds of control that have been used. I shall simplify these around basic ideal types for ease of understanding.

We can distinguish three kinds of control that can be employed to help extract more work—simple, technical, and bureaucratic. Simple control is exactly that, simply telling someone that you have decided what should go on and they should follow or else. Technical controls are less obvious. They are controls embedded in the physical structure of your job. A good example is the use of numerical control technology in the machine industry where a worker inserts a card into a machine and it directs the pace and skill level of the operation. Thus, the worker is meant to be simply as attendant to the machine itself. And, finally, bureaucratic control signifies a social structure where control is less visible since the principles of control are embedded within the *hierarchical* social relations of the workplace. Impersonal and bureaucratic rules concerning the direction of one's work, the procedures for evaluating performance, and sanctions and rewards are dictated by officially approved policy (Edwards, 1979, pp. 19-21). Each of these modes of control has grown in sophistication over the years, though simple control has tended to become less important as the size and complexity of production has increased.

The long period of experimentation by industry on the most successful modes of controlling production led to a number of conclusions. Rather than simple control where control is openly exercized by supervisors or persons in authority (and hence could possibly be subverted by blue or white collar workers), power could be "made invisible" by incorporating it into the very structure of the work itself. This meant the following things. The control must come from what seems to be a legitimate overall structure. It must be concerned with the actual work, not based on features extraneous to it (like favoritism and so on). Perhaps most importantly, the job, the process, and the product should be defined as precisely as possible on the basis of management's , not the worker's, control over the specialized knowledge needed to carry it out (Edwards, 1979, pp. 110). This often entailed the development of technical control.

Technical control and deskilling tend to go hand in hand. Deskilling is part of a long process in which labor is divided and then redivided to increase productivity, to reduce "inefficiency," and to control both the cost and the impact of labor. It usually has involved taking relatively complex jobs (most jobs are much more complex and require more decision-making than people give them credit for), jobs which require no small amount of skill and decision-making, breaking them down into specified actions with specified results so that less skilled and costly personnel can be used or so that the control of work pace and outcome is enhanced. The assembly line is, of course, one of the archetypical examples of this process. At its beginnings, deskilling tended to involve techniques such as Taylorism and various time and motion studies. Though these strategies for the division and control of labor were less than totally successful (and in fact often genrerated a significant amount of resistance and conflict (Noble, 1977; Burawoy, 1979), they did succeed in helping to legitimate a style of control based in large part on deskilling.

One of the more effective strategies has been the incorporation of control into the actual production process itself. Thus, machinery in factories is now often designed so that the machinist is called upon to do little more than load and unload the machine. In offices, word processing technology is employed to reduce labor costs and deskill women workers. Thus, management attempts to control both the pace of the work and the skills required, to more effectively increase their profit margins or productivity. Once again, as the history of formal and informal labor resistance documents, this kind of strategy—the building of controls into the very warp and woof of the production process—has been contested (Apple, 1980b; see also Aronowitz, 1978). However, the growing sophistication by management and state bureaucrats in the use of technical control procedures is apparent (Edwards, 1979).

I have mentioned that deskilling is a complex process as it works its way through a variety of economic and cultural institutions. Yet it really is not that hard to grasp one of its other important aspects. When jobs are deskilled, the knowledge that once accompanied them, knowledge that was controlled and used by workers in carrying out their day to day lives on their jobs, goes somewhere. Management attempts (with varying degrees of success) to accumulate and control this assemblage of skills and knowledge. It attempts, in other words, to separate conception from execution. The control of knowledge enables management to plan;[4] the worker should ideally merely carry these plans out to the specifications, and at the pace, set by people away from the actual point of production.

But deskilling is accompanied by something else, what might be called reskilling. New techniques are required to run new machines; new occupations are created as the redivision of labor goes on. Fewer skilled craftspersons are needed and their previous large numbers are replaced by a smaller number of technicians with different skills who oversee the machinery (Barker & Downing, 1979). This process of deskilling and reskilling is usually spread out over the landscape of an economy so it is rather difficult to trace out the relationships. It is not very usual that you can see it going on at a level of specificity that makes it clear since while one group is being deskilled another group, often separated by time and geography, is being reskilled. However, one particular institution—the school—provides an exceptional microcosm for seeing these kinds of mechanisms of control in operation.

In examining this, we should remember that capitalist production has developed unevenly, so that certain areas of our social institutions will vary in the kind of control being used. Some institutions will be more resistant than others to the logic of corporate rationalization. Given the relatively autonomous nature of teaching (one can usually close one's door and not be disturbed) and given the internal history of the kinds of control in the institution (paternalistic styles of administration, often in the USA on gender relations), the school has been partially resistant to technical and bureaucratic control, *at the level of actual practice*, until relatively recently. This "relative automnomy" may be breaking down today. (Dale, 1979) For just as the everyday discourse and patterns of interaction in the family and in, say, the media are increasingly being subtly transformed by the logic and contradictions of dominant ideologies (Gitlin, 1979),[5] so too is the school a site where these subtle ideological transformations occur. I shall claim that this goes on through a process of technical control. As we shall now see, these logics of control can have a rather profound impact on schools.

Controlling Curricular Form

The best examples of the encroachment of technical control procedures are found in the exceptionally rapid growth in the use of prepackaged sets of curricular materials. It is nearly impossible now to walk into an American classroom, for instance, without seeing boxes upon boxes of science, social studies, mathematics, and reading materials ("systems," as they are sometimes called) lining the shelves and in use.[6] Here, a school system purchases a total set of standardized material, usually one which includes statements of objectives, all of the curricular content and material needed, prespecified teacher actions and appropriate student responses, and diagnostic and achievement tests coordinated with the system. Usually, these tests have the curricular knowledge "reduced" to "appropriate" behaviors and skills. Remember this emphasis on skills for it will become rather significant later on.

Let me give one example, actually taken from one of the better of the widely used curricular systems, of the numerous sets of materials that are becoming the standard fare in American elementary schools. It is taken from *Module One* of *Science: A Process Approach*. The notion of module is important here. The material is prepackaged into cardboard boxes with attractive colors. It is divided into 105 separate modules, each of which include a set of pregiven concepts to teach. The material specifies all of the goals. It includes everything a teacher "needs" to teach, has the pedagogical steps a teacher must take to reach these goals already built in, and has the evaluation mechanisms built into it as well. But that is not all. Not only does it prespecify nearly all a teacher should know, say, and do, but it often lays out the appropriate student responses to these elements as well.

To make this clear, here is one sequence taken from the material which lays out the instructional procedure, student response, and evaluative activity. It concerns colors.

> As each child arrives at school, fasten a red, yellow, or blue paper rectangle on the child's shirt or dress.... Comment on the color of the paper and ask the child to say the name of the color he or she is wearing....
>
> Put thirty yellow, red, and blue paper squares in a large bag or small box. Show the children three paper plates: one marked red, one yellow, and one blue. (See *Materials* for suggestions on marking.) These colors should closely match those in the bag. Ask the children to come forward, a few at a time, and let each child take one square from the bag and place it on the plate marked with the matching color. [A picture of this with a child picking out paper from a box and putting it on a plate is inserted here in the material so that no teacher will get the procedure wrong.] As each child takes a colored square, ask him to name the color of that square. If the child hesitates, name it for him (*Science: A Process Approach*, 1974, pp. 3-4).

In the curricular material, everything except the bag or box is included—all the plates and colored paper. (The cost by the way is $14.00 for the plan and the paper).

I noted that not only were the curricular and pedagogical elements prespecified, but all other aspects of teachers' actions were included as well. Thus, in the "Appraisal" of this module, the teacher is asked to:

> Ask each of six children to bring a box of crayons and sit together.... Ask each child to point to his red crayon when you say the word red. Repeat this for all six colors. Ask each child to match one crayon with one article of clothing that someone else is wearing.... Before each group of children leaves the activity, ask each child individually to name and point to the red, blue, and yellow crayon (*Science: A Process Approach*, 1974, p. 7).

Even with this amount of guidance, it is still "essential" that we know for each child whether he or she has reached the appropriate skill level. Thus, as the final element, the material has competency measures built into it. Here the specification reaches its most exact point, giving the teacher the exact words he or she should use:

> Task 1: Show the child a yellow cube and ask, "What is the color of this cube?"

[This is done for each color. Then, after arranging orange, green, and purple cubes in front of a child, the material goes on.]

Task 4: Say, "Put your finger on the orange cube."

Task 5: Say, "Put your finger on the green cube."

Task 6: Say, "Put your finger on the purple cube" (*Science: A Process Approach*, 1974, p. 7).

I have gone on at length here so that you can get a picture of the extent to which technical control enters into the life of the school. Little in what might be metaphorically called the "production process" is left to chance. In many ways, it can be considered a picture of deskilling. Let us look at this somewhat more closely.

My point is not to argue against the specific curricular or pedagogical content of this kind of material, though an analysis of this certainly would be interesting.[7] Rather, it is to have us focus on the form itself. What is *this* doing? For notice what has happened here. The goals, the process, the outcome, and the evaluative criteria for assessing them are defined as precisely as possible by people external to the situation. In the competency measure at the end of the module, this extends to the specification of even the exact words the teacher is to say.

Notice as well the process of deskilling at work here. Skills that teachers used to need, that were deemed essential to the craft of working with children—such as curriculum deliberation and planning, designing teaching and curriculum stategies for specific groups and individuals based on intimate knowledge of these people—are no longer as necessary. With the large scale influx of prepackaged material, planning is separated from execution. The planning is done at the level of the production of both the rules for use of the material and the material itself. The execution is carried out by the teacher. In the process, what were previously considered valuable skills slowly atrophy because they are less often required.[8]

But what about the element of reskilling that I mentioned earlier was essential to understand how ideological forms can penetrate to the heart of institutions like the school? Unlike the economy where deskilling and reskilling are not usually found operating at one and the same moment withone and the same people, in the school this seems to be exactly the case. As the procedures of technical control enter into the school in the guise of pre-designed curricular/teaching/evaluation "systems", teachers are being deskilled. Yet they are also being reskilled in a way that is quite consequential. We can see signs of this at both teacher training institutions, in funding and enrollment patterns, and not the least in the actual curricular materials themselves. While the deskilling involves the loss of craft, the ongoing atrophication of educational skills, the reskilling involves the substitution of the skills and ideological visions of management. The growth of behavior modification techniques and classroom management strategies and their incorporation within both curricular material and teachers' repertoires signifies these kinds of alterations. That is, as teachers lose control of the curricular and pedagogic skills to large publishing houses, these skills are replaced by techniques for better controlling students.

This is not insignificant in its consequences for both teachers and students. Since the material is often organized around and employs specified outcomes and procedures and these are built into this kind of material itself (with its many workshops and tests often), it is "individualized" in many ways. Students can engage in it themselves with little overt interaction on the part of the teacher or each other as they become more used to the procedures, which are usually highly standardized. The students' progress through the system can be individualized, at least according to speed; and this focus on individualizing the speed (usually through worksheets and the like) at which a student proceeds through the system is becoming even more pronounced in newer curricular systems. Since the control is technical—that is, management strategies are incorporated into it as a major aspect of the pedagogical/curricular/evaluative "machinery" itself—the teacher becomes something of a manager. This is occurring *at the same time* that the objective conditions of his or her work are becoming increasingly "proletarianized" due to the curricular form's logic of technical control. This is a unique situation and certainly needs further thought. The possible effect of these forms of technical control on the students is just as serious and is something to which I shall return shortly.

Yet there are important consequences besides the deskilling and reskilling that are occurring. As the literature on the labor process reminds us, the progressive division and control of labor also has an impact at the level of social relations, on how the people involved interact. While this has had a momentous effect in factories and offices, its effects will undoubtedly be felt in the school too. And as in the workplace, the impact may have contradictory results.

Let me be more specific here. With the increasing employment of prepackaged curricular systems as the basic curricular form, virtually no interaction between teachers is required. If nearly everything is rationalized and specified before execution, then contact among teachers about actual curricular matters is minimized.[9]

If such technical control is effective, that is, if teachers actually respond in ways that accept the separation of planning from execution, then one would expect results that go beyond this "mere" separation. One would expect, at the level of classroom practice, that it will be more difficult for teachers to jointly gain informal control over curricular decisions because of their increasing isolation. In essence, if everything is predetermined, there is no longer any pressing need for teacher interaction. Teachers become unattached individuals, divorced from both colleagues and the actual stuff of their work. However, and here is part of what I mean by a contradictory effect, while this may be an accurate estimation of one of the results of technical control on one level, it forgets that most systems of control embody contradictions within themselves. For instance, while deskilling, forms of technical control, and the rationalization of work have created isolated individuals in, say, factories, historically they have often generated contradictory pressures as well. The use of technical control has often brought unionization in its wake (Edwards, 1979, p. 181). Even given the ideology of professionalism (an ideology that might make if difficult for collective struggles to evolve) which tends to dominate certain sectors of the teaching force, other state employees who in the past have thought of themselves as professionals have gained a greater collective sense in response to similar modes of control. Thus, the loss of control and knowledge in one arena may generate countervailing tendencies in another.

We cannot know yet how this will turn out. These contradictory results only emerge over long periods of time. In industry, it took decades for such an impact to be felt. The same will no doubt be true in schools.

Accepting Technical Control

So far in this essay, I have looked at teachers as if they were workers. That is, I have argued that the processes that act on blue and white collar workers in the larger social arena will and are entering into the *cultural forms* that are considered legitimate in schools. Yet schools, because of their internal history, are different in some very important ways from factories and offices, and teachers are still very different from other workers in terms of the conditions of their work. Products are not as visible (except much later on in the rough production of a labor force, in the production and reproduction of ideologies, and in the production of the technical/administrative knowledge "required" by an economy) (Apple, 1979a; Apple, 1979b; Noble, 1977)[10] as in offices and factories. Teachers have what Erik Olin Wright has called a "contradictory class location" and hence cannot be expected to react in the same ways as the workers and employees of large corporations (E. Wright, 1978). Furthermore, there are children who act back on teachers in ways an automobile on an assembly line or a paper on a desk cannot.[11] Finally, teaching does not take place on a line, but goes on in separate rooms more often than not.

All of these conditions do not mean that schools are immune or autonomous from the logic of capital. The logic will be mediated (in part due to the school as a *state* apparatus); it will enter where it can in partial, distorted, or coded ways. Given the specific differences of schools from other workplaces, a prime moment in its entry can be found less at the level of overt or simple controls (do this because I say so) or at the level of bureaucratic form (because individual teachers can still be relatively free from those kinds of encroachments).[12] These controls will go on, of course; but they may be less consequential than *the encoding of technical control into the very basis of the curricular form itself.* The level of curricular, pedagogic, and evaluative practice within the classroom can be controlled by the forms into which culture is commodified in schools. If my arguments are correct, then how are we to understand the acceptance and growth of this process of control?

These forms enter into schools not because of any conspiracy on the part of industrialists to make our educational institutions serve the needs of capital, as in the earlier mentioned Green Paper and Ryerson Plan. It occurs in large part because schools are a rather lucrative market. These sets of materials are published by firms who aggressively market where there is a need, or where they can create needs. It is simply good business practice in terms of profit margins to market material of this type, especially since the original purchase of the "system" or set of modules means increasing purchases over the years. Let me explain this by comparing it to another arena where similar techniques are employed to increase capital accumulation. Think of shaving. Large razor blade manufacturers sell razors at below cost, or even sometimes give them away as promotional "gimmicks," because they believe that once you buy the razor you will continue to buy their blades and their upgraded version year after year. In the curricular systems we are considering here, the purchase of the modules (though certainly not cheap by any stretch of the imagination) with their sets of standardized disposable material means the same thing. One "needs" to continue to purchase the work and test sheets, the chemicals, the correctly colored and shaped paper, the publishers' replacements of outmoded material and lessons, etc. Profits are heightened with every replacement that is bought. Since replacement purchases are often bureaucratically centralized, because of budget control, in the office of the administrator, the additional material is usually bought from the producer (often at exorbitant costs), not gotten from one's local store.

Thus, as with other industries, this "good business sense" means that high volume, the standardization of each of the elements of one's product and of its form, product upgrading, and then the stimulation of replacement purchasing are essential to maintain profits (Barker & Downing, 1979).[13]

Yet the notion of aggressive marketing and good business sense is but a partial explanation of this growth. In order to fully comprehend the acceptance of technical control procedures embodied in curricular form, we need to know something of why these kinds of materials evolved in the first place. Let me note these briefly.

The original introduction of prepackaged material was stimulated by a specific network of political, cultural, and economic forces, originally in the 1950s and 1960s in the United States. The views of academics that teachers were unsophisticated in major curriculum areas "necessitated" the creation of what was called teacher-proof material. The cold war climate (created and stimulated by the state in large part) led to a focus on the efficient production of scientists and technicians as well as a relatively stable workforce; thus, the "guaranteeing" of this production through the school curriculum became of increasing import (Spring, 1976). On top of this was the decision of the educational apparatus of the state, under the National Defense Education Act, to provide the equivalent of cash credits to local school districts for the purchase of new curricula created by the "private sector" to increase this efficiency. At the some time, the internal dynamics within education played a part since behavioral and learning psychology—on whose principles so much of these systems rely—gained increasing prestige in a field like education where being seen as a science was critically important both for funding and to deflect criticism (Apple, 1979a). In the more recent past, the increasing influence of industrial capital within the executive and legislative branches of government (O'Connor, 1973), as well as in the attendant bureaucracy, no doubt is an essential element here since there is recent evidence that the federal government has backed away from the widespread production and distribution of large scale curricula, preferring to stimulate the "private sector" to enter even more deeply into such production.[14]

This gives us a brief sense of history, but why the continued movement toward this today? A key element here is seeing the school as an aspect of the state apparatus. For the state's need for *consent* as well as control means that the forms of control in school will be encoded in particular ways (Donald, 1979, p. 44).

The strategic import of the logic of technical control in schools lies in its ability to integrate into one discourse what are often seen as competing ideological movements, and, hence, to generate consent from each of them. The need for accountability and control by administrative managers, the real needs of teachers for something that is "practical" to use with their students, the interest of the state in efficient production and cost savings,[15] the concerns of parents for "quality education" that "works" (a concern that will be coded differently by different classes and class segments), industrial capital's own requirements for efficient production and so on, can be joined. It is here that one can see how two important functions of the state can be accomplished. The state can assist in capital *accumulation* by attempting to provide a more efficient "production process" in schools. At the same time, it can *legitimate* its own activity by couching its discourse in language that is broad enough to be meaningful to each of what it perceives to be important constituencies, yet specific enough to give some practical answers to those who, like teachers, "require" it. The fact that the form taken by these curricular systems is tightly controlled and more easily made "accountable," that it *is* usually individualized, that it focuses on skills in a time of perceived crisis in the teaching of "basic skills," etc., nearly guarantees its acceptability to a wide array of classes and interest groups.

Thus, the logic of control is both mediated and reinforced by the needs of state bureaucrats for accountable and rational procedures and by the specific nexus of forces acting on the state itself. The curricular form will take on the aspects which are necessary to accomplish both accumulation and legitimation.[16] As Clarke puts it:

> Even where institutions meet a logic required by capital, their form and direction are never the outcome of a simple unidirectional imposition by capital. They involve a complex political work of concession and compromise, if only to secure the legitimacy of the state in popular opinion (Clarke, 1979, p. 241).

This is exactly what has occurred in the use of this kind of curricular form.

The Possessive Individual

So far I have examined the encroachment into the work of teachers of the technical control systems embodied in curricular form. Yet, teachers are not the only actors in the setting where we find this material. There are the students as well.

A number of writers have noted that each kind of social formation "requires" a particular kind of individual. Williams and others, for instance, have helped us trace the growth of the abstract individual as it developed within the theoretic, cultural, and economic practices of capitalism (Williams, 1961; MacPherson, 1962). These are not simply changes in the definition of the individual, but imply changes in our actual modes of material and cultural producing, reproducing, and consuming. To be an individual in our society signifies complex interconnection between our day to day meanings and practices and an"external" mode of production. While I do not mean to imply a simple base/superstructure model here, it is clear that in some very important ways there is a dialectical relationship between economic and ideological form. As Gramsci and others would put it, ideological hegemony sustains class domination; subjectivities cannot be seen as unrelated to structure. Yet the questions remain: How are they related? Where are the sites where this relationship is worked out? The school provides a critical point at which one can see these things working out. As Richard Johnson (1978, p. 232) notes, "It is not so much a question that schools...*are* ideology, more that they are the sites where ideologies are produced in the form of subjectivities."

But what kind of subjectivity, what kind of ideology, what kind of individual may be produced here? The characteristics embodied in the modes of technical control built into the curricular form itself are ideally suited to reproduce the possessive individual, a vision of oneself that lies at the ideological heart of corporate economies.

The conception of individualism located in the material we have been examining is quite similar to those found in other analyses of aspects of the cultural apparatus in our society. As Will Wright has demonstrated, for example, in his recent investigation of the role of cultural artifacts like film as carriers and legitimators of ideological changes, important aspects of our cultural apparatus represent a world in which the society recognizes each member as an individual; but that recognition is dependent almost entirely upon technical skills. At the same time, while heightening the value of technical competence, these films direct the individual to reject the importance of ethical and political values through their form. They portray an individualism, situated in the context of a corporate economy, in which "respect and companionship are to be achieved only by becoming a skilled technician." The individual accepts and does any technical job that is offered and has loyalty to only those with similar technical competence, not primarily "to any competing social and community values" (W. Wright,1976, p. 187).

An examination of these curricular "systems" illuminates the extent to which this kind of ideological movement is occurring in increasingly dominant curricular forms. Here, the *rate* at which a student proceeds is individualized; however, the actual product as well as the process to be accomplished are specified by the material itself.[17] Thus, it is not "just" the teacher who faces the encroachment of technical control and deskilling. The students' responses are largely prespecified as well. Much of this growing arsenal of material attempts as precisely as possible to specify appropriate student language and action as well, often reducing it to the mastery of sets of competencies or skills. Here Wright seems correct.

The notion of reducing curriculum to a set of skills is not unimportant in this regard since it is part of the larger process by which the logic of capital helps build identities and transforms cultural meanings and practices into commodities (Aronowitz, 1973, p. 95). That is, if knowledge in all its aspects (of the logical type of that, how, or to—i.e., information, processes, and dispositions or propensities) is broken down and commodified, like economic capital it can be accumulated. The mark of a good pupil is the possession and accumulation of vast quantities of skills in the service of technical interests. As an ideological mechanism in the maintenance of hegemony this is rather interesting. In the larger society, people consume as isolated individuals. Their worth is determined by the possession of material goods or, as Will Wright noted, of technical skills. The accumulation of such goods or of the "cultural capital" of technical competence—here atomistic bits of knowledge and skills measured on pre-tests and post-tests—is a technical procedure, one which requires only the mastery of the prior necessary technical skills and enough time to follow the rules, at one's own pace, to their conclusion. It is the message of the new petty bourgeosie writ large on the ideological terrain of the school.

In fact, one might hypothesize just this, that this kind of movement speaks to the increasing importance in the cultural apparatus of the ideologies of class segments with contradictory class locations, in particular what I have called the new petty bourgeosie—those groups who make up middle management and technical occupations (E. Wright, 1978, p. 79). The particular kind of individualism we are witnessing here is an interesting shift from an ideology of individual autonomy, where a person is his or her own boss and controls his or her destiny, to a careerist individualism. Here the individualism is geared towards organizational mobility and advancement by following technical rules. As Eric Wright puts it, for the petty bourgeosie, "individualism is structured around the requirements of bureaucratic advancement" (E.Wright, 1978, p. 59). It may also be a coded "reflection" of the increasing proletarianization of white collar work. For, while previously individualism signified some serious sense of autonomy over how one worked and what one produced, for a large portion of white collar employees autonomy has been trivialized (E. Wright, 1978, p. 81; Braverman, 1974). The rate at which one works may be individualized, but the work itself, how it is accomplished, and what the exact specifications of the final product will be, are increasingly being specified.

At this stage, we are left with many questions. When technical control means that the form that the curriculum takes is highly specified, that it is individualized to such an extent that there is little required interaction among the students so that each activity is by necessity viewed as an individual intellectualact of skill, that answers often take the form of simple physical activities (as we saw in the module I discussed earlier), that answers are either correct or incorrect based on the application of technical rules, and this kind of form is what one follows throughout one's elementary school life, what impact does it have on the teachers and students who interact with it at the level of practice each day?

We do have evidence to suggest what procedures of this type do to workers in industry and in offices.

Increasing rationalization and a more sophisticated level of control tends to encourage people to manifest an interesting array of traits: a "rules orientation"—that is, an awareness of rules and procedures and a habit of following them; greater dependability—that is, performing a job at a relatively consistent level, being reliable and getting the job done even when rules have to be modified a bit to meet changing day to day conditions; and, the "internalization of the enterprise's goals and values"—that is, conflict is minimized and slowly but surely, there tends to be a homogenization of interests between management and employees (Edwards, 1979, pp. 150-151).[18]

Will this happen in schools as well? This clearly points to the significance of engaging in analyses of what actually happens within the black box of the school. Do teachers and students accept this? Will the gradual introducton of the logic of technical control generate resistances, if only on a cultural level? Will class and work cultures contradict, mediate, or even transform the expected outcomes? (Apple, 1980a, 1980b, 1981). It is to this that we shall now turn.

Resistances

I have not presented an optimistic appraisal here. As the activities of students are increasingly specified, as the rules, processes, and standard outcomes are integrated through and rationalized by the materials themselves, so too are teachers deskilled, reskilled, and anonymized. Students work on material whose form both isolates individuals from each other and establishes the conditions of existence for the possessive individual; the form of the material and the embedded nature of the technical control process does nearly the same for the teacher. Surrounded by a specific logic of control, the objective force of the social relations embodied in the form itself tends to be quite powerful.

Yet I am not arguing for a crude kind of functionalist perspective, where everything is measured by, or is aimed toward, its ability to reproduce an existing static society. The creation of the kind of ideological hegemony "caused" by the increasing introduction of technical control is not "naturally" pre-ordained. It is something that is won or lost in particular conflicts and struggles (Johnson, 1979, p. 70).

On the one hand, teachers will be controlled. As one teacher said about a set of popular material even more integrated and rationalized than the ones I have pointed to here, "Look, I have no choice. I personally don't like this material, but everyone in the district has to use this series. I'll try to do other things as well, but basically our curriculum will be based on this."

On the other hand, resistances will be there. This same teacher who disagreed with the curriculum but used it, also was partially subverting it in interesting ways. It was employed only three days a week instead of the five days which were specified. As the teacher put it, "Listen, if we worked hard we'd finish this stuff in two or three months and besides it's sometimes confusing and boring. So I try to go beyond it as often as possible, *as long as I do not teach what is in the material to be covered by this series next year*." Thus, as we can see from this last part of her comment, internal conditions make such overt resistances more difficult.

Yet these internal conditions need not preclude teachers from also making these commodified cultural forms their own, to generate their own creative responses to dominant ideologies, in a manner similar to what the counter-cultural groups studied by Marxist ethnographers have done to commodified culture. These groups transformed and reinterpreted the products they bought and used so that they became tools for the creation of alternative pockets of resistance (Willis, 1978). Students and teachers may also find ways of creatively using these systems in ways undreamed of by state bureaucrats or corporate publishing. (I must admit, however, that my repeated observations in classrooms over the last years make me less than totally optimistic that this will always or even very often be the case.)

Other elements in the environment may provide the site for different meanings and practices to evolve, though, even within the curricular form itself. For we should remember that there may be progressive elements within the *content* of the curriculum that contradict the messages of the form.[19] And it is in the interaction between the content, the form, and the lived culture of the students that subjectivities are formed. No element in this set of relations can be ignored.

This last point about the lived culture of the actors, the students themselves, needs to be stressed. One would expect resistances on the part of students as well, resistances that will be *specific by race, gender, and class*. My earlier quote from Johnson is correct here. The formation of ideologies—even those of the kind of individual I have examined in this analysis—is not a simple act of imposition. It is produced by concrete actors and embodied in lived experiences that may resist, alter, or mediate these social messages (Johnson, 1978). As Willis demonstrates, for instance, segments of working class youth partially defeat the ideology of individualism. The same may be true for many women and "minority" students. While we can and must focus on these resistances, though, their actual meaning may be unclear. Do they, like those of the lads in Willis' book, also reproduce at an even deeper level ideological meanings and practices that provide quite powerful supports to relations of domination? (Willis, 1977).

Take teachers, for example. While technical controls could possibly lead to unionization, within the school most resistances that occur will be, by necessity, on an individual not a collective level because of the very social relations generated by the curricular form itself (Edwards, 1979, p. 154). The effects, hence, can be rather contradictory.

We must remember as well that, as I mentioned earlier, these more "invisible" modes of control may be accepted if they are perceived as coming from a legitimate overall structure. The fact that curriculum selection committees give teachers a say in the curriculum they will employ means that some of the prior conditions for the consent necessary for this kind of control to be successful have already been laid. The choice is made, in part, by the teachers themselves. It is hard to argue in the face of that.

It is easy to forget something else. This is not a good time, ideologically or economically, for teachers who engage in overt resistances. Given a difficult ideological climate and given the employment situation among teachers today—with thousands having either been laid off or living under the threat of it—the loss of control can progress in a relatively unthreatened way. Deskilling and reskilling, progressive anonymization and rationalization, the transformation of educational work, somehow seem less consequential than such economic concerns as job security, salary, etc., even though they may seem to us to clearly be part of the same dynamic.

When all is said and done, though, we must recognize that these powerful social messages, while embedded in the actual experiences of teachers and students as they go about their day to day lives in classrooms, *are* highly mediated by other elements. The fact that individual teachers like most other workers may develop patterns of resistance to these patterns of technical control at the informal cultural level alters these messages. The contradictory ideologies of individualism and cooperativeness that are naturally generated out of the crowded conditions of many classrooms (you can't be an isolated individual all the time when there are twenty or thirty other people around with whom one teacher must cope) also provide countervailing possibilities. And lastly, just as blue and white collar workers have constantly found ways to retain their humanity and continually struggle to integrate conception and execution in their work (if only to relieve boredom) so too will teachers and students find ways, in the cracks so to speak, to do the same things. The real question is not whether such resistances exist—Aronowitz, myself, and others have claimed at length elsewhere that they are never far from the surface (Aronowitz, 1978; Apple, 1980b; Burawoy, 1979)—but whether they are contradictory themselves, whether they lead anywhere beyond the reproduction of the ideological hegenony of the most powerful classes in our sociey, whether they can be employed for political education and intervention.

Our task is first to find them. We need somehow to give life to the resistances, the struggles. What I have done here is to point to the terrain within the school (the transformation of work, the deskilling and reskilling, the technical control, and so on) over which these struggles will be fought. The resistances may be informal, not fully organized or even conscious; yet this does not mean that they will have no impact. For Gramsci and Johnson (1979) remind us, hegemony is always contested. Our own work should help in this contestation.

FOOTNOTES

[1] I wish to thank Linda McNeil for bringing this material to my attention.

[2] This is not to deny the importance of analyzing official documents, especially those emanating from the state. Donald (1979) provides an excellent example of the power of discourse analysis, for example, in unpacking what these documents mean and do.

[3] See also the impressive discussion in Braverman (1974) and Burawoy (1979).

[4] I have discussed the school's role in producing this knowledge in Apple (1979b).

[5] The work of Philip Wexler (1983) of the University of Rochester on the commodification of intimate relations is important here.

[6] This is not only an American phenomenon. The foreign subsidiaries of the companies who produce these materials are translating and marketing their products in the third world and elsewhere as well. In many ways it is similar to the cultural imperialism of Walt Disney Productions. See, e.g., Dorfman and Mattelart (1975).

[7] See, for example, my analysis of science curricula in Apple (1979a).

[8] I do not mean to romanticize that past, however. Many teachers probably simply followed the textbook before. However, the level of specificity and the integration of curricular, pedagogical, and evaluative aspects of classroom life into *one* system is markedly different. The use of the system brings with it much more technical control of every aspect of teaching than previous text-based curricula. Obviously, some teachers will not follow the system's rules. Given the

level of integration, though, it will undoubtedly be much more difficult to ignore it since many systems constitute the core or only program in that curricular area in the entire school or district. Thus, accountability to the next grade level or to administrators makes it harder to ignore. I shall return to this point later on.

[9] This may be similar to what happened in the early mills in New England, when standardized production processes drastically reduced the contact among workers. See Edwards (1979, p. 114).

[10] One could also claim that schools operate to produce use value, not exchange value. Erik Olin Wright, personal conversation.

[11] Therefore, any outcomes of schooling must be analyzed as the products of cultural, political, and economic resistance as well as determinations. See Willis (1977) and Apple (1980a).

[12] I do not want to ignore the question of the relationship between capitalism and bureaucracy. Weber and others were not wrong when they noted that there are needs for rationalization specific to bureaucratic forms themselves. However, neither the *way* bureaucracy has grown in corporate economies nor its effects have been neutral. This is treated in considerably more detail in Clawson (1978). See also Wright (1978).

[13] See also Noble (1977) for his account of standardization and its relationship to capital accumulation.

[14] Among the reasons for the fact that the state has slowly but surely backed away from such production and distribution is the contoversy surrounding "Man: A Course of Study" and, no doubt, the intense lobbying efforts on the part of publishing firms. Corporations will let the government socialize the costs of development, but obviously would prefer to package and distribute the curricula for themselves. See Apple (1977).

[15] This is not meant to imply that the state always directly serves the needs of industrial capital. It, in fact, does have a significant degree of relative autonomy and is the site of class conflict as well. See Donald (1979), Wright (1978), and Dale (1982).

[16] We should remember, however, that accumulation and legitimation may be in conflict with each other at times. See Wright (1978) for a discussion of these possible contradictions and for an argument about the importance of understanding the way the state and bureaucracies mediate and act back on "economic determinations".

[17] Bernstein's work on class and educational codes is interesting here. As he notes, "The pacing of educational knowledge is class based." (Bernstein, 1977, p. 113).

[18] This does not mean that important resistances and countervailing practices do or will not occur. But they usually occur on the terrain established by capital.

[19] Geoff Whitty has been particularly helpful in enabling me to see this point. It should also be recognized that the very fact that industrialists *are* interested in content speaks to the import of content as a contested area.

REFERENCES

Apple, M. Social structure, ideology, and curriculum. In M. Lawn & L. Barton (Eds.), *Curriculum: Self and Structure*. London: Croom Helm, 1981.

Apple, M. Analyzing determinations: Understanding and evaluating the productions of social outcomes in schools. *Curriculum Inquiry*, 1980, *10*, 55-76. (a)

Apple, M. The other side of the hidden curriculum: Correspondence theories and the labor process. *The Journal of Education*, 1980,*162*, 47-66. (b)

Apple, M. *Ideology and Curriculum*. Boston: Routledge & Kegan Paul, 1979a.

Apple, M. The production of knowledge and the production of deviance in schools. In L. Barton & R. Meighan (Eds.), *School, Pupils, and Deviance*. Driffield, England: Nafferton Books, 1979b, pp. 113-131.

Apple, M. Ideology and form in curriculum evaluation. In G. Willis (Ed.), *Qualitative Evaluation*. Berkeley: McCutchan Publishing Corp., 1978, pp. 495-521.

Apple, M. Politics and national curriculum policy. *Curriculum Inquiry*, 1977, *7*, 351-361.

Aronowitz, S. Marx, Braverman, and the logic of capital. *The Insurgent Sociologist*, 1978, *8*, 126-146.

Aronowitz, S. *False Promises*. New York: McGraw-Hill, 1973.

Barker, J. & H. Downing. Word processing and the transformation of patriarchal relations. Unpublished paper. Birmingham, England: University of Birmingham Centre for Contemporary Cultural Studies, 1979.

Bernstein, B. *Class, Codes, and Control, Volume 3*. Boston: Routledge & Kegan Paul, 1977.

Braverman, H. *Labor and Monopoly Capital*. New York: Monthly Review Press, 1974.

Burawoy, M. Toward a marxist theory of the labor process: Braverman and beyond. *Politics and Society*,1979, *8*, 3-4.

Clawson, D.C. Class struggle and the rise of bureaucracy. Ph. D. dissertation. Stony Brook: State University of New York at Stony Brook, 1978.

Clarke, J. Capital and culture: The post-war working class revisited. In J. Clarke, C. Critcher, & R. Johnson (Eds.), *Working Class Culture*. London: Hutchinson, 1979, pp. 238-253.

Dale, R. Education and the capitalist state: Contributions and contradictions. In M. Apple (Ed.), *Cultural and Economic Reproduction in Education*. Boston: Routledge & Kegan Paul, 1982.

Dale, R. The politicization of school deviance. In L. Barton & R. Meighan (Eds.), *Schools, Pupils, and Deviance*. Driffield, England: Nafferton Books, 1979, pp. 95-112.

Donald, J. The Green Paper: Noise of a crisis. *Screen Education*, 1979, *30*, 13-49.

Dorfman, A., & A. Mattelart *How to Read Donald Duck*. New York: International General Editions,1975.

Downing, D. Soft choices: Teaching materials for teaching free enterprise. Austin: The University of Texas, Institute for Constructive Capitalism, 1979.

Edwards, R. *Contested Terrain*. New York: Basic Books, 1979.

Finn, D., N. Grant, R. Johnson, & the C.C.C.S. EDUCATION GROUP. Social democracy, education, and the crisis. Birmingham, England: University of Birmingham Centre for Contemporary Cultural Studies, 1978.

Gitlin, T. Prime time ideology: The hegemonic process in television entertainment. *Social Problems*, 1979, *26*, 251-266.

Jameson, F. *Marxism and Form*. Princeton: Princeton University Press, 1971.

Johnson, R. Histories of culture/theories of ideology: Notes on an impass. In M. Barrett, R. Corrigan, A. Kuhn, & J. Wolf (Eds.), *Ideology and Cultural Production*. New York: St. Martin's Press, 1979, pp. 49-77.

Johnson, R. Three problematics: Elements of a theory of working class culture. In J. Clarke, C. Critcher, & R. Johnson (Eds.), *Working Class Culture*. London: Hutchinson, 1978, pp. 201-237.

Macpherson, C. B. *The Political Theory of Possessive Individualism*. New York: Oxford University Press, 1962.

Noble, D. *American by Design: Science, Technology, and the Rise of Corporate Capitalism*. New York: Alfred A. Knopf, 1977.

O'Connor, J. *The Fiscal Crisis of the State*. New York: St. Martin's Press, 1973.

Ryerson, J., & Son, Inc. The Ryerson plan: A teacher work-learn program. Unpublished advertisement. Chicago: Joseph T. Ryerson & Son, Inc., no date.

Science: A Process Approach. Module One. Lexington, MA: Ginn & Co., 1974.

Spring, J. *The Sorting Machine* New York: David McKay, 1976.

Wexler, P. *Critical Social Psychology*. Boston: Routledge & Kegan Paul, 1983.

Williams, R. *Marxism and Literature*. New York: Oxford University Press, 1977.

Williams, R. *The Long Revolution*. London: Chatto & Windus, 1961.

Willis, P. *Profane Culture*. Boston: Routledge & Kegan Paul, 1978.

Willis, P. *Learning to Labor*. Westmead, England: Saxon House, 1977.

Wright, E. O. *Class, Crisis, and the State*. London: New Left Books, 1978.

Wright, W. *Sixguns and Society*. Berkeley: University of California Press, 1975.

7

Our own being-as-wholeness, says Kenneth R. Beittel in this paper, we can potentially discern as we become conscious of our qualitative experiencing. We experience both dis-integration and integration, but by the art of metaphoric expression, of love and dialogue, we can bind up these "contraries." There is a mythic or spiritual quality to this adventure, to this art of qualitative thinking, which requires a depth hermeneutic, no mere surface understanding. The self is transformed, as is the world about us. Learning to be competent must grab us at this profound level of experiencing and move us toward consciousness of our real being-as-wholeness.

Beittel gives us lessons in this art of qualitative thinking and does so in extraordinarily artful language that taps his meanings in ways no ordinary language could evoke. In this poetic/metaphorical expression, Beittel reminds us of the central role metaphors play in integrating our experience into meaningful wholes. The key elements in Beittel's lessons are: qualitative experiences, expressions of them through iconic and/or literary "texts,"deep structure in these experiences and "texts," process as dialogic and organismic, distancing and recovery, interpreting, self-awareness through reflexivity, and critical evaluation.

After reading Beittel's artistic work on competence, you should apply his guidelines for qualitative thinking to your own experience of competence and see how wholistic it becomes. If you find it difficult to express such competence-as-being in verbal or poetic form, as Beittel is able to do, you can enact your understanding of it, for example, as a teacher, by being a living icon or image of the competent teacher. Perhaps a second and a third reading of this complex paper will be necessary in order to grasp its full meaning.

Professor Beittel is Professor of Art Education in the College of Arts and Architecture, The Pennsylvania State University.

Great Swamp Fires I Have Known: Competence and the Hermeneutics of Qualitative Experiencing

Kenneth R. Beittel
The Pennsylvania State University

To speak of competence from within a hermeneutical and phenomenological perspective and as an art educator, artist, and sometimes scholar imposes a heavy burden on one who likes most to be deadly playful. "O rose," meaning O self, O being-of-education, "thou art sick," I want to say with Blake. The rose, the self-culture whole, is simultaneously beautiful and harbors a worm. How to expel the worm from the rose and round out a full blossoming? How to knock the implicit negation in the heart of experience and like a blithe spirit embrace the contradictories within our very bosom?

A stick has two ends. Without them, one has nothing—at least not a stick—to get a handle on. "White must win," as Watts[1] puts it, reveals a mind not on to the Tao of things. The late Heidegger[2] could not speak of coming-into-being without the celebration of poetry, the divine dance performed in the midst of the mystery. "Truth" pulled out of its contemporary tailspin for him just in time to pull the rip-cord, where it took on the pre-Socratic shining forth from concealment, the compatible incompatibility of light and darkness as one. Shining forth conceals, and concealment is the adumbration of the light. At the heart of the mystery of coming-into-being is a unity of contradictories, of warring members, of conflicting nexuses, that form an indissoluble whole, insofar as we permit ourselves to experience and treat it as whole.

The memory of wholeness antedates conscious recollections of our infancy. Is it the organismic, tissue memory, of a community of cells exploding from the impact of the contradictories of conception? The body has its memories. The body-mind has its memories. The body-mind-consciousness has its memories. What are the symbols, the myths, the flickering flames from the murky smoke of unextinguishable swamp fires that light the darkness of our habituated dis-integration?

So with competence. It is not worth an artist's attention. "Be gifted," he will say; "don't tell me your un-wholesome problems. Who cares when there is dancing to be done?" On the other hand, he implies, "be yourself, see yourself, free yourself."[3] Or, with Suzuki,[4] he says: "right practice, right attitude, right understanding." Or quotes Dogen-Zenji:

> To study Buddhism is to study oneself.
> To study oneself is to forget oneself.[5]

So with competence. It is a sick rose that merits all of our attention. It teases out any complacency to believe that politics is not there, that hidden strategies are not whispering to one another like evil spirits in the night. It says that to believe otherwise is to be already totalized, to be politicized in unacknowledged ways. It says that there is no hiding place, that self and culture alike synergistically incubate a common cancer.

Strict phenomenology, strict science, and strict hermeneutics—to expand our strictures—conspire to make of man an endangered species. All of these slide into a positivism which turns man's mind against his body (or against body-mind-consciousness, which is "love's body"[6]) and against nature (or against body-mind-consciousness-in-the-world, which is qualitative experience). The mind, as mere tool of consciousness of body-mind, attacks the whole of which it is a fragment—the ultimate technological reversal and put-down. Existential and hermeneutic phenomenology attempt to heal this dangerous condition, as does post-Einsteinian Taoistic physics, but these remain lopsidedly mental, like a Gregory Bateson or a Bucky Fuller. It was Kierkegaard who told us that the purpose of talk is to keep us from action, just as it was Kafka who showed us where mere talk could lead, taking us within the Castle, or rather, losing us within the labyrinth of collective mind at the end of its tether.

Only qualitatively, adrift in the qualitative immediate present, does man grasp his Eden-like potential and discern the scope of his Adamic fall. The wholeness we remember, the wholeness we bring back with us, the wholeness we discern when and only when we are experientially and qualitatively whole, reveals the Eden, the rose, of self-plus-culture as one, before the reversal of mind, the knowledge of good and evil, the separation of light from darkness, splits asunder that moving wholeness into fragments forgetful of their origin, like the faithless art critic who forgets that what he took apart to make a point was really done through an act of violence demanding reaffirmation or, at the least, an apology.

The deep structure of the qualitative adumbrates a self and a culture before "world" crashes down on it. The world that comes with being-as-wholeness is not the one we want to stop to get off of. It is the unpresupposed world our assumed, dead-metaphor worlds are always trying to play footsie with. Pre-symbolic, iconic, pregnant with meaning, it moves us to break the totalitarianism of language to sound the bronze bell of ordinary speech. In the early world, in the qualitative world of experence, there are only poets, lovers, artists.

The myth of the fall, the metaphor of the rose and the worm, is the myth of the everday life-in-death of our qualitative experience. Redemption exists only through the death and renewal that an uncorrupted consciousness passes through within qualitative experiencing—that is, of overcoming negation to bind up the contraries; that is, of expression, as art; that is, of being, as love and dialogue; that is, of expression with thought, as the art of qualitative thinking. How else is the simultaneous renewal of self and culture possible?

In the latter, the *art* of qualitative thinking, the life instinct, or wholeness within qualitiative experience, eventually overcomes the two-headed worm, the inner politics of self and the external politics of culture, as these operate through their constraints and distortions on the former, producing a clash between life and death instincts out of which new powers of body-mind-consciousness are born by the circling back movement of expressive thought toward renewed wholeness. This is a politically dangerous doctrine, for it is the only one that I can find that truly fits or makes free men.

Hence self and culture, as existents, politically conspire, as tacit accomplices, a C.I.A. of the spirit, to keep potentially dangerous and thus unwanted wholeness from happening. One of the best ways to do this, of course, is to preach wholeness and offer techniques for it, thus moving to control or technologize what is out of control and not under techniques. What are we left with? The words are not enough: be yourself, see yourself, free yourself; right practice, right attitude, right understanding; no withdrawal from the senses; no *a priori* hierarchy of qualities; no Hegelian spiritual ladder; no mind-fucking. Actually, there is no danger. One cannot ever wallow in quality, alas! The waves are of the ocean. They reveal deep structure. They neither stay still nor respect the surfer.

Recently a student questioned why I said a two-headed political worm abides within the rose of qualitative experiencing. But she was willing to explore with me a Socratic question-and-answer excursion into what assumptions we could agree upon. We agreed that we have internalized the memory and the expectation of wholeness, as kind of a prerequisite toward experiencing it. We agreed that in the center of qualitative experiencing is a consciousness witnessing our very involvement; that being *in*-volved is connected somehow with our becoming *e*-volved; that we cannot *in*-voke what has not first been *e*-voked; that we cannot distance without first being near. Further, we retain an awareness that the quality of our conscious experience could always be both extended and deepened. This led to the question of what could limit us at the heart of what we so desire and yearn for. Enter the two-headed worm of self and culture, what I have called the politics of the internal and of the external. Here, at the heart of experience, a teleology of the spirit tenses against an archaeology of the spirit, a progressive view with a regressive one; here, purpose, insight, intentionality, bias, and renewal compete with evaluation, judgment, coping, and assessment. Here we see that a reconciliation of surface and hidden strategies of inner and outer standards requires a depth hermeneutic. We cannot escape ideology, but only resist totalization.

We learn, at least from within the art education tradition, that personal art must remain within highart. We sense that no art worthy of that name can be taught, and yet, paradoxically, that there is a way of being which, at all times and places and levels, requires that it be learned ever anew and at once—that is, wholistically.[7]

The entropy of un-loving is the great law of spiritual thermodynamics. When I write too much, I secretly fear my environment may be falling apart. What will happen to my pottery studio, to the weeping cherry now blooming outside my window? If my eyes and feelings and acts do not go out to these, will not they partially wither and crumble away? The International Institute of Yoga Science and Philosophy has taken over a former Catholic theological seminary outside of Honesdale, Pennsylvania, as its national headquarters. In this beautiful spot, the farm buildings are deteriorating from dis-use and the landscape has itself become introverted from the lack of contact between inner and outer paths.

Where do we start? To be congruent, artists and thinkers taking up the art of qualitative thinking must find a parallelism, synchronistic at the very least, between their circumlocutions and their moving feet.

But, what do you do, preacher man? Start with practice. Shut up and drink your tea, wedge your clay. Make love—that is, bind together the contradictories into wholeness—not war—that is, avoid yielding to the worm which hates the other: the alchemical self and the mythic culture.

In talk, in dialogue, we can invoke the language of practice.[8] In this language a dialectic occurs in which what is implicit is brought to first words, which enlarges awarenesss to include what was tacit, or bodily participative, thus enlarging again the language of practice. We cannot speak our doing except as we can do our saying. The mythic resides in the commonplace, the everyday. We see that:

The bamboo shadows sweep the stairs
But raise no dust.[9]

We begin to learn the pine from the pine, and the bamboo from the bamboo.[10] We are toppled by a feather and transfixed by a ray of light.

Recently one of my students brought a game of his invention to class. It was about the potential existence within our presence of a mythic being. He had tape-recorded a series of 50 responses to yes-no questions in which four alternatives were possible: yes, no, I don't know, I don't want to say. These and their order were arrived at through the four movements of Chevreuil's pendulum: back and forth, sideways, clockwise circular, and counter-clockwise circular. The assignment of meanings to these four was random. We decided to play the game as a group instead of individually. With seven in the group, we went around the group seven times, twice magical thus, trying not to pre-think the questions that would arise. Two students acted as secretaries as well as participants.

The outcome of this psychic parlor game was an enigmatic "text" ripe for playful, and therefore serious, interpretation, if anyone wished to pick it up. The participative ingredient, the unfolding blind game of strategy, stains the text with meaning and a deep structure. We were only playing, but we became involved. Tarot cards and the I Ching only carry this game a bit further by supplying structural complexity, interpretive metaphors, and a tradition of usages which make the synchronistic lasso more binding. How can nothing be determined and yet all revealed? Events and works are reinstated for what they are (which we would often sooner forget): spring lambs autonomously materializing and cavorting on a green meadow at the edge of a dark abyss.

Here is a mystery. The pygmalion myth is imperfect. Within the creative process the forming work is like a dialogue partner, taking us to otherness, away from ourselves, so that something can be at stake between us. So the dialogue metaphor has meaning here. But, in addition, the dialogue progressively transforms into a structure and the dialogue partner into a work. This is a subtle alchemy shaking us from the comfort of even a dynamic single vision. Blake says it thus:

> Twofold always, May God us keep
> From single vision and Newton's sleep.[11]

The twofold vision of creating, of qualitative experiencing, accepts the paradox and the contraries that make up one unity. Both the dialogue and the organism analogy are sustained. The work, as process play transformed into structure, is flesh of our flesh and radical otherness simultaneously. Like breathing in and breathing out, like subject and predicate, these two things are one; this one thing is two.

Here also is the double target of the two-headed worm. The self, that unique personhood seen as unbounded metaphor, narcissistically gravitates toward the organism analogy: we return to our origins, we become what we always were, our endless potential (always envisioned as "in there") is progressively unveiled, we are ful-filled in love and art and qualitative thought. The other, the world as unbounded metaphor, pluralistically gravitates toward the dialogue analogy: we lose ourselves, our potential is only seen by the other, love and art and the qualitative encounter us. The problem of the one and the many is hidden deep within the rose. "The self," said Mead, "is an other."[12]

This is enough of a challenge for the best of heads. It is as though experience breaks down our mental computer by confusing us with: here's how I see you seeing me seeing you seeing me.[13] There is one too many complicating twist for us to follow. Here, at our most vital, we cannot even be sure of our ground, let alone find a ground for a concept such as "competency." But let us put this problem aside as we look at the *art* of qualitative thinking.

I propose to turn my back on hermeneutics and phenomenology proper while borrowing heavily from the complex language lore these traditions have given me. There is something I must do beforehand so that I dare both to use and misuse these traditions. Were I in theological or scriptural hermeneutics, this would be equivalent to saying that before getting bogged down in the niceties of methods and arguments, I would like to face the issue of implicit faith and the kerygma.

First, I would like to say that the twofold vision which the joint metaphors of dialogue and organism bestow upon us, is the surest ground of a unity of dynamic contraries I can find. It is the ground of the free-becoming-of-being[14] which is art and which is qualitative experiencing. In isolating the artist and the artist-in-us, I set off this archetype from others possible—for example, the saint. Therefore I do not claim completeness, but convenience and power through a focus. There are many ways to do in competence, but this one will do nicely. I even suspect that it will do so most tellingly, for the side of unity I find most enthralling is the progressive side where, as coming into being, we cannot be sure of the idealist side *a priori*.

What I further propose to do is to perform a hermeneutic analysis of the *art* of qualitative thinking. By this clever dodge, I think to talk conceptually, as befits a professor of education and art; but also artistically, as befits a professor of art and education, for in stressing that it is an art of qualitative thinking which will be both our "pre-text" and our "text," I resist the single vision which would allow the conceptual to extend so far that its connection with the qualitative would be tenuous or token. This analysis will take on some of the direction of a book now under way by my wife and me, called *The Art of Qualitative Thinking: Celebrating, Interpreting, and Renewing Human Vitality*. If follows that I cannot give you a book in a few paragraphs, but I believe that the flow of arguments represented by its emerging structure will help our thinking together. There will be eight pointers.

1. There is a qualitative basis to our experience. I would like to say at the beginning, with no thanks to Thorndike, that whatever exists, existed as some quality and therefore cannot be measured. Quality, consciousness, and experience are separate words for what is one whole, as one lived-process. Current metaphors for consciousness tend toward the dialogue analogy, away from the earlier wax and stamp metaphor, or the somewhat later container and contents metaphor.[15] Our reality, as experienced, would seem to be dynamically interactive, two-fold, from the start. The two-fold witnessing effect of consciousness during our most in-volved participative states further points to a constantly reflexive and self-formative process ongoing within us. There is a natural, organic, and esthetic unity in our experiencing when it has most presence and vitality for us. This is experience as Dewey[16] described it, *an* experience, with a beginning, middle, and end; a rounded-out, event-full, consummatory whole. If we are up for it, we can extend the qualitative immediate present through our participation, the way a poet does.[17]

William James kept shifting his metaphors for consciousness.[18] He called it a stream to get at its change with continuity. He switched to a sculptor finding a single figure in a stone to accentuate the way consciousness has both selectivity and unity. Still again, to show the tender care and authorship the mind has for its thoughts he spoke of it as a herdsman herding his sheep.

In this example, we see how James gravitates to metaphor, to a language of presence, imagery, and feeling, to remain in touch with an elusive quality. By so doing, he creates for us an expressive "text" or qualitative event surrogate which mediates the quality for both him and us. I will use the word "text" for this surrogate in what follows, but it should always beenvisioned as in quotation marks. Further, I will make a functional distinction between "originary quality" and "dependent quality," thus further shifting from the hermeneutic tradition. By this I simply mean, as originary, that no text or work exists as the start for our hermeneutic round-trip, but that we will have to supply one by our direct participant-participation (as I now call it) in our qualitative experience. I thus set our focus away from those cultural objectivations called works and texts without quotation marks, for in the consumer's mentality these inspire they cause us more political, academic, and language problems than does originary quality. This distinction, again, is purely functional and didactic. I see text interpretation in the traditional sense as also an art of qualitative thinking, but it helps me to cleanse my thought to set it aside for now.

There is indeed a world-view and a knowledge interest implicit in the art of qualitative thinking. What it is about is the disclosure of being itself. Through it we enhance our vitality, our community, our self-actualization, and our praxis. It opens us up to love and dialogue and change, to what Bachelard called "the contact between two poetries."[19] Its interest is also political: to give meaning to life, to learn from its mystery, to enhance autonomy, to liberate thought through action, to become expressive vehicles for newness of being. But it is apolitically political; it detests totalization of any kind and cannot really make even the claims I have made for it. It is humble and grandiose. If the poet is a legislator, he is certainly, as Shelley said, an unacknowledged one. But, if "poetically man dwells,"[20] as Hoederlin claims, what choice do we have short of extinction or alienation?

In the analysis that follows, the art of qualitative thinking will be presented as a dialectical process composed of four moments: (1) expression or "text'; (2) distancing as the start of an analytical effort; (3) interpreting as itself a dialectic between explanation and understanding; and (4) renewing as a process where evaluation, speculation, and expressive return occur. These will constitute the round trip of this artistic journey.

2. "Text" in this perspective appears in artistically expressive and expressive descriptive forms. For convenience, these can be schematized into expressive modes, of which I see two, iconic (or non-verbal) and literary, and into descriptive modes, of which there are also two, phenomenological and historical. The general importance of "text" in the originary art of qualitative thinking cannot be overestimated. I myself also feel that the expressive modes have a priority in this regard, for, as closer to art already at the "text" level, they are also closer to the event. They are also more omnivorous of the remaining three moments

of our hermeneutic voyage—that is, in them, expression, distancing, interpretation, and renewal are often intricately entwined into one large work of conceptual art. Besides, in these times of hidden politics, the artist must be his own hermeneut. The descriptive modes (which do not give up all claim to expression by any means) are more distanced from the event, receptive of depth rather than symbolic (pre-symbolic) of it. They are also more prone, because more self-conscious, to acknowledge from the start the separation of the "text" from the other moments. In an era when scientism and technology enjoy center stage, descriptive modes are inclined to be pseudo-scientific in their language or admit to a proto-scientific interest ready to be abandoned where "true science" can take over. This is, of course, a misplaced emphasis within what I am characterizing as an art, and it hides the artful and expressive nature of descriptions, narratives, and chronicles.

It turns out that unless we can imaginatively enlarge our capacities to create in responding, to engage more fully the qualitative immediate present, we will not be able to open up to the profundity and potential meaning of our lived experience. We will not, that is, experience dialogue as transformed into organism, and we will lack the impetus to correct the perpetual enfeebling of self and culture, the inner and outer politics, hidden in the heart of our rose. This can be put as a maxim: the more we move "from" in order to move "to," too quickly, the less there is to move "towards." To move in haste away from the qualitative immediate present is to move toward the weakening of self and culture.

What I am here separating for discussion's sake occurs integrally and organically in instances of qualitative thinking. If space permitted I would present here a longish excerpt from Proust's *Within a Budding Grove.*[21] The first person narrator in the novel is on a carriage ride in Combray with an aging countess. All of a sudden, at a turn, they come upon three trees and he is, as we now say, both "spaced out" and "wiped out." The image of the three trees constitutes a separate reality within the narrator's life-world, triggering off a qualitative immediate present of great scope, depth, and import. The ongoing narration, measuring out to the beat of the horse's hooves and through the charging spatial perspectives from the carriage, establishes the qualitative event in its context. Without a break, but with mounting agitation, a distancing movement, within the heart of experiencing, sets in. What can these three trees signify? The narrator searches through six alternatives: (1) they are from the remote and nearly forgotten past; (2) they belonged to repetitive "dream landscapes"; (3) they brought mystery back to a place that knowledge had denuded of meaning; (4) they were a dream residue from the night before; (5) they hid a meaning so obscure that the narrator searches in the past when the idea is actually a new one; and (6) they had no concealed thought or message for the author. Then comes a direct surge into interpretation (almost like Swedenborg's dream journal, where he glides smoothly from description to interpretation—easy, alas, for one who talks with angels, tells his neighbors when they are going to die, and smells a great fire a thousand miles away). The narrator says: "*I choose rather to believe* that they were phantoms of the past, dear companions of my childhood, vanished friends who recalled our common memories." (Italics added.)

We recognize in this interpretation the direction which Proust seems destined to take. It will take him seven volumes to round out his research into the vanished past, wherein he finds the rich golden vein of significance. He suggests to the reader that he will eventually succeed in penetrating into this kind of mystery in what lies ahead, but, he laments "...of those trees themselves I was never to know what they had been trying to give me nor where else I had seen them." Hence Proust turns himself, and the reader, back into the mystery unfulfilled (a perfect literary device to move the reader on with him). Says he: "...I was as wretched as though I had just lost a friend, had died myself, had broken faith with the dead or had denied my God."

Short of the expressive, we are bound to fail in establishing a vital "text." The failure of language to capture quality straight on needs little detailing. Dewey[22] says it clearly:

> Language comes infinitely short of paralleling the variegated surface of nature.... The unique quality of a quality is found in experience itself; it is there and sufficiently there not to need reduplication in language.... But words serve their poetic purpose in the degree in which they summon and evoke into active operation the vital responses that are present whenever we experience qualities.

So whether, at the"text" level, we do a poem or a phenomenological description in "gray, anonymous language,"[23] both will reveal a spontaneity within discipline, both will have to be expressive, will have to be able to in-voke what was e-voked. Both will have to back away from surface interpretations, premature cause-and-effect language, and laundry lists of factual details.[24]

3.*There is a deep structure to the qualitative.* I have already explicitly presented this concept in the form of the two-fold vision, self and culture, dialogue and organism, inner and outer politics, and the primordial unity where seemingly estranged elements are synthesized through a conflict which remains as a vital force in the whole. Metaphorically, I have spoken of it as a rose with a phantom two-headed worm at its heart. I will add only one new item here: that of the autosymbolism[25] which the fringe areas of the body-mind complex provide consciousness for intuitive insights during states of qualitative experiencing. One of the girls in a graduate seminar of mine recently had a dream. The seminar was on evaluation and assessment in Art Education. In it we jointly engaged in a workshop and in theoretical discussions on the art of qualitative thinking. In her dream, a group was gathered around an L-shaped pond into which they intently peered. She vaguely sensed a large, pickerel-like fish with a long nose hidden in the dark shadows of the pool. The dream changed then and among other things presented a boy in a butcher's apron who was confronted by a large fish which started to blow upon him, pushing him backward. As the dream faded, she had an uneasy feeling that the fish might actually have devoured him. She woke and it was early morning. She felt the dream had something to do with our seminar, but felt no inclination to interpret it. Instead she wrote the following:

> The silhouette of quality in thought is cut from an elusive aptitude—the ability to recall image/experience, to savor them in combination and to join them in relevant patterns. Quality as such is reflected as a certain depth, a clarity and definition, a sense of the one in many. Some people are more sensitive than others to aspects of a particular experience—the rhythm, color, and form of an event and the suggestions of past and future experience suspended within the event. These configurations become images in memory.
>
> Created meaning is the bridge joining the profound moment with the construction of what-would-happen-if models. It rises from the appreciation of particular experience and moves to invent what-if models from this body of stored images. These models can then be turned at various angles. We see how they catch the light of present circumstances.
>
> Meaning has to do with the relatedness, the purposefulness of acting in the world. Without created meaning as a kind of spine in the body of experience, even the most sensitive appreciation of particular moments can be shattered. It has an internal consistency built on values that are believed to enlarge men's awareness. It is a commitment to reunite the many in one.
>
> balance: joy—purpose
> marry: others—self
> merge: body—mind[26]

This girl did not usually write philosophically. Here she was able to integrate images of power and danger, the one and the many, into one "text" which also became, obliquely, a distanced interpretation and a renewal in touch with the autosymbolism of a dream. The reference to the "spine in the body of experience" gave me the image of my seminar as a chiropractic of the qualitative where we worked out the various "subluxations" to keep our experience whole and hearty.

I prefer not to inflate such happenings, but to court and use them. They are happy synchronistic self-discoveries with which, if we are relaxed enough, we can spontaneously collaborate.

Another student of mine made the autosymbolic miasma of the hypnogogic state just prior to falling asleep the joint event and "text" of an exercise in the art of qualitative thinking. He settled down to go to sleep in a relaxed frame of mind, but he first pushed the record button of a tape recorder. Insofar as possible, he spoke out what images floated through his mind, sometimes forgetful to do so, eventually drifting off into sleep until the click at the end of the tape awakened him.

Later he typed out the recorded words of images. Then he took this paragraph apart and positioned phrases and words on successive pages to approximate the temporal spatiality of actual gaps on the tape and remembered or forgotten gaps in his experience. You might call this "text" number two. As it went on, words lost their belongingness to phrases and to each other, and plain blank pages began to be inserted to show complete dissociation of word with word, image with image, and of memory with both.

Here is a kind of reversal. The event is only partially accessible. Qualitative explorations in expression reconstruct it.

4. *Process itself has quality and structure and also leads to new structure.* The example just cited reveals the structural-existentiality of process.[27] Process is deep; process is dance and dream and play; and process is both dialogue and, as transformation into a structure—that is, as emerging work and "text"—is also organism. It is a music that sounds without a score and yet produces one. The artist-in-us, in qualitative experiencing, does the same. The extension of the dialogue of process is the best preparation for the "poetic purpose" of the work and the "text," for it is in the qualitative immediate present of experiencing that the "active operation" of "vital responses" occurs.

5. *Distancing of the qualitative is a tacit preparation for interpretation and renewal.* By invoking an art of qualitative *thinking*, I simultaneously invoke the image of the artist as reflective and reflexive rather than as an innocent child or as an unreigned intuition ripe for possession. Paradoxically, we must become as little children to enter into the heaven of the hermeneutics of qualitative thinking. In other words, we are called to do both. We lose and regain our cool only, we will find, to lose it again in a renewing return. Positing enlarged self-awareness and its assimilation as healthy and good, distancingis inevitable. We saw it happen in the heart of Proust's narrative. Without it, I suspect, the two-headed worm will eat the heart out of our rose. We will eventually say, with Pogo, we have met the enemy and he is us, but add, and he is also our friend.

I see two ways of distancing. One is through *reduction* by selection and paraphrase. The other is through *expansion* by selection and substitution. Whether we reduce in numbers or expand in numbers a distancing can occur. We acknowledge this in our imagery of the retreat and the crowd, or more positively put, in the hermitage and the community.

I am inclined to be more suspicious of reduction than of expansion. The clearer we talk, through reduction, the more we lose the "poetic purpose" of what we are saying. As Norman Brown [28] has put it: "Mysteries display themselves in words only if they can remain concealed: this is poetry, isn't it?" In expansion it is as though we realize that we cannot talk the dance well, so we seek out the community of other dances, other dancers. But both reduction and expansion employ selection and a kind of paraphrase, even if only in the crowding of metaphors one with another.

There is, however, no necessity to choose. Expansion and reduction can go together. Expansion can be facilitated by reduction, that is, by highlighting what is significant we can see how it might spread to a community of expression. It is like exhaling before inhaling. Conversely, spreading out or extensionalizing qualitatively allows for family resemblances to accrue which can lead to felt reductions. Parenthetically, educational practitioners are most turned off by so-called qualitative evaluation because they don't know what to do with a mass of descriptive and poetic life-world material. Usually, an inexpressive "text" has led to unfelt distancing, and these provide no basis for the dialectic of interpretation, which is the point where a panic occurs in the scramble to pick up some phantom theory or method to bail them out. There is no ready-made theory or method importable into the art of qualitative thinking.

Distancing is of course backing off, and this implies both in time and away from the "thickness" of expression and expressive description which provide us a viable "text." A space of time is often the route to *qualitative selection*. There is no external authority operating legitimately on qualitative selection. Relaxed attention is another way, much as one squints to see the big patterns in a painting or the large masses in a sculpture.

In the example of the hypnogogic event, repeated and different "texts" aided both distancing and recovery of the event. We can also invite multiple passional viewpoints—the so-called Rashomon effect. Myths are suggested from within a community of works or "texts," thus preparing the ground for later myth analysis or a formative hermeneutics through mythic parallels.[29]

There is, however, a key question to be posed for all distancing if it is to move us profitably toward interpretation and renewal: *are the norms of action implicit in qualitative experiencing*? Yes, I say, if we stick to the *art* of qualitative thinking. The qualitative base both guides and reabsorbs the round trip. For it we need not posit ideal universals or essences or hierarchies of these. Loving, arting, dialoguing are their own energy and life, and deal most vitally with what is other. Experience is greater than all Scriptures. Only what we have stood in the heart of can we really distance. Whether we use the knife or the harvest basket, distancing has the same function. The only way we can bind up the potentially qualitative in education is through live tradition, which permits us as teachers to engage in a depth hermeneutic of another's self-formative process within that common tradition. But that is a step beyond the complexity of my present simple focus.

6. *Interpretation is a dialectic of explanation and understanding*. But though I sharewith Ricoeur[30] the belief that there is a hermeneutic arc which moves from naive understanding through explanation to a

knowledgeable understanding, I feel that the art of which I am speaking throws a different accent on "explanation" than does philosophical hermeneutics. As art it "does not assume a philosophical stance."[31] It is, thus, pre-symbolic, revelatory, world-making, and world-revealing.

In the present context it is still, nevertheless, a crisis stage, for it teases out from hiding our hidden motivations and our personal causation. We interpret to make clear what eluded us in our intuitive understanding. This moment is only arbitrary to an uninvolved external eye, for while the mind may seem biased, nevertheless it is doing all it can. It can, for example, extend alternatives, but at the crossroads we are constrained, as creatures of Eros, to make existential choices which seem more destined than arbitrary. From inside Proust's life-world, as I have said, he chose the alternative of the six we would expect.

Ever since Freud, we find commonplace that there is a manifest and a latent, or a surface and a depth, interpretation to dreams. So it is with qualitative experiencing. Were we sufficiently involved, we would be unsure whether we were men dreaming we were butterflies or butterflies dreaming we were men. Stained by our existential projects, our mind probes experience and offers alternatives and uncertain explanations. A deep structure between us and the event takes over. Our autosymbolic processes become involved. There is a welling up of interest, politics, and myth.

If we are daring and believing, we encourage the mind to over-intrude, secure that the greatest contest will yield the greatest revelation. The pinch of self and culture here does its damnedest. One could call this moment a "downer," a descent, a depression. The two-headed worm becomes a dragon. To go on requires the St. George in us.

If we were to stop there, explanations would never be convincing where quality is concerned. Explanation means that our dialogue is blocked, our understanding clouded. To escape an impasse, we propose mental fictions and alternatives, choose among these what will set us in motion again, and what will allow us to assimilate the concealed biases of self and culture implicit in the "text," further revealed in distancing, and unavoidable in interpretation. Qualitative interpretation should be deadly playful, for that is deadly serious enough. Tensing up or an approach-avoidance conflict will not help.

This third moment of one artistic process does not take well to a search for cause and explanation outside its own movement. To do so would be as useless as leaving a painting three-quarters on the way to seek external counsel for the finish. Even in art school, as Collingwood[32] well knew, one doesn't enroll to learn to paint, but to learn to watch oneself painting. The clues for the end of the painting are in the first three quarters. So, too, with this art: "text," distancing, and interpreting are the ground for evaluating, speculating, and renewing.

Distancing and interpreting are reciprocal processes. Like two active fragments they form a nexus which clashes then with the "text" to allow a resolution which moves behind the "text" itself. For the "text" is only a proxy, a stand-in. There is nothing to prove, only something to express and reveal. It is not about proving but im-proving. It is both an adventure and an in-venture.

All "texts" are distorted and require a depth hermeneutic. In confronting them, we sink into a dialogue with a dialogue, with an understanding of our understanding. But this is no infinite regress. We come to a rock bottom which is life, experience, the disclosure of being. So seen, the art of qualitative thinking is basic inquiry into the disclosure of being,[33] the complete horticulture of the rose of qualitative experience. In Bergson's[34] terms, interpretation is a minding of intuition, a "going-around," an "entering-in."

7. *The reflexivity of interpretation moves into self-discovery and self-awareness.* All experience makes one sadder but wiser, says Gadamer.[35] But wisdom is its own kind of deep tranquility and unfettered joy. There are innumerable tales about a mystical reversal which occurs unbidden when, in the midst of a crisis, we truly give up. It is like the clarity of perception I had when I was shot and thrown to the ground in a German courtyard in World War II.

If we slay the two-headed worm (latterly a dragon), we begin to reconcile standards of the inside with standards of the outside and to acknowledge the distortions from both. We are ready for a depth hermeneutic, acknowledging that we are simultaneously on the path and standing within a common tradition. As an art educator, the lore I have inherited has it that self-insight and self-awareness precede acceptance of tension with tradition's standards. This is because even if we fail from an outside view, we can be fulfilled through enlarged self-awareness and self-renewal. Thus I have called the art of qualitative thinking a great work of conceptual art. By being oneself in it (that is, by losing myself in the qualitative immediate present), one can see oneself in it, and one can free oneself through it.

8. *The fourth moment is simultaneously an advance and a return to origins, through evaluation, speculation, and renewal.* Celebration, interpretation, and renewal are synonymous for this artful round trip.

For Ricoeur,[36] interpretation is "where language prepares to die." But it is also where it prepares for resurrection. In the language of faith, for example, the very failure of even speculative thought gives rise to an "in spite of" which strengthens into a "thanks to," while both of these are englobed by the "how much more." Implicit faith and the art of qualitative thinking are life-affirming, upward surging. They say, with Claudel, "still the worst is never sure."[37]

I will deliberately play down the more mentalistic and philosophical expressions of this moment for there is a vast literature on these. Having come this far, the experienced evaluator, critic, and judge will have cause for personal fear and trembling and desire for renewal. The political will have been sorted out. No longer will a brain for hire come across as a higher brain. "Competence" will appear as mere wisps, or even thickened up billows of smoke from forgotten swamp fires. When it comes to the question of competence, an interesting reversal occurs. The healthful wholeness of the qualitative deservedly clashes headlong with any conceptual or political *a priori*. For power and thought presume to decide what shall be encouraged to come into existence. It's almost a case of cultural eugenics. From the side of experience, it is fair to ask a series of questions. Whence the standard? What is the politics of experience it supports? How does it limit the freedom of the experiencer? How much does the experiencer want what power controls—e.g., credential, certification, position, recommendation? What is the fit between the context for experience and the constraints of assessment? Who are those who have access to the system as reward seekers?

In all these questions, the experiencer is a passive object. Judgment is here the match between experience and pre-existent ideal. Truth is that of correspondence. Consciousness is a container to be filled with contents.

But where truth is organic, revelation, unveiling, search, then the wholeness of the movement from within experience takes over. No imput-output model, no closed system, will suffice. Truth is revealed. Consciousness is the self and its context or circumstance. Dialogue is the appropriate metaphor, organism the appropriate extension or transformation of dialogue into structure or new being. Judgment here is justice tempered by understanding and the reflexivity, the limit, of the judge himself.

In educating, a different goal system then appears, and it must be wondrously lacking in that precision which permits technologizing. To acheive within the being of educating: a depth hermeneutic of an other's self-formative process according to a common tradition. Such an art of qualitative experience and qualitative thinking fits no systems management hegemony suffering from an advanced case of "legitimation crisis."[38]

In art a new being, a new world, comes forth. What was dialogue as process becomes work as organism. Play becomes art when there is a transformationinto structure. Self becomes self, and other becomes other, and both co-exist. The metaphors of dialogue and organism overlay one another. The new rose is always healthy.

Critical reflection is the liberation empowered by the fullest play of the art of thought. Application is the living forward of meaning as praxis, constructive action. Judgment is the interpretation of the law for this case, with all of history and the present community as witnesses. But all of these are especially the renewal of an expressive return, a return with wholeness to the whole, a love which is the continuing contact between two poetries. If I were to place competence within the art of pottery which I practice, seeing it wholistically from the perspective of a great tradition of planetary and historical scope,[39] I would only say: competence, your name is mud.

FOOTNOTES

[1] Alan Watts. *In My Own Way*. New York: Vintage Books, 1972.
[2] Martin Heidegger. *On the Way to Language*. New York: Harper & Row, 1971.
[3] Munishree Chitrabhanu. The philosophy Jainism, Chapter 4. In Sri Swami Rama & Others, *Inner Paths*. Honesdale, PA: Himalayan International Institute of Yoga Science and Philosophy, 1979, pp. 49-66.
[4] Shunryu Suzuki. *Zen Mind, Beginner's Mind*. New York: Weatherhill,1974.
[5] Ibid.
[6] Norman O. Brown. *Love's Body*. New York: Random House Vintage Books, 1966.
[7] Kenneth R. Beittel. The artist's perception of the affective domain, Chapter 7. In Louise M. Berman & Jessie A. Roderick (Eds.), *Feeling, Valuing, and the Art of Growing: Insights into the Affective*. 1977 Yearbook of the Association for Supervision and Curriculum Development. Washington, D.C.: The Association, 1977.
[8] Kenneth R. Beittel. The teaching of art in relation to body-mind integration and self-actualization in art. *Art Education*, 1979, *32*, 7, 18-20.
[9] Alan Watts. *Op. cit.* (reference 1), p. 426.
[10] Kenneth Yasuda. *The Japanese Haiku*. Rutland,VT: Charles E. Tuttle Co., 1971, p. 24.
[11] William Blake. *Letters*. (Edited by Geoffrey Keynes) New York: Macmillan, 1956, p. 79.
[12] George Herbert Mead. *Mind, Self, and Society*, Part 3. Chicago: University of Chicago Press, 1934.
[13] Paul Watzlawick, Janet H. Veaven, & Don D. Jackson. *Pragmatics of Human Communication*. New York: W. W. Norton & Co., 1967, pp. 261-266.
[14] John M. Anderson. ...Since the time we are a dialogue and able to hear from one another. Man and World, 1978, *10*, 115-135.
[15] S. R. Harper & D. L. Miller (Eds.). *Interpretation: The Poetry of Meaning*. New York: Harcourt, Brace & World, 1967, p. 51.
[16] John Dewey. *Art as Experience*. New York: Capricorn Books, 1958. (Reprint Edition)
[17] Stephen C. Pepper. *Concept and Quality*. La Salle, IL: Open Court,1967.
[18] Richard Eder. Metaphor's role at core of thought. *The New York Times*, Tuesday, April 15, 1980, pp. C-1 and C-4.
[19] Gaston Bachelard. *The Poetics of Reverie*. (Translated by David Russell) Boston: Beacon Press, 1971.
[20] Martin Heidegger. *Poetry, Language, Thought*. New York: Harper & Row,1971.
[21] Marcel Proust. *Within a Budding Grove*. New York: Random House (The Modern Library). (Original copyright, 1924.) Part II, pp. 20-23.
[22] John Dewey. *Op. cit.* (reference 16), pp. 215-216.
[23] M. Foucault. *The Order of Things: An Archaeology of the Human Sciences*. New York: Pantheon Books, 1971.
[24] Max van Manen. An experiment in educational theorizing: The Utrecht school. *Interchange*, 1978-79, *10*, 1, 48-66.
[25] Wilson van Dusen. *The Natural Depth in Man*. New York: Harper & Row, 1973.
[26] Kay Shamalla. Graduate student paper, Art Education 545, Spring, 1980, The Pennsylvania State University.

[27] Joan Novosel-Beittel. Inquiry into the qualitative world of creating: The J-E model. *Studies in Art Education*, 1978, *20*, 1, 26-36.
[28] Norman O. Brown. Apocalypse: The place of mystery in the life of the mind. In Harper & Miller (Eds.), *Op. cit.* (reference 15), p. 9.
[29] Carl G. Jung. *Psychology and Alchemy*. New York: Pantheon Books, 1953.
[30] Paul Ricoeur. *The Philosophy of Paul Ricoeur*. Boston: Beacon Press, 1978, p. 154.
[31] Gregory Battcock (Ed.). *Idea Art*. New York: E. P. Dutton & Co., Inc., 1973, pp. 91-92 (quotation is by Joseph Kosuth).
[32] R. G. Collingwood. *The Principles of Art*. New York: Oxford University Press Galaxy Books, 1958. (Reprint Edition)
[33] Martin Heidegger. *On the Way to Language*. New York: Harper & Row, 1971.
[34] Henri Bergson. An introduction to metaphysics, from *The Creative Mind*. In William Barret & Henry Aiken (Eds.), *Philosophy in the Twentieth Century: Vol. 3, Contemporary European Thought*. New York: Harper & Row, 1962.
[35] Hans-Georg Gadamer. *Truth and Method*. New York: The Seabury Press, 1975.
[36] Paul Ricoeur. *The Conflict of Interpretations: Essays in Hermeneutics*. Evanston, IL: Northwestern University Press, 1974.
[37] Paul Ricoeur. *Op. cit.* (reference 30), p. 58.
[38] Jurgen Habermas. *Legitimation Crisis*. Boston: Beacon Press, 1975.
[39] Kenneth R. Beittel. *The Way of the Potter: East and West of the Great Tradition*. Tokyo: John Weatherhill, 1984 (in press).

8

William E. Doll, Jr., conceives of competence as much more than behavior or performance, rather, as a state of being, a capacity, or an intellectual power. Doll traces the contributions of Noam Chomsky, Jean Piaget, and Jerome Bruner to our understanding of competence. From this analysis he generates a model of competence based on cognitive structuralist assumptions rather than on behaviorist ones. This model has clear pedagogical implications, and Doll identifies some of these: principles of action, skills, and structures; the role of contrast, play, and mastery; and the development of experience, all of which are explicated in greater detail in his 1979 *Theory into Practice* article, volume 18, December issue, pages 336-348. Doll ends by exemplifying the practical process of implementing this way of developing competence in actual learning situations related to developing mathematical competence in children. By contrast with "copying" or "remembering" models, this cognitive structuralist approach has, as Doll believes, many exciting possibilities for facilitating the effort to learn to be competent.

Professor Doll is Associate Professor and Chair of the Department of Elementary Education, State University of New York, Oswego.

Developing Competence

William E. Doll, Jr.
State University of New York, Oswego

In keeping with the theme of this conference—that of reassessing competence—I would like to argue that competence can and should be developed in the schools, and that the curriculum design needed for such development will be radically different from the design now in use. I will begin my argument by recapitulating the competence-performance distinction I've made elsewhere,[1] and then move on to an analysis of the competence concept in Chomsky, Piaget, and Bruner. I will conclude with curriculum recommendations, including an outline of the model I believe should be employed for developing competence. I am excited about the possibilities such a model holds for American schooling but pessimistic about its adoption.

All of us in education are, of course, knowledgeable about the now-waning competency-based education movement. This movement was—I like to put it in the past tense—but another variation of the knowledge-copy view of learning which dominated American schooling and curriculum during so much of the twentieth century. Others at this conference have drawn connections between this view of learning and the industrial-mechanistic society in which we live. For myself I wish only to point out that the competency-based movement equated, wrongly, competence with performance, and in so doing did disservice not only to the word and notion of competence, but also to a very exciting idea which I believe holds great pedagogic potential.

It hardly seems necessary today to cite examples from the competency movement equating competence with performance, or to state that the movement was a part of a broader behaviorist-positivist perspective. However, lest some be unaware of these connections let me cite two quotations. Both come from the Hall and Jones book, *Competency-Based Education: A Process for the Improvement of Education*. With a title like that and carrying an imprimatur from Robert Howsam, it is obvious the authors believed strongly in the movement and its efficacy. The first quotation comes from a section analyzing the foundations of the movement and states that the prime characteristic of competency-based education is: "an emphasis on specification of learner outcomes in terms of behavioral objectives."[2] The second quotation defines competency as: "a statement that describes the observable demonstration of a composite of the specific skills."[3] The sentences following this second quotation state that competency (a word which in this form bothers me) is "a description of performances," performances that somehow are "integrated" with "a set of related skills and knowledge." This quotation shows that at the very time leaders in the movement were equating competence with performance they were also realizing that competence was somehow not merely performance; that it was at least "a composite...greater than the sum of the individual skills."[4]

The words themselves—competence and performance—are, as any etymological dictionary will show, and as I've argued previously,[5] of quite different origin and have different thrusts or senses. Performance refers essentially to a "doing," particularly to a "doing" which is "completed, finished, achieved." It originated as a word to distinguish between promises made but not completed and those completed. Hence performance is a task finished. It carries no judgment of value as to how well the task is done, just that it is done. Competence refers essentially to a state of being or to a capacity. One who is competent is one who has a certain "fitness, sufficiency, or aptitude;" or to take the word's Latin derivation, a competent person is one who possesses a certain confluence, "symmetry, conjunction, or meeting together" of powers which allow him or her "to adequately deal with a situation." In short, performance is the outward and public manifestation of underlying and internal powers. The problem, of course, lies in determining just what these powers are, and in determining the relation which exists between them and their performance manifestations. Unfortunately these powers cannot be determined directly, but must always be inferred from observable performances. The simple solution, which certain radical behaviorists like Skinner have taken, is to deny the efficacy of the competence concept and to work exclusively at the level of performance. Those in the competency movement have not, to my knowledge, made such a strong theoretical statement; but they are operating out of a similar framework. That is, they are simplistically equating competence with performance and assuming that those who perform well are competent and those who perform poorly are incompetent. This is evidenced in their development of performance checklists as indicators of competence. But as Chomsky has said:

> A person might memorize the performance table and perform on various simple-minded tests exactly as the performer who knows the rules of arithmetic, but this would not, of course, show that he knows these rules....
> The deeper question concerns the kinds of structures the person has succeeded in mastering and internalizing....
> For anyone concerned with intellectual processes...it is the question of competence that is fundamental. Obviously one can find out about competence only by studying performances, but this study must be carried out in devious and clever ways, if any serious result is to be obtained.[6]

As a structuralist I agree with Chomsky that there are internal structures of competence underlying performance, and I wish to argue that a curriculum model based on this assumption will be more exciting and productive than the current performance model. Evaluation of this model will require the "devious and clever ways" Chomsky mentions, for competence cannot be assessed easily or directly from performance. As Nel Noddings points out, performance is neither a necessary nor a sufficient criteria for competence.[7] Yet the two are related, and to possess or pursue one without the other is to possess or pursue little.

Chomsky

Noam Chomsky has undoubtedly done more than anyone else to illuminate the competence-performance distinction. In doing so he has been operating on at least three levels: that of linguistics, that of rules, and that of humanness. Each of these levels gives a sense of competence that cannot be found by taking performance at its face value. Linguistically, Chomsky has been impressed with the fact that mistakes in performance are not necessarily mistakes in competence. A stutterer may well know the rules of grammar, or a concert pianist may well give a poor performance, because of fatigue, nervousness, or other personal factors. Of even more import for Chomsky is the fact that in their grammatical development young children acquiring a native language evidence both a type of logic and a sense of generative creativity in their mistakes (i.e., the boy "runned" the dog). Further, all children, regardless of experience and genetic inheritance, go through this process. Thus for Chomsky there must be some sort of innate patterning, universal to all people, underlying language acquisition. This innate or deeper patterning is far more important, Chomsky believes, than the experience-response patterns behaviorists rely on so heavily.

This structural patterning is indicative, Chomsky believes, of some principle other than the behaviorist ones of associations and experiences operating when an individual speaks. This principle he calls "mind," and for its history he refers back to the Cartesians of the 17th century.

> The Cartesians tried to show that when the theory of corporeal body is sharpened and clarified and extended to its limits, it is still incapable of accounting for facts that are obvious to introspection.... In particular, it cannot account for the normal use of human language...(nor can it explain) the basic properties of thought. Consequently it becomes necessary to invoke an entirely new principle—in Cartesian terms to postulate a second substance whose existence is thought.[8]

This new principle has a "creative aspect" to it, and can be found in "the distinctively human ability to express new thoughts" and to understand new thoughts, all "within the framework of an 'instituted language'."[9] This framework, Chomsky believes, is formed by the grammar rules underlying a language. Knowledge of these rules is knowledge of the language's competence or structure, and individuals display this competence when they perform with language. But since performance brings in many factors other than competence, what is important in performance is not the "correctness" or "incorrectness" of the performance, but the connection between the rules and the performance. Chomsky's reason for emphasizing the rule-performance connection is that he believes the correctness of a performance to be cultural and hence arbitrary, while the rule-performance connection he believes to be universal, innate, and indicative of the very essence of human thought. In this generating aspect of linguistic competence, humans are displaying the nature of mind.

> The most striking aspect of linguistic competence is what we may call the 'creativity of language,' that is, the speaker's ability to produce new sentences, sentences that are immediately understood by other speakers although they bear no physical resemblences to sentences which are "familiar."
> Normal use of language involves the production and interpretation of sentences that are similar to sentences that have been heard before only in that they are generated by the rules of the same grammar.[10]

Young children acquire this competence or knowledge of rules at a very young age and without specific training. Once acquired they are able to convey to others thoughts, feelings, judgments, and perceptions of a subtle kind.[11] Thus the real power of a language, or of a person, lies at the competence level. This competence allows one to generate an infinite variety of sentences from a finite set of basic structures and rules. The educational task then, as Chomsky has been saying, is to get beyond performance to competence.

In working at this second level—that of the universality and power of rules—Chomsky has posited a specific attribute to human beings, the ability to understand and generate language. On one hand this ability is language specific; on the other hand it is reflective of the more universal powers of the human mind. At the language level Chomsky believes humans are "wired," or genetically programmed, to understand a language. Fancifully, Chomsky calls this ability a Language Acquisition Device (LAD), or a "black box." However, at another level this language ability is not language specific, but is indicative of those more universal traits of thought called mind. Thus, Chomsky speaks of a vision competence and a mathematics competence. As he says:

> Language is a mirror of the mind in a deep and significant sense. It is a product of human intelligence, created anew in each individual by operations that lie far beyond the reach of will or consciousness.[12]

All this leads to a third level in Chomsky's competence-performance distinction. Quite simply Chomsky believes there to be something unique about the human species:

> Any objective scientist must be struck by the qualitative differences between human beings and other organisms, as much as by the differences between insects and vertebrates.

> Even the most superficial observation suffices to show that there are qualitative differences between humans and other complex organisms which must be explained.[13]

This explanation will come only when we are willing to posit the notion of mind and to study this notion in terms of the competence which underlies human acts. It is this knowledge which is of most worth.

Piaget

In the section just finished I tried to show that Chomsky's notion of competence introduces qualitative distictions between competence and performance, and that competence while taking a particular form in regard to language is also indicative of more universal powers of human intelligence, those we call mind. In reintroducing mind as a concept for serious study, Chomsky is urging us to look beyond the performance level of human actions to a deeper, structural, more generative level. The pedagogical corrollary to this, of course, is that as educators we should pay more attention to competence (and mind) than to performance (and behaviors). For competence is the well-spring of all action, although not easily discovered in such action.

In this section I should like to look at Piaget's view of competence, particularly as this relates to the biological model of change he proposes. In so doing I am asking you, the reader, to throw away previous conceptions about Piaget and to consider him in a new light. First, I will ask you to transpose those things Piaget calls "structures-of-the-whole" into a notions of competence as abilities underlying, and partially controlling, performance. This is necessary because Piaget does not concern himself directly with the word competence, but his notion of structures-of-the-whole is essentially a competence notion. Second, I will ask you to consider Piaget not just as a child psychologist, but as a broad-based intellectual—a scientific philosopher, if you will—who began his career in biological science and whose recent work, from *Biology and Knowledge* on, has come back to this origin.[14] This shift is necessary if we are to understand not only what Piaget is saying about cognitive development in children, but also his basic assumptions underlying those sayings. In short, Piaget's own structure is a biological one. One key quote should bring both of these points in focus.

> My one idea...has been that intellectual operations proceed in terms of structures-of-the-whole. These structures denote the kinds of equilibrium toward which evolution in its entirety is striving...(and whose) roots reach down as far as biological morphogenesis itself.[15]

I will deal with structures-of-the-whole first, and then with Piaget's biological model of change, or development.

The idea of structure is an important one for Piaget, and it is one which separates him so definitely from those psychologists labelled behaviorists. These behaviorists—J. B. Watson, E. L. Thorndike, B. F.

Skinner, etc.—in their desire to make psychology "scientific" adopted the model used by the physical sciences in the 19th century. In this model only the observable and measurable is dealt with, and then in a manner where the complex is reduced or factored into the simple. In aggregate the parts are assumed to equal the whole, and the whole is assumed to be divisible into its parts. Behavioristic psychology, in order to be scientific also, adopted this model without question. It decided to deal only with the events that were observable and to isolate the independent variables of human behavior in a reductionist and atomistic manner. Educationally this model advocated that children be taught discrete behaviors, and assumed that once these behaviors were learned they would form themselves into an overall developmental whole. To behaviorist psychologists the concept of structures as organizational patterns of mind, underlying and controlling behaviors was, and is, anathema. But for Piaget these structures are very much a reality, and all learning must be framed in structural terms. That is, it is structural patterns or schemas which control learning, and "not vice-versa...."[16]

The four main structures, those which dominate the intellectual development of the child, and which Piaget labels structures-of-the-whole, are the sensory-motor, the pre-operational, the concrete operational, the formal operational. Each of these structures has its own mode of operation—action, representation, relations, systems (to over-simplify a bit)—and while the child is in a particular stage these structures govern his actions, his perceptions, his thoughts. As Piaget says:

> (the child) cannot proceed in any way he likes. He finds himself, as it were, in a field of force governed by the laws of equilibrium, carrying out transformations or operations determined not only by occurrences in the immediate past, but by the laws of the whole operational field of which these past occurrences form a part.[17]

In simple terms development explains learning more than learning explains development. And while Piaget does not use the word competence here these structural levels are competence levels. Each level has its own competence pattern, and these patterns underlie behaviors in much the way Chomsky's rules underlie performance.

The foregoing has been a simplified view of Piaget's stage theory, that for which he is famous in America. However, the question of how a child or adolescent moves from one stage of competence to another—in short how competence is developed—has not been answered. For this it is necessary to go beyond Piaget's stage theory to his biological model of change. In simple terms change can be looked upon as being internally or externally directed. That is, change can be seen as proceeding according to some sort of inner, genetic, innate mechanism, or it can be seen as emanating from the environment and then passed on to, or copied by, the organism. Historically the former has been known in biological circles as preformation. It was a popular doctrine in the 17th century when it was commonly believed that the image of a person could be seen in the male sperm. In recent years the doctrine has received renewed emphasis with the concept of DNA containing all the genetic codes an individual would possess in his lifetime. The other view, an environmental one, has been championed by Lamarck and Darwin. In its extreme form, one attributed to Lamarck, the environment causes the organism to make changes, which changes are then passed on genetically in a direct manner to succeeding generations. In its less extreme form, that attributed to Darwin, and that which Piaget comes closest to adopting,[18] the environment provides the trigger or motivation for change, but the change itself is an internal or genetic occurrence.

This environmental view of change is one Piaget adopted early in his career. In 1918, the year he took his doctorate in natural science, he states: "The heredity of acquired traits is an experimental fact."[19] But he rejects the Lamarckian version as putting too much emphasis on the environment, and he rejects the Darwinian version, especially the neo-Darwinian, for unjustifiably emphasizing the elements of randomness and competition (or struggle) in the organism's internal adjustments to the environment. For Piaget there is an internal sense of telos or purpose in an organism's interaction with its environment,[20] and there is a sense of harmony, or integration, among the various systems in an organism, and between these systems and the environment. Thus instead of accepting either a Lamarckian or Darwinian form of environmentalism Piaget proposes a third way (or "tertium quid") of dealing with change. In this view it is not the internal or the external which receives emphasis, but the interaction between them. The heart of this alternative is the notion of autoregulatory systems maintaining an equilibrium or a balance both among themselves and between themselves and the environment. As Piaget says:

> Life is essentially autoregulation...(and there is need for) a third solution which is cybernetic and is, in effect, biased toward the theory of autoregulation.
> The central problem of contemporary biology...(is) the question of equilibration or autoregulation.[21]

This notion of equilibration or autoregulation, framed as it is within a view of biological systems, is what underlies Piaget's view of development, including knowledge construction and his recommendations for education.

This alternative view of change, with its emphasis on autoregulation, can be found in Piaget's earliest writings and has remained with him. When he was working on his doctorate at the University of Neuchatel, studying the mollusks of Valais, one of the issues was whether the mollusks of the deep waters were of the same or of a different species from the mollusks of the shallow marshes—eating, breathing, food gathering habits of the two being quite different. Piaget argued[22] that the two were of different species, but that each had evolved from a common ancestry, and that in time and with the right conditions either could evolve into the other. The "right conditions" were those of autoregulation, where the mollusks would be able to integrate their new habits of breathing and food gathering with some of their old (or "natural") habits. In short there must be a balance between old habits, or behaviors, and new ones in such a way that harmony among the mollusk's systems and sub-systems is preserved. Piaget says:

> Time alone will have a real effect. Moreover, it is not the factors which must be new, but the ensemble of factors, their relationships, their synthesis. In other words a new species is from its beginnings, not characterized by its properties, its acquired characteristics, but by its tendencies....[23]

This model of change is central to all of Piaget's thinking. He believes it applies to human cognition as well as to lower order biological organisms. This is not to deny the major structural differences between humans and invertebrates, but it is to say that while the structural forms are different the process of change each undergoes is similar. Thus in later writings, in describing the development of thought, Piaget argues that the process is still autoregulatory. Specifically he asserts that development occurs when (l) an individual establishes an equilibrium with his environment, so that he is comfortable with his own ways of operation and can (at least tacitly) understand those operations. Then (2) a disturbance must be introduced to unbalance this equilibrium. Finally, (3) a new, higher level, equilibrium must emerge, resolving the conflict or inbalance. This balance-disturbance-rebalance process is akin to John Dewey's transformation of experience, and even to Thomas Kuhn's paradigm change. As Piaget says of the process:

> We can observe a process (hence the term 'equilibration') leading from certain states of equilibrium to others, qualitatively different, and passing through multiple 'non-balances' and reequilibrations. It is worthwhile to note that however the nonbalance arises, it produces the driving force of development. Without this, knowledge remains static. But nonbalance also plays a release role, since its fecundity is measured by the possibility of surmounting it, in other words, of reaching a higher equilibrium.... Without the nonbalance there would not be 'increasing reequilibration.'[24]

It is via this process of change that Piaget believes individuals move from one level or stage of competence to another. The curriculum implications inherent in this view are, of course, radically different from the ones now in practice. The teacher must help the student, and give the student time, to establish an equilibrium with the curriculum. Then that equilibrium must, gently but definitely, be disturbed. Finally a synthesis must be produced where a new higher level, equilibrium is established. This equilibrium-disturbance-reequilibrium process is labelled by Piaget "equilibration," or "reequilibration," to distinguish the process of movement from the static state of balance. The teacher's task is to bring this process to fruition and consciousness, without destroying its naturalness. Or as Nel Noddings has said:

> The aim of instruction becomes the transformation of cognitive structures not just the mastery of a task.[25]

Bruner

While Jerome Bruner does not directly draw on Chomsky or Piaget for his own view of competence, he does raise (and extend) issues they raise. Thus when Bruner is discussing the role of culture in assessing differences among peoples, his argument rests heavily on the type of competence-performance distinction Chomsky makes. And when he talks of "competence motivation" he is alluding to the same sort of internal drive Piaget is when he speaks of biological homeorhesis. Bruner's view of competence then brings forward some of the key aspects of Chomsky's view and of Piaget's view. This is especially true at the pedagogic level.

In his essay "Cultural Difference,"[26] Bruner raises the competence-performance distinction to counteract the notion that Blacks or minority students who perform poorly in school are therefore incompetent. In doing so he "extends" the competence-performance distinction by asserting that the teacher's task is: (1) to find a performance outlet suitable for an individual's competence to emerge, and (2) to help that individual transfer his or her competence-performance skill in one area to another area. The "deficit hypothesis" of the 1960s argued that those groups which showed linguistic or intellectual differences as categorized by standardized testing or usage were evidencing a deficit—a deficit which could be made up by nutritional additives and intellectual stimulation. Bruner was bothered by the arrogance of this "difference is deficit" hypothesis and drew heavily on the work of William Labov, and others, to show that the performance differences among groups were more indicative of differences in social contexts than of underlying competence differences. In making this case Bruner brings to mind Chomsky's assertion that many factors other than competence come to play when an individual expresses his competence via performance. And Bruner also draws on the linguist's assertion "that languages do not differ in their degree of development," possessing instead a "functional equality."[27] Differences that do exist then are superficial, performance differences governed by the situation or culture in which the language is developed. As Bruner says:

> The crux of the argument...is that those groups ordinarily diagnosed as culturally deprived have the same underlying competence as those in the mainstream of a dominant culture, the difference in performance being accounted for by the situations and contexts in which the competence is expressed.[28]

In making this assertion Bruner is not only reminding us that "it is difficult if not impossible to infer competence directly from performance,'' but he is extending the notion of competence by saying that competence needs to have a performance outlet, and the teacher's task is to find that outlet. Not only should the teacher find a performance vehicle for the expression of competence; he should also help the individual transfer the competence-performance relation he has from a task he knows and can do to one he does not know and cannot do. In this way competence will be developed by extending it from one social milieu (or performance framework) to another.

Indeed this is quite a different role for the teacher from the traditional behaviorist one of presenting material in a clear, concise, and logical way. But then as Piaget says, the knowledge-construct view of learning is different from the knowledge-copy view.

Bruner's other use of competence, that coming fromRobert White's article, ''Motivation Reconsidered: The Concept of Competence,''[29] also presents some definite pedagogic principles, and is compatible with Piaget's notion of homeorhesis. In the Piaget section just read the difference between equilibrium, as a steady state, and equilibration, as an on-going process, can be described as the difference between homeostasis and homeorhesis. In simplified terms homeostasis is that internal balancing of systems and subsystems within an organism that keeps the organism in harmony with its environment. Homeorhesis is the progressive balance-disturbance-rebalance process whereby an organism (or individual) attains control over its environment. One of the balances Piaget is talking about in his system of balances, or ''hierarchy of regulations'' as he calls it,[30] is the balance between homeostatsis and homeorhesis. In more general terms this is a balance between an organism's desire or drive to be comfortable with its environment and an organism's desire to conquer or control its environment.

This sense of balance between the stable and the dynamic has similarities with Bruner's balance between internal and external motivations; and the notion of homeorhesis as a driving force to control the environment is similar to White's concept of ''competence motivation,'' which Bruner uses heavily. White's argument is that if one wishes to view motivation in terms of drives and reinforcement then it it necessary to posit another drive for humans—the drive to deal effectively, or to control, the environment. As White says:

> I shall argue that it is necessary to make competence a motivational concept; there is a 'competence motivation'.... It is directed, selective, and persistent, and it continues not because it serves primary drives...but because it satisfies an intrinsic need to deal with the environment.[31]

Bruner goes beyond this notion of White's by arguing that there are ''forms of activity...(which) develop the competence motive...and make it the driving force behind behavior.''[32] In short, competence as ability to control the environment is natural, but can and should be developed. The first principle for development is to maintain the nature of this internal drive. Competence is its own reward, and should not be obliterated or lessened with too many external rewards. The balance, or essential tension between internal and external motivations should always weigh in favor of the internal, and work to develop the internal. The second principle for development is that growth in competence occurs via the balance-disturbance-rebalance process Piaget describes. To quote Bruner:

> I am convinced we shall do better to conceive of growth as an empowering of the individual by multiple means for representing his world, multiple means that often conflict and create the dilemmas that stimulate growth.[33]

A Competence Model

In the foregoing section I have had two aims. The first has been to separate competence from performance, lest we confuse one with the other. I have tried to show that the words have different meanings, thrusts, histories. My second aim has been to show that in the idea of competence there lies a pedagogical field rich enough to support a new model of education. This model would provide a direct challenge to the behaviorist one which has dominated American schooling for the past century. The behaviorist model comes essentially from an empiricist or positivist paradigm. In this paradigm there is no need for mind, behaviors alone are adequate; or, if one insists on positing mind as as organization of habits, this mind can be seen as a "blank tablet" ready to receive the impressions experience and schooling provide. The learning theory is associationist with a strong predilection towards stimulus-response techniques. The whole is always considered equal to the sum of the parts, thus allowing for the factoring of the whole into discrete units, with the assumption that once the units are mastered then the whole, naturally or automatically, takes shape. Performance becomes the goal, the product, and the process in this model.

The competence model not only assigns a very different role to performance—as an entry point for the study of competence—but brings with it, or arises from, a different set of paradigmatic assumptions. The overall framework is a rationalist one, positing the existence of mind, and seeing all behaviors as interpreted by or screened through this mind. Development occurs, not by direct associations, but in terms of structural patternings. Those things which can easily be assimilated into existing structural levels are learned without much struggle; other things which are not assimilated are either ignored or act as catalysts to disturb the old equilibrium and reestablish the new. This process is equilibrative and forces a good deal of interaction between teachers and students, and among both groups. Goals are not so much firmly pre-set as they emerge from the interaction and reflection on past and immediate past experiences. The whole is not considered as merely an aggregation of parts, but is believed to have a structure and unity of its own. This unity, in terms of a person or a field, lends direction and coherence to activity. These three—mind, equilibration, holism—form the heart or foundational base of the competence model. I will not elaborate on these three, although much work needs to be done with them, but rather will refer the interested reader to my paper, "A Structural View of Curriculum."[34] Nor will I elaborate on the five pedagogic principles of action, skills and structures, role of contrast, play and mastery, development of experience, which I have also described elsewhere.[35] Rather I will turn to personal experiences working with primary grade children both in and not in a structural curriculum. My intent is to make practical my foregoing remarks by focusing on curriculum development, and to highlight some differences between a structural curriculum and a non-structural or traditional one.

I became interested in this project of curriculum development when, a few years back, I read David Olson's *Cognitive Development*.[36] There he shows, quite dramatically I believe, that in teaching young children (4 to 7 yearsof age) to do a set task (placing checkers in a diagonal sequence) it makes no difference whether the teaching model is a traditional-performance one or a structural-competence one. However, in asking them to extend their learning, either in terms of time or in terms of transfer to other tasks (here placing the checkers in the other, or opposite, diagonal), the teaching model makes an enormous difference. One example: In a traditional group, none out of fourteen children were able to transfer the skill of checker placement along one diagonal to the opposite diagonal. Whereas twelve out of fourteen children in the structural group did so the first time.[37] Examples like this intrigued me and my graduate students. Thus some of us set up the Oswego-Sodus Structural Arithmetic Project.

The Project began with a number of primary school teachers (K-3) in Sodus, New York, and has now been expanded to include a primary group at the S.U.N.Y.-Oswego, Swetman Learning Center. The heart of the project is to develop a curriculum and teaching methodology based on the notion that the student and the field each possess structures or types of competence. As Bruner says, the task is to bring these two structures together:

> At each stage of development the child has a characteristic way of viewing the world and explaining it to himself. The task of teaching a subject to a child at any particular age is one of representing the structure of that subject in terms of the child's way of viewing things.[38]

The device we use for developing the student's structures, particularly those structures relating to arithmetic, is a sense of patterning. The whole curriculum-teaching part of the Project is built around patterning: copying patterns, building patterns, extending patterns, and finally transferring and transforming patterns. Kindergarten children work with a simple ABAB pattern. First graders examine the relations between

ABAB and BABA, or AABB. Second graders build all the possible combinations—six—of ABAB, and begin to notice the concept of closing the system. Third graders compare the ABAB system with other systems such as ABCABC.

Traditional skill work with adding, subtracting, multiplying, and dividing is also put into this structural or competence framework. Thus the kindergarteners begin—with the aid of rods, cubes, blocks—simple addition and subtraction combinations. First graders relate addition and subtraction, multiplcation and division as opposites, and explore non-traditional combinations, (2x5)-1 equals ?. Second graders look for structures within groups of numbers:

1 plus 7 plus 1 equals 9
2 plus 5 plus 2 equals 9
3 plus 3 plus 3 equals 9
4 plus 1 plus 4 equals 9
? plus ? plus ? equals 9

Third graders analyze these combinations in terms of operating systems—in the foregoing (3x3) is a perfect square, the (2x5) combination requires a negative one(-1), or the introduction of subtraction. They also manipulate the symbols within the system for their purposes—12x15 being transformed to 6x30, or 101 minus 49 being changed to 102 minus 50. Throughout this work with numbers in terms of patterns, there is the assumption that children do have minds, competence, organizing abilities. The pedagogical task is to develop these abilities so that, over years, the child becomes aware of these abilities (his competence) and gains insight into the way a field is structured (its competence).

It is too early to make any definitive remarks about the success of the Project in developing competence. Years of longitudinal study and numerous case examples will be necessary before such statements can be made. But some personal, preliminary observations appear in order. The children like the program very much—the challenge is both exciting and rewarding. The teachers find that curriculum construction gives them a new feeling about teaching. It is hard to imagine that any of them will adopt the common practice of turning pages in a text or workbook. The experimental groups are outperforming the control groups on virtually all (but not all) measures of performance testing.

I would like to close this paper with a counter-illustration, one taken from my work with my own son, age seven, who goes to a traditional school in the town in which we live. Here much of the second grade arithmetic curriculum has been devoted to learning how to subtract one two digit numeral from another. The process of "borrowing" has been the culmination of the curriculum. The beginnings were started in early October, after a month of review addition, with drill on the subtraction "facts"—1 minus 0 through 19 minus 9. The second step was to introduce subtraction of two digit numerals from two digit numerals, with the subtrahend *always* smaller than the minuend (i.e., 56 minus 23, not 53 minus 26). In fact, at the time the comment was frequently made that "a larger number cannot be taken from a smaller." The third step was to introduce "regrouping," one ten being converted to ten ones (97 always became 80 plus 17, never 100 minus 3, nor 95 plus 2, not 75 plus 22. The fourth step was "to cross out, borrow, and subtract" (i.e., 53 minus 26 would be 4 13 minus 2 6).

During all this time, and the process took months, form October to March, each segment was isolated from the other. Thousands of separate examples were done, but never was subtraction related to addition, never were the children shown the difficulty involved in 53 minus 26, and never was regrouping explained in terms of need. The textbook, and this almost totally controlled the curriculum, merely presented the procedure and asked the children to copy. Neither the structures of arithmetic nor the child's own competence motivation were ever brought forward as pedagogical devices. The result of all this was that at the end of Easter vacation, when Will had some make-up work to do, he could neither solve 72 minus 17 nor make an appropriate beginning. He sat trying to remember. After a time lapse I suggested he forget how he had been "taught" and try to figure out the example any way he could. "I could add," he said. "O.K. Add!" "Three plus seventeen equals twenty and fifty...two more equals fifty...five!" "Can you do another?" "Sure!"

I conclude with this example to bring home, again, the point that children do have minds; but the performance model used in the schools does not recognize this point. It seems doubtful the schools will give up their performance model and adopt a competence one, but the model is there for those wishing to develop and use it. And I believe it has exciting pedagogical possibilities.

FOOTNOTES

[1] William E. Doll, Jr., The role of contrast in the development of competence. In Alex Molnar & John Zahorik (Eds.), *Curriculum Theory*. Washington, D. C.: Association for Supervision and Curriculum Development, 1977, pp. 50-63.

[2] Gene Hall & Howard Jones. *Competency-Based Education: A Process for the Improvement of Education*. Englewood Cliffs, NJ: Prentice-Hall, Inc., 1976, p. 6.

[3] Ibid., p. 29-30.

[4] Ibidem.

[5] William E. Doll, Jr., *Op. cit.* (reference 1), pp. 52-53.

[6] Noam Chomsky, Formal Discussion, in response to Miller & Ervin, The development of grammar in child language. In U. Bellugi & R. Brown (Eds.), *The Acquisition of Language*. Chicago: The University of Chicago Press, 1964, 1971, p. 36.

[7] Nel Noddings, Competence, A paper presented to Curriculum Inquiry Conference, The Pennsylvania State University, May 18-20, 1980. (Published in this volume.)

[8] Noam Chomsky, *Language and Mind*. Enlarged Edition. New York: Harcourt, Brace, Jovanovich, Inc., 1968, 1972, p. 6.

[9] Ibidem.

[10] Noam Chomsky, *Topics in the Theory of Generative Grammar*. The Hague: Mouton, 1966, p. 11.
[11] Noam Chomsky, *Reflections on Language*. New York: Pantheon Books, 1975, p. 4.
[12] Ibidem.
[13] Noam Chomsky, *Language and Responsibility*. New York: Pantheon Books, 1977, p. 95.
[14] Piaget's most important works in this area are his magnum opus, *Biology and Knowledge* (Chicago: The University of Chicago Press, 1967, 1971), and his follow-up works, *Behavior and Evolution* (New York: Pantheon Books, 1976, 1978) and *Adaptation and Intelligence* (Chicago: University of Chicago Press, 1974, 1980). It is also interesting to note that in his Foreword to *The Essential Piaget*, edited by H. Bruber & J. Voneche (New York: Basic Books, 1977), Piaget states that he "was extremely happy not to appear only as a child psychologist." He then goes on to say that this period was for him "only a link" between biological adaptation and "the analysis of that higher form of adaptation which is scientific thought." Gruber and Voneche then devote, appropriately, the first section to Piaget's early biology writings.
[15] Jean Piaget, Autobiography. In S. F. Campbell (Ed.), *Piaget Sampler*. New York: John Wiley & Sons, Inc., 1976, p. 136.
[16] Jean Piaget, Development explains learning. In *Piaget Sampler* (reference 15), p. 76. The quotation runs: "In other words, learning is subordinated to development and not vice-versa...." He then goes on to say that while it is indeed possible to teach individual learnings three questions must be asked: (1) Is this learning lasting? (2) Is it transferable? (3) How does it relate to other learnings?
[17] Jean Piaget, Logic and psychology. In *The Essential Piaget* (reference 14), p. 473.
[18] The only review of Piaget's biological thrust that I have found is by Sophie Haroutunian, *Harvard Educational Review*, 1979, *49*, 1, 93-99. There she labels Piaget's position as essentially Darwinian. This would be correct if one were to neglect Piaget's own alternative—neither Darwinian nor Lamarckian. Although Piaget lays out his position frequently and carefully, many prefer to place him in an either-or dichotomy.
[19] Jean Piaget, Biology and war. In *The Essential Piaget* (reference 14), p. 40.
[20] This sense of telos or purposeness in the organism is brought out strongest in Piaget's *Behavior and Evolution* (reference 14).
[21] These two quotes are from Piaget's *Biology and Knowledge* (reference 14). The first is from p. 26; the second from p. 10.
[22] See Part I, Early Biology. In *The Essential Piaget* (reference 14), pp. 3-22.
[23] Ibid., p. 4. Notice not only the words ensemble, relationships, and synthesis, but also the emphasis on tendencies as opposed to properties. This is but another variation on the competence-performance distinction I've been making.
[24] Jean Piaget. *The Deveopment of Thought*. New York: The Viking Press, 1975. 1977, pp. 3 and 13.
[25] Nel Noddings, Competence theories and the science of education, *Educational Theory*, 1974, *24*, 4, 360.
[26] Jerome Bruner, Cultural differences. In J. M. Anglin (Ed.), *Beyond the Information Given*. New York: W. W. Norton & Company, Inc., 1973, pp. 452-466.
[27] Ibid., pp. 454-455.
[28] Ibid., p. 458.

[29] Robert W. White, Motivation reconsidered: The concept of competence, *Psychological Review*, 1959, *66*, 297-333.
[30] Jean Piaget.*The Development of Thought* (reference 24). Ch. 1, especially p. 21.
[31] Quote in Jerome Bruner, The act of discovery. In *Beyond the Information Given* (reference 26), p. 407. Also in White (reference 29), pp. 317-318.
[32] Jerome Bruner, The act of discovery. In *Beyond the Information Given* (reference 26), p. 407.
[33] Jerome Bruner, The growth of representational processes in childhood. In *Beyond the Information Given* (reference 26), p. 323.
[34] William E. Doll, Jr., A structural view of curriculum, *Theory into Practice*, 1979, *18*, 5, 336-348.
[35] Ibid., and The role of contrast in the development of competence, *Op. cit.* (reference 1), and Play and mastery, *The Journal of Curriculum Theorizing*, 1980, *2*, 1, 209-226.
[36] David Olson. *Cognitive Development*. New York: Academic Press, 1970.
[37] Ibid., Ch. 4, especially pp. 46-55, and Table 4-14.
[38] Jerome Bruner. *The Process of Education*. Cambridge, MA: Harvard University Press, 1960, 1977, p. 13.

9

This final paper concerning the process of acquiring competence focuses upon the qualitative character of the relationship between the teacher and the student, between parent and child. In so doing, Max van Manen illuminates another dimension of pedagogic competence—the existential, phenomenological dimension—how we are present to children. How this perspective is translated into pedagogic existentials van Manen reveals through his inquiries into the phenomenological experiences of both pedagogues and children. Where the relationship works for the good of both, we recognize pedagogic competence.

Van Manen begins by pointing to the ontological core of teacher competence—the beingness of teaching—which lies within the doingness of teaching and lets us *be* competent teachers. He explores the kind of theorizing which causes us to get behind the what and how of "doing" teaching and allows us to "see" the experience of "being" a teacher.

Van Manen then outlines a whole method of pedagogic theorizing related to Aoki's definition of competence as reflective praxis. It is not a descriptive theorizing aimed at explaining pedagogic action, but it is a phenomenological theorizing aimed at deep re-collection of our individual pedagogic existence in search of the ground of our relationships with children. This attainment of pedagogic competence is not only a caring for the beings of our children but also a minding, a theorizing about what is fundamental, essential in such relationships.

Van Manen explores dozens of nuances in this fundamental search. He shows us the value of phenomenological inquiry. He points out traps we get into when we do not touch base with the essentials of the pedagogical relationship, such as when we impose a theory on a child without recognizing that the child brings his own schemes and frameworks to the pedagogic situation. He also shows us how certain acts we employ, such as listening, chuckling, leading, are meaningful beyond the mere behaviors displayed only as they reflect a deeper pedagogic concern which the child recognizes.

This beautifully expressed inquiry by van Manen into pedagogic competence is both inspiring and frightening to think about. It will grip you as possibly none of the other papers will. Its mode of inquiry into pedagogic competence is an example of the kind of qualitative thinking we have been invited to engage in about our own pedagogic competence by several of the earlier writers. Van Manen says to us, as he thinks the good, the competent pedagogue says to the child, "Come, I shall show you the world."

A revised and expanded version of part two of this paper appears in *Curriculum Inquiry*, 1982, *12*, 3, 283-299, under the title, "Phenomenological Pedagogy." The copyright for those portions included here is held by John Wiley & Sons, Inc., with whose permission they appear.

Professor van Manen is Professor of Education in the Faculty of Education, University of Alberta.

Reflections on Teacher Competence and Pedagogic Competence

Max van Manen
University of Alberta

1

The idea of teacher competency is complex even though the appeal of the concept of competency lies probably precisely in its seductive suggestion of simplicity. The idea of competency implies a promise that, reasonably speaking, anyone who wishes to become a teacher can acquire the skills to become one. But competency does not only refer to the more technical skills of teaching. The true significance of competency has more to do with the real meaning of the being of teaching: what a teacher *is*.

From a phenomenological point of view we like to know how we can come to a deeper and fuller understanding of a phenomenon by returning to the lived experience itself. And a curious thing happens with the notion of teacher competence in that it is a concept which is virtually alien to teacher life. Students, young or old, seldom if ever speak of teacher competence, neither do teachers. And it seems to be the same for parents. We may speak of good teachers, bad teachers, excellent even lousy teachers, but the words "teacher competencies" and "teacher skills" belong to a peculiar language that is life-world strange as far as the school is concerned. Although this may not be an earth-shattering way of beginning a discussion on competency, it is nevertheless an important lesson which phenomenology teaches us, namely that much of the language by way of which teachers are forced to think about themselves and their teaching may be forgetful of the very life they live with children.

And yet the notion of competency has a sense of practical urgency about it that teachers recognize. "Competency" is a word that reminds us that the pedagogy of teaching and parenting is a profoundly practical vocation. To the extent that we theorize or do research on teaching, we do not only study it to know how things are; we wish to understand teaching better precisely in order to know how to act. As a beginning teacher, some twenty years ago this urgency with teaching as always having to act, having to *do* things, was even more important for me. Oh sure, it felt gratifying to be able to stand in front of a class of students who were only slightly younger than I was, and know the thrill of mission and importance I felt then to be able to tell them what was important to learn and what they should do. But sometimes this was somewhat frightening as well because I soon realized that in order to be able to tell *them* what to do I always had to know what *I* was doing. Did I really know what I was doing in a deeper sense? Did I really have a sensitive grasp of how what I did was to fit into the lives of the students I taught, when I hardly knew what life or even my own life was about?

To teach is to act. And when we stand in front of the class or better when we stand quite literally in the very midst of it we know this incredible pressure of always having to do just the right thing. What could be more alive and more demanding of a person's constant, active attention than a class of some thirty young people? Is it strange therefore that teacher life, together with the life of surgeons and air traffic controllers, has been found the most pressure laden vocation in modern society? And is it strange, therefore, that in the preparation of young men and women for the teaching profession we, at universities or schools of education, tend to focus almost exclusively on the principles (or methods) from which the practical activities of teaching are derived? To teach is to act and anyone who wishes to speak of what it is to be a good teacher better speak of teaching competence in a manner that is responsive to our pragmatic predicament. A teacher must know what to do and how to do things right in the lives of those with whom he or she stands in a pedagogic relationship.

And yet when we allow ourselves to reflect more thoughtfully on teacher life, we may come to the recognition of a more profound truth: that more important than what we do is how we are present to children. Competence does not only refer to objective abilities and skills; it more essentially refers to the quality from which the knowledge of how to act somehow springs. This is the theme I want to make central to my discussion: *More important than what we do is how we are present to children.* But is the way we are present to children not already a form of doing or acting? No doubt this is true. But what is displayed in this reminder is our inclination forever and again to turn being (ontology) into doing (epistmology). The distinction between being and doing is thus a more profound issue than the often discussed distinction between what we *say* and what we *do*. It may be true that it is usually more important to consider what people do than what they say (they do). It is even more important that people's language as well as their behavior must ultimately be interpreted and understood in terms of what they are, that is, how they *are* in the world.

A powerful teacher is a man or a woman who has power of presence. But do we know what it means to be present as teacher to someone, to some child or some adult? It is said that we know a person by his deeds. And it is easier to observe or to describe what we do than what we are. Administrators and managers of human affairs know this and that is why we are always told in so many words that you may not be able to do anything about what you are but you can do something about what you do. And for this reason too teachers are faced with never ending series of two hour or two day workshops which are so many, mostly futile attempts to alter what we do rather than what we are. Traditional educational theory not only does not know how to distinguish between being and doing; it even fails to notice the very possibility of this distinction. And yet we know that the difference between the modalities of doing and being is a real way of knowing ourselves and knowing others. We (and our children may be more so than we) know it especially in the lived experience of a contradiction between what we say or do and what we are.

If a teacher competently adheres to a set of curriculum objectives but in a deeper sense does not know where he is going; if a teacher discusses poems but is unable to poetize life; if a teacher always talks about responsibility but does not live a responsible life; if a teacher constantly assigns grades or marks but fails to make perfection the standard of his own striving; if a teacher works hard at being liked by his students but then forgets what teaching is really to be like; if a teacher knows many jokes and can amuse the students but lacks a true sense of joy of being; if a teacher demonstrates a flair of knowing things but on closer inspection fails to embody what is thus falsely stylized; if a teacher shows an eloquent command of the language but produces mostly empty chatter; if a teacher effectively individualizes the curriculum but fails to really know the children; if a teacher gives evidence to know the world but does not take responsibility for the world; if a teacher can cite important educational aims and goals but is unable to live a deep sense of hope for each child; if a teacher integrates his subjects into a whole but lacks a vision of the idea of the whole; if a teacher asks his students lots of questions but does not know how to be truly addressed by a question; if a teacher acts with authority but does not know what pedagogically authorizes him in the first place; if a teacher...(I could go on almost forever)...then the observable teacher behavior, what the teacher is overtly doing, is in profound contradiction to the way the teacher is in the world, or better, in this school, in this classroom with these young people. Or maybe we should say that when a teacher fails to *be* what ostensibly he *does* then he really is an absence, he *is* not at all. Thus we may be physically present to children but something essential is absent in our presence. Similarly, we may be physically absent from the children but in a different sense they remain present in our lives after school and we remain present to them. The difference then between a true teacher and a false teacher lies not in an observable set of behavioral or technical competencies but rather the difference lies in the presence or absence of the experience of pedagogy itself. A phenomenology of teacher competency must therefore consist in the reawakening or the recovery of the lived experience of the pedagogy of teaching. And similarly, pedagogical theorizing from a phenomenological point of view is not the working out of some abstracted theoretical principles but rather a showing of how the deep principle of pedagogy forever animates our practical ways of acting and doing things with children. Theorizing is interpreting life. But the aim of pedagogical theorizing is not primarily to produce forms of knowledge with which we now can (technically) *do* something. Rather, we theorize so that hopefully this form of knowledge can do something with *us*, transform us, by edifying our pedagogic tactfulness, or better by inspiring that which at the core of our being lets us be effective teachers in the first place.

For brevity sake let me now change pace and make suggestions how the phenomenological concern with returning to the lived experience can provide us insight also into the nature of specific aspects of the competency of the teaching task. Let me take an example from the field of teaching reading. Reading theory too has been motivated largely by epistimological concerns, with finding sure methods, strategies, and knowledge principles which ensure both teachers and students of no fail competencies in the teaching and learning of reading. In research and theorizing of reading processes both the so-called linguistic or word-centered approach as well as the cognitive processes or reading for comprehension approach to reading is ultimately oriented to producing teaching skills for teaching reading skills rather than producing understandings of what the lived experience of reading itself consists. This dominant epistemological orientation of reading research has led to the peculiar situation where the very act of reading is cut off from the world. Reading researchers have had very little interest in the seemingly trivial observation that to read is always to read something. Reading specialists have been so busy with focusing on the technical aspects of the reading act that the very idea of competency inherent in the conceptualization of the activity of the act tends to be reduced to a literally lifeless orientation to doing rather than to being. The majority of the principles of reading research lack life. And yet when we hear public accusations that some or maybe many young people leaving high school do not know how to read or write this accusation is always grounded in life. It is books, newsletters, job descriptions, poetry, correspondence, public announcements, guides, and consumer directions that young people cannot read. And do we after all really know what reading *is*? Young children may know this better than their teachers. A reading specialist at my university asked her nine year old daughter coming home from school what she had done in reading today and was a bit taken back when her daughter told her that they had not had any reading. What they had done was worksheets and workbook exercises which the reading specialist recognized as belonging to the reading curriculum. It was only some time later that my colleague began to be somewhat bothered by that innocent exchange between herself and her daughter. Have teachers been trained so well in the busy-busy doing workbook syndrome that they themselves have forgotten what really counts for reading? A recent study in Toronto showed that in the schools that were studied children actually read only for four minutes out of every hour devoted to reading. Do we really know what reading it? What it is like? For what purposes we read? What the significance is of being lost in a book? How the body partakes in reading? How we look for a good place to read? How reading a story is done in a different modality than reading an assigned study text? What reading is like while underlining or writing notes in the margins? How time is experienced while being absorbed in a book? How being absorbed in a book is always being absorbed with one's life?

Recently I heard an internationally known scholar of reading say that "everything considered the best exercise for learning to read may well be to simply let children read something." This pronouncement is astonishing. But hardly for its depth of insight. The specialist went on to say that her main advice to schools would be that "teachers should simply provide children with the opportunity to read, to read anything, no matter what." The last recommendation is as astonishing as the first one. Does it really not matter what it is that children read, when they read something? Or have the real questions of the nature of the reading experience hardly begun to be asked? Returning to the main theme of this discussion, I guess we should ask what does it mean to be a competent teacher of reading if a teacher lacks a true understanding of the full meaning of reading?

What can we learn when we engage children from elementary and secondary schools in conversations about outstanding teachers they have had, teachers they learn best from, the kind of teacher they would like to be themselves, how you can tell a good teacher from a bad one, and so forth? And as one learns to listen to the undertones of what young people say, certain themes begin to emerge. These themes are hidden behind stories which commonly would lead to certain generalizations such as the importance for teachers of being fair, being patient, being able to communicate, keeping good discipline, having a sense of humor, knowing the children, knowing what you teach, being interesting, and generally liking kids. But the themes behind these generalizations are less easily abstracted into concluding statements. At a deeper level teacher competency has more to do with something one could refer to as pedagogic tactfulness, having a sensitivity to what is best for a child, which also means having a sense of this child's life including those aspects of life that lie deeply within, or in a different sense those aspects that draw the curriculum of Math, English, Social Studies, Art, or Science to the curriculum of life itself.When a child tells real life stories of how he "wanted to be trusted and believed" by a teacher, he also touches on a deeper sense of trust and belief in children without which a teacher no longer can be an educator. When children say that "teachers should like what they teach" and "have a sense of humor" but that "they should not always try to be funny or tell dumb jokes," then they point us in the direction of what it really means "to be what you say or do" as a teacher, to have a sense of joy and deep commitment to life, to this world, and to the subject matter that draws the teacher and students to the world. When children say that "teachers should know what students need," "help them with homework," "be available to them" and "not hand out classroom work and then walk out of the door," that "teachers should have patience" and "not give up on kids," then they have again pointed us to the essence of pedagogic competence: a teacher who gives up on a child, such teacher who no longer knows how to have a sense of hope for that child, such teacher immediately abdicates his essence. When children say that "good teachers know how to make you learn," "good teachers know how to make you like Math or Science or English even though you always hated it," "good teachers are enthusiastic about what they teach," then they refer us to another essential aspect of teaching: good teachers do not just happen to teach Math or poetry; a good teacher embodies Math or embodies poetry. Or better yet good teachers *are* what they teach.

It is true that no matter what anyone says, teaching, like parenting, is a profoundly practical vocation. The pressing Monday morning question for teachers always evolves around "What am I going to do?" But reflection on the experiential significance of the idea of competence teaches us that this question should be brought in deep harmony with a neglected more primordial question: "What am I going to be?" And for pursuing this question we need a form of research and theorizing which constantly turns us back from reductionist abstractions and technical methodologies to the world of lived experience of doing and acting. This is also what a deeper notion of action research might mean. We engage in action research to make a difference in our pedagogic practices but without a certain thoughtfulness how are we to tell whether the difference between this approach and that approach is indeed a difference that makes a real difference?

In the works of great phenomenologists the essence of phenomenology emerges as the practice of thoughtfulness: a minding, a heeding, a caring attunement—a heedful mindful preoccupation with the project of living with children, of what it means to live a life as an educator. So in some strange sense, the theoretical practice of phenomenological research like the mundane practice of teaching or pedagogy is a ministering of thoughtfulness. To be full of thoughtmeans not that we have a whole lot on our mind but rather that as teachers we recognize our lot of minding the whole—it is a being given over to some quest, a true task, a deep questioning of that which restores an original sense of what it means to be an educator and what it means to be a researcher. Phenomenological research aims to establish a renewed contact with the original experience of pedagogy. This turning to the things of our lived experience is a becoming full of the world, full of lived experience. "Being experienced" is a wisdom of the practice of living which results from living our lives with children deeply or thoughtfully. Phenomenologists often speak of themselves as perpetual beginners. By this they mean that phenomenology is constantly oriented to the primoriality of lived experience of which every conceptualization is always an abstraction. Maybe teacher competency involves such phenomenological attitude of always being inclined to reject ready made answers for pedagogical problems and situations; of always returning to life itself in order to question the significance of any particular encounter or experience we have with a child. Teacher competence does not consist of some systematic set of teaching skills and classroom management techniques which once mastered takes the mystery out of teaching children. Teacher competence is that which a teacher resorts to when he or she tactfully converts just any kind of experience into a true learning experience—and in so *doing* he or she restores the mystery of *being* a teacher.

2

Some people bring children into this world and then abandon them. Others hold on to them but do not know how to love. Again others may be well intentioned but they make a mess of it. And so we need laws to protect the child from neglect, or worse, from child abuse. And then there are parents who do love and make an effort but they make a mess of it anyway. The same kind of scenario can be sketched for teachers. It seems easier to talk about pedagogic incompetence than about competence. (We might boldly say that those who do *not* find the topic of competence difficult do not know in a serious way what they are talking about). What makes it possible for us to speak (theorize) of competence when it comes to raising or teaching (educating) children? It means that we are *able to do* things in children's lives and that we are *able to do things right*. But modern (positivistic) conceptions of theorizing no longer permit us to speak of certain forms or kinds of theories as right or wrong, good or bad, reasonable or unreasonable. Modern conceptions of theorizing are more often guided by the useful than by the good. Indeed Nietzsche, Heidegger, and others have shown that our conception of knowledge and rational thinking has been detached from its traditional affiliation with the conception of the "good." And yet it is essentially the "good" we have to understand in order to give content to the meaning of competence when we speak of an adult as a "good" teacher or "good" parent.

We are interested in pedagogic competence because we realize that it is not enough to bring children into the world and to love them, or to accept a job as a teacher and to lecture about history or science. We also have to be able to help the child grow up and give shape to life by learning what is worthwhile knowing and becoming. So we are interested in competence because we want to know what to do: as pedagogues we must act and in acting we must be true to our calling. If we are expected to do the right thing in our pedagogic relationship with children we may require an idea of pedagogic competence which makes pedagogic praxis possible. However, to spell out the conditions of adequate pedagogic performance by formulating a concept, theory, or model of pedagogic competence is an inane endeavor. Because it presumes that we know conceptually what is essentially unknowable in a conceptual or positive sense. But we do know in what directions the significance of pedagogic competence must be sought.

On the one hand pedagogic competence involves an answering to the fundamental existentials of the pedagogic relationship. We see this answering at work in the lives of parents and teachers with children. We see it at work in the mother who engages in playful "conversations" with her infant. Although the little one has not developed a formal vocabulary as yet, it nevertheless knows how to "converse" by way of smiling, eye contact, bursts of laughter, hugging and hitting, babbling and silence, and crying of various sorts, whimpering, weeping, wailing. Early childhood psychologists who have made micro-studies of the "hidden" skills of social initiation, response behavior, mediation, etc., between mother and child call this interaction "reciprocity behavior." Giving names to the fundamental existentials of the pedagogic relationship no doubt is helpful. So we say that a competent parent or teacher knows when and how to provide a child in concrete situations with proper "security," "love," "reciprocity," "stability," "continuity," and so on. But by assigning words to pedagogic existentials we inevitably convert into discrete entities (as if "security," "stability," etc., is something that could be "administered" or "delivered") what functions much more dynamically.

Mark is playing on the floor while his mom is reading a magazine. But the little boy has begun to crawl speedily toward the door while chuckling with pleasure. Then he stops, sits up and looks at his mother who casts a furtive glance. The next moment Mark is back on all fours and now his movements are even faster while his laughter turns into an excited panting. Mark stops again and looks back at his mom. The excitement is impossible to ignore and mother tears herself out of her reading and proceeds noisily and playfully into the direction of Mark. The chase is now fully on! And Mark is getting beyond himself with excitement, so that his laughter turns into high-pitched screams. "I'll get you! I'll get you!" laughs Mom and stamps her feet and claps her hands. Mark can hardly control himself. His delighted laughter virtually immobilizes him and instead of crawling faster his limbs now move awkwardly slowly. He just cannot get away from his mother!—who'll grab him in her next move. And then she fetches him and pulls him into a playful embrace. "I gotch'a!" This is all too much and the little boy shrieks with pure exaltation. It's good that Mom's kisses are so sweet because one gets the uncanny feeling that Mark's joyful excitement could have climaxed into a confused crying bout. Some more hugging and face rubbing in Mom's hair and Mark is back on the floor. Mom sits down but she leaves the magazine alone. She knows the next "come and get me" is only a few seconds away.

Are we still talking of pedagogic competence here? But of course! A good mother knows that Mark's so-called "initiation behavior" is really an invitation. An invitation to show that she really cares—enough to drop what she is doing to show the little boy that he cannot get away as yet. And so mother's confirmation of her care turns into an adventurous pursuit. When Mark "runs away" from his mother his escape experience turns into a primitive mock-up of independence. Although being chased and caught borders on playful fright, it would be more frightening if no one cared enough to come and claim you. Both mother and child are showing each other that they cannot do without each other. So the chase becomes a testing of Mom's dependability. And yes, also "security," and "love," and "independence" are the pedagogic existentials of this relationship. But if these words are to communicate more to us than theoretic-didactic precepts of child development, then we need to learn that pedagogic competence involves a form of praxis (thoughtful action: action full of thought and thought full of action) wherein the requirements of the pedagogic existentials are actualized in real and concrete situations. Competence means that mother knows when to do what and how, and when to stop the chase game, "because too much excitement is too much."

Secondly, pedagogic competence is the anticipatory and reflective capacity of fostering, shaping, and guiding the child's emancipatory growth into adulthood: what you should be capable of, how you should have a mind of your own, and what you should be like as a person. The emancipatory interest of pedagogy in the educational development of children does not require that children are "educated" to become like the adults who educate them. Adults themselves are challenged by the emancipatory interest to see their own lives as a potentiality, that is, as an oriented being and becoming. The transition from childhood to adulthood is therefore not "merely" a change of status, from primitive or undifferentiated to more perfect or complex cognitions and competencies. If emancipatory adulthood implies a being oriented toward actualizations of a deep sense of the Good then pedagogy requires that children develop a transformed (i.e., emancipated) orientation to the question of what they potentially may become.

Pedagogic competence manifests itself not only in praxis, in our concrete relationships, activities, and situations with children. It manifests itself as well in theorizing, where the parent or professional educator reflectively brings to speech the meaning of pedagogic thought and actions. This usually happens when the children have been tucked in bed or when the class has been dismissed; then the pedagogic life of parents and teachers finds reprieve. Friends come over for a visit, teachers retire to the staffroom, or join their spouses at home. It is on these occasions that adults talk "kids" with adults—a mundane form of pedagogic theorizing.

The distinction of pedagogic competence as praxis and as reflective theorizing does not imply that praxis is unreflective. In fact, parenting and teaching are often highly reflective activities. I may deal with a child in a particular situation in a probing fashion (How can I let her realize more deeply the significance of what she has done?); or in an exploratory way (I have tried this, now I'll try that); or in a more routinized manner (Now I come to think of it, I usually have more impact on this child by simply overlooking this sort of thing); and so forth.

Pedagogical theorizing in a phenomenological sense is not some kind of "born again" pedagogy, nor some sort of self-help method for teachers who need to learn to care deeply about children. Rather theoretical pedagogy is a constant searching out of the beginning. In a modern positivistic context theoretical pedagogy is paradoxically pre-theoretic. It refuses to leave the concrete situation wherein pedagogues and children find themselves. And since it is situation bound and situation specific, pedagogical theorizing does not develop testable hypotheses, abstracting frameworks, or categorical schemas. The pedagogue as theorist makes a difference in the sense that he shows the difference between what is essential and what is inessential in concrete pedagogic situations. The contemporary confusion of educators about that which really matters in curriculum and teaching marks a decaying sensitivity to the pedagogic ground of educational theory and practice. Theorizing for the sake of theorizing, like art for art's sake, is not a superfluous self-serving exercise as it is sometimes supposed. Theorizing contributes to one's resourcefulness—not in a simple means-ends or applied, technical pragmatic sense, nor in an attitudinal or subjectivist psychological sense. Theorizing contributes to one's resourcefulness by directing the orienting questions toward the source itself; the source which gives life or spirit to (inspires) our pedagogic life.

In reflectively bringing their thoughts and actions to speech, students of pedagogy are challenged to formulate their auspices: what it is that grounds their pedagogic life with children. So that, to theorize is to get to know oneself. Not in the superficial sense of self-awareness as reflected in the narcissistic literature of popular psychology, but in the phenomenological sense of anamnesis. To theorize is to struggle to achieve one's limits, to find one's origin, one's grounding in that which makes our pedagogic life possible. Phenomenological pedagogy is not simply an "approach" to the study of pedagogy. It does not simply yield "alternative" explanations of educational phenomena. Rather, it bids to recover reflectively the grounds which, in a deep sense, provide for the possibility of our pedagogic concerns with children. The phenomenological attitude reminds us that children are already or mundanely a pedagogic concern to us prior to any systematic inquiry, indeed prior to any epistemological choice point.

Inquiry as pedagogic theorizing is expressed in the effort to keep a pedagogic question alive. Truly significant questions ask for the grounds of the pehenomenon which the question interrogates. Thus, pedagogic questions ask for answers—but they do not ask for answers which annihilate, do away with the questions. As Heidegger would say, the answer to a question of relevance is not exhausted in an affirmation which answers to the question by completing it. Such an answer sees itself successful only when it has put the quest of our question to a permanent rest—when it has made the question unnecessary so to speak. Rather, an answer which is responsive to a question is reflectedin the adequacy of bringing to light the full force and immanent direction of the question. Competence as pedagogical theorizing is an enabling process. It enables us, because it permits us as educators to ground ourselves in pedagogy. But in what ways can we speak of adequate or correct answers? What does a correct answer correct? The word "correct" derives from the Latin "corrigere" which means "to lead straight" (*regere*) with "vigor" (*com*). Correct answers lead us with vigor from the erring ways in which we may tend to follow a question. A correct answer straightens us out and leads us more accurately to the source, the grounds of the question. Speaking or writing in the sense of correct answering is a process (theorizing) which brings to speech our successes and failings of addressing the question in the ways it wants to be addressed. It prevents us from straying, erring off the path of the question.

So every time that a question is addressed phenomenologically the answering becomes an occasion for us to recollect, that is, to *re-collect* the collectedness: that which owns our connectedness with children, that which brings pedagogic actions into being. Being oriented in a questioning way to the grounds of our pedagogic existence becomes our way of formulating answers. There is this powerful heuristic sense, in which the dwelling in the question that captures us, is the answer to our question. The answer to the question "what it is like to be a pedagogue?" is, therefore, not a proposition or a set of generalizations. Rather, the answer is something that "shines through" when our reflective questioning respects the grounds of the inquiry by heeding that which gives rise to our care for children.

The function of this foundational, recollective or poetic thinking or speaking is to return us to the origin—to remind us as pedagogues of the worth of minding. This does not "merely" imply that as educators we need to care for and take care of the children who are entrusted to us. It means more than that. Our "pedagogic" caring needs to be anchored more deeply than in the loving gestures of wiping Mark's nose or taking Joan aside for extra help with her math. Pedagogic theorizing, as minding, is a caring for that which draws us as parents, as teachers to children. The educator who attempts to be fundamentally accountable (for his work with children and to himself as pedagogue) therefore, is also fundamentally accountable to that which "lets him be" pedagogue. By "fundamentally accountable" I mean being accountable, responsible or answerable to the fundamental, that is, to the foundational, the essential or the recollective. Indeed, we cannot say anything fundamental unless our speaking speaks to the foundations.

We might say that at any time in the history of thought about parenting, schooling, or educational theorizing the degree of absence of foundational or recollective minding constitutes a form of nihilism, pedagogic indifference. Nihilism implies a lack of commitment, a lack of moral will or desire to be reflectively responsive to the calling of pedagogy—a sort of vocational amnesia. Some educational thinkers find the source of their research methodology in foundational philosophy or in so-called alternative research approaches. But they too tend to suffer from this forgetfulness—a forgetfulness about that which draws pedagogy to its liking, that which makes pedagogy possible in the first place.

With phenomenology we are guided back from theoretical abstractions to the reality of lived experiences—the lived experience of the child's world, the lived experience of schools, curricula, and so on. Phenomenology asks the simple question, what is it like to have a certain experience? (For example, an educational experience). An innocent question indeed. We may know that we have a certain experience, that we feel alone, afraid, in love, bored, amused, but we are quickly at wits end when we are pressed to describe what such feeling consists of. Yet, in the field of curriculum we confidently talk about "selecting, planning, or organizing learning experiences." This confidence begs a question, whether we really know what it is like when a child "has an experience" or when the child "comes to understand something." Husserl's phrase "back to the things themselves" means that the phenomenological attitude is mindful of the ease with which we tend to rely on a reconstructed logic in our professional endeavors. We read theories into everything. And once a theoretical scheme has been brought to life we tend to search for the principles that seem to organize the life to which the theory was brought. In our efforts to make sense of our lived experiences with theories and hypothesizing frameworks we are forgetting that it was living human beings who bring schemas and frameworks into being and not the reverse.

The phenomenological attitude towards the concerns of our daily occupation compels us to constantly raise the question: What is it about being an educator which makes a pedagogic existence different from other pursuits? As adults we meet children socially in many situations where pedagogy is not permitted or encouraged to enter. My interest in a child may be primarily for reasons of coaching a sporting event or selling pop records. But to say this, challenges the question what difference there is between hockey coach, sales person, boy-scout leader, math teacher, or school principal. No doubt there are commonalities between a coach and pedagogue. Both may be teaching the child different things. So that there are essential and inessential differences between those who teach children. To ask how a teacher shows a difference which makes a pedagogic difference is to ask how the essence of pedagogy can be made intelligible. And now the simple and innocent phenomenological question "What is it like?" assumes a deeper dimension. Because now we are led to address the question what kind of answer would meet the phenomenological requirement of intelligibility. How can we come to a deep understanding of that which makes it possible to say that between this teacher and this child pedagogy is in attendance? What kind of speaking would satisfy such understanding? In phenomenology what kind of speaking counts as an answer? Or, more precisely, in phenomenology what counts as knowledge?

One way of dealing with this question is to theorize about knowledge; to epistemologize our answer by theorizing, for example, about the distinctions between different types of knowledge (such as empirical, hermeneutic, and other types of social science). But if we wish to remain responsive to the commitment of phenomenology then we should try to resist the temptation to develop positivistic schemas, paradigms, models, or other categorical abstractions of knowledge. Instead we should refer questions of knowledge back to the life world where knowledge speaks through our lived experiences. We, therefore, wish to ask: How can we pursue the question of what constitutes (phenomenological) knowledge in such a way that our way of addressing this question may become an example of what the question seeks to bring to clarity? In other words, how can we show the what-ness of the pedagogic experience, at once in an iconic and in a recollective sense?

Phenomenological writing succeeds there, where it lets us see that which shines through, that which tends to hide itself. And how can phenomenology "let us see"? Phenomenology is heedful of our propensity to mistake what we say (our words) with what we talk about (the Logos). Phenomenology is not found in the colorful words of the story-teller, nor in the fanciful phrases of the person with a flair for writing. The words are the thing. And yet, it is to our words, language, that we must apply all our phenomenological skill and talents. Because it is in and through the words that the shining through (the invisible) becomes visible.

The language of phenomenological pedagogy discloses reflectively ("shows us") how phenomenological knowledge is held and what it is like to know things pedagogically. In other words, pedagogical theorizing requires a responsive reading. One does not read poetry as if it were a mathematical treatise, or a logical argument, or even a story line. He who reads poetry as if it were prose misses a full "understanding" of the poem. Similarly, he who cannot see how a phenomenological use of words is a function of the things being described in the words will, therefore, be unable to "understand" the description. The occurrence of dramatic irony in phenomenological language use means that the reader must be prepared to be attentive to what is said in and through the words: What the content of the words may leave unspoken as silence is revealed through their form. Content may be visible as form but for that reason concealed as content. Phenomenology is like poetry, in that it speaks partly through silence: it means more than it explicitly says. Phenomenology, like poetry, intends to be silent as it speaks. So, to read or write phenomenologically requires that we be sensitively attentive to the silence about the words by means of which we attempt to disclose the deep meaning of our world. For this reason Norman O. Brown says that,

> Speech points beyond itself to the silence, to the word within the word, the language buried in language, the primordial language, from before the Flood or the Tower of Babel; lost yet ready at hand, perfect for all time; present in all our words, unspoken. To hear again the primordial language is to restore to words their full significance. [p. 258, *Love's Body*, 1966]

A phenomenological description is like an icon: it refers us back to what stands behind it. The Greek word "icon"carries the meaning "likeness," "to be like." When we strive to think phenomenologically, we are striving to think of knowledge iconically, we ask, "What is this or that like?" "And how can we let it show itself in its very essence?" And so, as educators every phenomenological questioning is always a form of being oriented towards what it is that makes it possible for us to be pedagogues, teachers in the first place. The function of the icon is to let pedogogic being make itself manifest in the things about which we reflectively speak as pedagogues. To recognize phenomenological descriptions as iconic is to recognize the difference between description and the recollective as revealed by the description. Indeed, Heraclitus points at this difference when he admonishes his listeners away from his words towards the logos which make the speaking possible.

Heidegger, Merleau Ponty, and others talk of the comportment which enables us to keep open to the logos as "openness to the mystery." But this desire for openness is not a recommendation for submitting to mysticism as a way of pedagogical theorizing. Rather, it is a recommendation to cherish a notion of truth in the fullest sense—not as a property of propositions or icons, but instead as the attempt to let the living sense of pedagogic being speak profoundly in and through language.

What then is pedagogy? The question as to the essence of pedagogy does not summon an answer as might be provided in the form of a set of propositions about teaching in a methods textbook on curriculum and instruction. Rather pedagogic questions call for answers which are responsive, responsible to the calling of our pedagogic being with children.

Pedagogy as a calling or vocation discloses itself to the pedagogue in the experience of being called upon to educate. In the re-cognition of the calling, we re-call that which has summoned us to put aside any particular interest we may have in the world in favor of our interest in this child or these children. It is visible in the surging the mother or father feels in the spontaneous hugging of the infant. "You and me, we belong together." It is in the "you my child belong to me" and "I belong to you." It is exactly in the truth experience of this strong impulse we feel for the child that the true nature of pedagogy remains hidden. It is in the being called that we sense both the showing and the hiding of pedagogic being. The clearer pedagogic being presents itself in our lives as parents or teachers the more perplexing its true nature recedes from our intelligibility. There is indeed mystery in the being commanded by the calling to apply oneself to goodness in our lives with children. The newly born comes into the world as an appellation. And so it names us to the vocation of parent or guardian. But more deeply it is the calling of the vocation which names us. This naming is an authoritative invocation to act authoritatively (because authorized by the heeding of the calling) in the personal becoming of the child: to act pedagogically in the lives of children.

The pedagogic calling is universal in the sense that it calls anyone who cares to listen. Not every mother or father has a parental orientation to his or her child. About someone we might say, "He just never grew up and so he does not know what it means to be a father." The same is true for school teachers. A teacher says, "I found out that I do not really like children, and so I decided after a few years that I should try my hand at some other career." This is not an uncommon confession among teachers. Of course, some teachers find the prospects of a new job more threatening than getting out of their present one. So they persist and struggle on. Others may never have felt right about the choice of making a career in education, but they keep blaming the Faculty of Education, parents, the administration, or some other culprit (even the children) for their apparent lack of pedagogic dedication.

But how can we know that pedagogy is largely absent in the lives of some teachers (or parents)? Our positivist orientation tends to confuse pedagogy with what teachers or parents do. We judge teachers almost entirely in terms of the ability to demonstrate certain productivity, effectiveness, or the competencies which are presumed to serve these values. Positivism has difficulty discerning whether the contact a teacher has with his children is indeed a "real" contact, a pedagogic contact. For example, positivism could teach teachers of the effectiveness of eye-contact in the "management of classroom behaviors." And positivism can assess the incidence of eye-contact in empirical situations, by means of categorical interaction analysis systems or other such instruments. However, the function of optimum frequency of eye-contact in the completion of specific learning tasks entirely glosses over the pedagogic meaning of the "meaningful look" between teacher and students.

So positivism in educational research and theorizing suffers from a certain blindness. It mistakes categorical or operational instances of some rational conceptualization of pedagogy for the "real" thing. It fails to see that we cannot "see" pedagogy if "to see" means to observe operational or experimental instances of pedagogic teaching. It fails to see that the meaning and significance of pedagogy remains concealed behind our inability to approach pedagogy pre-theoretically. It remains concealed as a consequence of the theoretical overlays and perspectival frameworks we construct in the paradoxical effort to see more clearly the significance of certain pedagogic practices (usually called "teaching behaviors,""curriculum effects," etc.).

The positivist notion of practice as the testing ground of theory is maintained in the term "practice teaching." We say, "practice makes perfect." Indeed practice makes perfect a particular technique or skill—but practice as applied theory in an instrumental sense does not necessarily contribute to pedagogic wisdom. Wisdom is something that does not flow from practice. Our narrow, positivistic preoccupation with methods (witness the so-called"methods courses" in teacher preparation institutions), with teaching strategies and techniques paradoxically has led to obsessive interests in the interpretation or usage of such methods. But to be original is not to be merely different. The originality of creative or novel methods and constantly changing teaching techniques is a vulgarization of the idea of originality, that deprives it of all serious meaning. We could ask, what is it like to overcome the forgetfulness of behavioral objectives or a performance oriented pedagogy which has lost the concern (care) from which the interest in objectives, techniques, and methods in curriculum and instruction originally issued? To be original is to be true to the meaning which originates from our pedagogic relationship with children.

As teachers we use so-called techniques, strategies, or instructional approaches in helping our children learn. But the much abused word "techniques" has a richer history than the simple instrumentalist interpetation of a technique as an instructional means to a curricular end. The etymology of the term "technology" carries the meaning of "producing," of "bringing forth" in the sense of "being responsible for." In this sense the idea of the technical is akin to the Greek concept of truth (aletheia): it brings something forth from hiddenness into unhiddenness. The Greek word "techne" is connected to "episteme," both are modes of knowing, meaning, "being versed in," as well as "modes of disclosure" (Aristotle, *Ethics*). So rather than a mere skill or procedure, a teaching technique can be understood as the act of ably letting something come into presence, into unconcealment. Why then should, in the formulation of the idea of competence, the emphasis on techniques and skills be reprehensible? For sure, it is not the productive relation of didactics as bringing forth in children what belongs to them as possibilities of essential becoming that is reprehensible. But it is the disposition to transform the transformation of bringing forth, as well as the whatness of what is thus brought forth, into positivistic objective quantities—visibles, tangibles, definables—that is deserving of our disquietude. It is the thing likeness of the objects to which our technical concept of competence applies which should be of concern to us. Because this vulgarization of the objectification of pedagogic competence denies the interplay between disclosure and hiddenness in our understanding of the meaning of pedagogy.

Man encounters himself in all his making. In a highly modernistic world man (homo faber) sees himself reflected in the technological objects of his productive activities. Even in the way we go about educating our children we constantly are faced with students and their curricula as of our making. We plan programs, construct, select knowledge, formulate objectives, evaluate children and their doings as projects of our own hands. We see ourselves constantly in this process. But in a deeper sense we fail to see more essentially who we are. Because in making the curriculum thinglike and in distancing ourselves from the essentials of the pedagogic life, we radically cut ourselves loose, into a truncated existence, from the possibility of "really" knowing ourselves, our children, and our possibilities.

In a mundane sense we confuse pedagogy with what we see pedagogues do. If pedagogy were absent in a particular situation, positivism would not be able to tell the difference. But positivism fails to see, in a *deep* sense too, the absence of pedagogy. It fails to see the absence of pedagogy by mistaking concrete descriptions or case studies of pedagogy with that which constitutes its ground. Positivism fails to see that in a deep sense pedagogy absents or "hides" itself by virtue of its own activity: in the process of showing itself it also shows its hidden character.

This implies that one can *be* a pedagogue and yet not *have* pedagogy.Pedagogy is not something that can be "had," "possessed" in the way that we say that a person"has" or "possesses" a set of specific skills or performative competencies. Rather pedagogy is something that a pedagogue continuously must redeem, retrieve, regain, or recapture in the sense of recalling. Every situation in which I must act educationally with children requires that I must continuously and reflectively be sensitive to what authorizes me as pedagogic teacher. Exactly because pedagogy is fundamentally unfathomable it poses the unremitting invitation to the creative activity of pedagogic reflection which brings the deep meaning of pedagogy to light.

So, in spite of what we think parents or teachers do or don't do, pedagogy is something that is cemented deeply in the nature of the relationship between adults and children. But not so much as a certain kind of relationship or a particular kind of doing; rather, pedagogy is something that lets an encounter, a relationship, a situation, or a doing be pedagogic. All our pedagogic being with children is a form of speaking with them. Even when we quietly listen, raise eyebrows, nod encouragingly, embrace, turn away, sing, chuckle, or hold a child's momentary attention with our eyes, we may do so out of a pedagogic concern. So that in everyday concrete situations where we speak with children, pedagogic being is something that occurs as a showing in our being.

From an etymological point of view, a pedagogue is a man or woman who is a leader or teacher (agogos) of children (paides). But the deep meaning does not unambiguously lie in the example of the watchful Greek slave or guardian, whose responsibility it was to lead the young child to school. Rather, in the "leading" or "guiding" there is a "taking by the hand," in the sense of a watchful encouraging: "Here, take my hand!" "Come and I shall show you the world." That is why education or teaching has been likened to initiation and guidance. The pedagogue is the adult who shows the child the way into a world. My world, and yours. I know something about being a child. Because I have been there, where you are now. I was young once. But childhood is something one must grow out of. And so my adulthood becomes an invitation, a beckoning to the child. This is the meaning of leading: going first. And in the "going first" there is a promise: that you can trust me, for I have tested the ice. I have lived. I now know something of the rewards as well as the trappings of growing towards adulthood and making a world for yourself. And although my going first is no guarantee of success (because the world is not without risks and dangers), in the pedagogic relationship there is a more fundamental guarantee: that, no matter what, I'm here. And you can count on me!

Afterword

10

The inquiries in this volume were intended to generate conceptual and practical knowledge concerning the nature of competence and its acquisition. The individual papers have indeed provided some new understandings related to the notion of competence and have furnished several new possibilities for further inquiries. Each inquiry was, however, initiated quite independently from the others, and each used a distinct form of inquiry by which to generate this knowledge. The question to be answered at the conclusion of this volume is whether collectively these inquiries provide any consistent basis for drawing implications about the use of the concept of competence in educational settings and for distinguishing between appropriate and inappropriate practices related to its acquisition. The diversity and complexity of the inquiries presented here make it difficult to summarize the knowledge that may be derived collectively from them regarding the adoption and use of viable and adequate conceptions of competence. Nevertheless, the reader may have already recognized some of the valuable insights that come through these papers when competence is viewed from multiple perspectives. The editor, in this final chapter, attempts to identify some of these ideas and to suggest ways by which they may be applied in future educational practice and inquiry.

Gleanings and Possibilities

Edmund C. Short
The Pennsylvania State University

The papers in *Competence: Inquiries into its Meaning and Acquisition in Educational Settings* address a domain of significant problems related to thinking about the idea of competence in educational policy and practice. Few issues in education have aroused greater controversy in recent times than those surrounding the nature of competence. Significant questions have been raised about what the term *competence* really means and whether its use in the context of education is really appropriate and fruitful. Many current usages of the term *competence* appear to be based upon concepts that differ widely from one another, ranging from very narrow understandings of the term to very broad ones, thus obscuring effective communication and veiling differences in views of competence that are subscribed to or accepted by various people.

The effort to translate the rhetoric surrounding the term *competence* into concrete educational programs and practices is thereby made extraordinarily complicated, if not impossible. Consider the dilemmas faced when such practical questions as the following are raised:

1) What specific forms does competence take in particular contexts—those related, for instance, to program goals, life-role projections, school subject areas, concrete educational or training activities, evaluation criteria, and reports to the public on attainments by students?

2) Can competence be taught?

3) How can competence be detected?

4) Can the public hold schools accountable for developing competence in students?

5) Can legislative mandates to guarantee minimum levels of competence in school graduates be effective?

6) Are the prevailing notions of competence adequate bases for curricular and instructional planning?

7) How is teacher competence related to student competence?

Answers to these questions invariably depend upon what is meant by the term *competence* and how it is construed in various contexts.

It is the view of those scholars represented in this volume, and of others engaged in inquiry into the nature of competence, that much remains to be done to clarify what current usage of the term implies and what conceptions might be asserted that would enhance educational thinking and practice. It has been the special purpose of the scholars represented in this volume to examine the idea of competence by methods of analysis, criticism, and empirical synthesis, with a view toward illuminating new ways of thinking about and employing the term *competence.* This effort has *not* been one of boldly asserting from one perspective or another what are deemed appropriate conceptions and directions that education should adopt with respect to the notion of competence, though there is evidence that some of these writers are considerably disenchanted with what has been said and done in the past in the name of competence. Their more modest goal has been to try to inch gradually toward firmer scholarly knowledge upon which such projections might be constructed in the future.

From a variety of scholarly perspectives, some tentative understandings of the idea of competence have been introduced. This work helps push outward the boundaries of inquiry on competence, both substantively and methodologically. It is to be hoped that the pursuit of these and other lines of inquiry may eventually extend our understanding of various conceptions of competence and enable those who work with this concept to employ it more discriminatingly in light of this fuller understanding. Strictly speaking, however, it has not been the primary intention of these scholars, in the work reported here, to suggest new programs or lines of inquiry or to summarize definitively what has been generated so far within any one of them. Rather, each one has simply chosen to report an individual inquiry undertaken within a particular scholarly tradition, with the hope that others, both within and outside these particular traditions, may find his/her work illuminating. The task that falls to the editor in this final chapter is to scrutinize the work of all these scholars as a whole and to identify what, if anything, has been cleared up by this group of inquiries about the meaning and acquisition of competence.

Before launching into this editorial review and analysis, it is appropriate to say something about the reasons for offering a series of inquiries on competence that is interdisciplinary in character, and to indicate the special requirements that this kind of collection places upon the process of summarizing and interpreting such a diverse range of work. It should be understood, first of all, that problems such as the meaning of competence and how it is acquired are too broad and holistic to be adequately dealt with by any one of the common forms of disciplinary inquiry (scientific, historical, philosophical, phenomenological, or any other), all by itself. Each of these forms of inquiry, of necessity, must address relatively narrow research questions of the kind that its particular methods and procedures are designed to address, and such questions are never as broad or holistic as are those about the nature and acquisition of competence, for example. Yet these broader phenomena have to be understood in their wholeness, as entities, and not simply as unarticulated parts, if they are to be recognized and handled intelligibly within the real world of education. Consequently, interdisciplinary knowledge is the kind that must be sought in these circumstances.

Interdisciplinary understanding does, however, require the services of the various disciplines. Studies must be conducted on questions that each of these disciplines can address, as they relate to certain dimensions of the whole, and the results must be related in some way to one another so as to enable us to grasp something intelligible about the whole. It is clear from the work done on the methodology of interdisciplinary study that these separate disciplinary studies cannot logically be related to one another, except as certain ones dealing with the exact same question using the same mode of inquiry can be combined through processes of generalization, or as conceptually related studies in the same discipline can be integrated into meaningful configurations.[1] Across disciplines, however, the limitations of logic and language make it impossible to integrate knowledge generated under different conceptual and methodological systems. The mind, however, seems to be able to grasp the totality of meanings from these separate disciplinary findings when laid out side by side. This is what Michael Polanyi refers to when he describes the abstract meaning we are able to derive from using subsidiary clues elicited by the two parts of a focal metaphor, though logically they cannot be related.[2] This is surely what Joseph Schwab means by our taking a "polyfocal conspectus."[3] This is the advantage of what Alfred Schutz calls a "reciprocity of perspectives,"[4] where one sees from a multiplicity of different perspectives or vantage points.

While this kind of understanding cannot be articulated in the familiar linear forms of ordinary discourse, it can be expressed poetically (metaphorically) or iconicly and thereby understood publicly, just as Kenneth Beittel has demonstrated so well in his chapter in this volume. Even without attempting to re-express these meanings publicly through the visual or literary arts, we often act on the implications of their meaning as we have gained them from others who have expressed them in these forms to us. They have practical significance for us. So, too, can there be practical, professional significance for us as educators when interdisciplinary inquiries on competence are laid out side by side and examined and interpreted from various perspectives. What we learn from them, as we view them in this fashion, is more than what any one of them means when focused upon separately, one at a time. And even if we cannot easily convey to others what we find meaningfully present to us by this method (except as we become artists and deliberately create messages in iconic or metaphoric modes), we can utilize what we have acquired by this method in whatever situations may arise that call for an application of our holistic understanding of competence. That is, this is possible if we really use the inquiries subsidiarily while focusing upon some other immediate task to which they are relevant.

It is for these reasons that perhaps this book should end without a final chapter that tries to capture the significance of these inquiries. The editor certainly cannot do for the reader the kind of holistic interpretation of the entire series of papers that has been suggested is necessary in gaining interdisciplinary understanding. Each reader has to do this for him/herself, and it will occur not at the time of the reading but as situations arise in which they can be put in perspective and drawn upon to nourish the focus of attention at the time. Perhaps it will cause different decisions to be made about some matter in which the meaning or acquisition of competence figures than would have been made without such knowledge in waiting from multiple research perspectives. Of course, the knowledge provided in this book is not the whole of what is available, and yet may become available, from within various disciplines of inquiry on this subject. The sum total of such knowledge should be what is drawn upon in attempting interdisciplinary understanding, not just what is here.

The editor can, however, try to perform two services for the reader in these final pages: 1) a kind of extracting of some of the key ideas that are presented in these nine papers and relating or organizing them, insofar as that is possible, into some sort of coherent summary, and 2) offer some implications of these ideas on how they might influence educational thought and practice. A selection process will be at work; not all the key ideas to be found in these papers can be reiterated. What is taken note of by the editor represents, as was stated earlier, an attempt to see what has been made clearer, what has been illuminated, what new conceptual paths have been opened up that might be pursued with merit. Because the editor may have approached these inquiries with a different stock or level of knowledge about competence at his command than does the reader, his estimate of what contributions these writers have made may differ from that of the reader. Therefore, this analysis and review should be seen as a personal one and not taken as a substitute for the reader's doing the same sort of thing on his/her own. There is plenty to survey here, in any case.

The first set of observations I want to make is derived less from the content of the papers themselves than from what I discovered as convenor of the group about the authors' interest in this kind of interdisciplinary enterprise. I think it it fair to say that all of them believe that studying *competence* is a highly important and timely activity, which can have considerable practical pay-off in the world of education. Their intent seems to be to help remove some of the intellectual constraints surrounding the uses of the idea of competence in educational settings and to free up intelligent policies and practices that relate to this idea.[5] This scholarly intent, I think, has been achieved, at least in some measure. They also see that reporting their work in an interdisciplinary context has special value as well. There can be no doubt that as each person discovers from fellow researchers something about the historical development of teacher competence, the results of careful rhetorical or conceptual analyses of the term *competence*, the existential and philosophical values people place on competence, and the difficulties and dynamics of its learnability, a new perspective on one's own line of research is found. Put another way, there is a recognition that what is being done in one mode of inquiry on a broad topic like competence can and should affect what is done in another. New research directions are often stimulated, and some less fruitful ones are sometimes more quickly abandoned. Perhaps a format that permits this sort of interpenetration of perspectives should be utilized more frequently in research on educational problems.

Second, please note that the assessment of arguments for and against competency-based education (CBE) or competency-based teacher education (CBTE) were not central to the purpose of the inquiries presented in this volume, even though some of the authors have expressed or implied their views on these issues. Readers should be cautioned not to look for any authoritative guidance on these issues from whatever the authors have said on the subject, and I will not attempt any sort of summary of these arguments. Much more direct and systematic analysis of the issues involved would have to be done before useful policy guidelines could emerge about CBE or CBTE. In fact, I would judge that the authors generally believe that, before such issues can be meaningfully argued and recommendations for action offered, some basic inquiry has to be done about the nature of competence, its meaning and acquisition, and it is to this sort of inquiry that they have given their attention in these papers. What then do they say? What have their inquiries yielded?

The Meaning of Competence

As a basis for much of the constructive analytic work done by these scholars, several of them have first noted and attempted to deal with the confusion that exists over the definition of the word *competence*, and its derivatives, *competent*, *competency*, and *competencies*, as they are currently being used in ordinary educational discourse, policy, and practice.

A *competent* person is one who is described as having *competence* (in some particular realm of thought or action). This adjective form of the word is seldom confused or misused. The word *competency*, however, does not always seem to be used as a synonym for *competence*, though dictionaries commonly define it as such. Rather, *competency* has come to refer to a specified attribute that may be possessed by someone, perhaps within a series of related *competencies*, connoting both a concrete *category* on which a person's adequacy or sufficiency may be judged and that *quality* or *state of being* which characterizes a person as being competent, able, adequate, or sufficient within such a category. The word *competence* has normally been reserved for the second of these connotations, a quality or state of being competent, and when one is said to have *competence* in some realm, it ordinarily means that he/she possesses this general quality or state of being but we do not know specifically what he/she is capable of doing. Thus, confusion occurs when the word *competency* is coupled with the first connotation, that of a concrete category more specific than that usually meant when the word *competence* is used.

It is one thing to say that someone has *competence* in conversing in

Spanish; it is quite another thing to say that someone has mastered the *competency* of using the subjunctive mood in Spanish, or the *competency* of using appropriate Spanish inflections, or any one of a number of other concrete categories (*competencies*) that may be related to conversing in Spanish. Mastering particular *things* is not the same as possessing certain *qualities*, as an examination of any taxonomically organized thesaurus will remind us.

For many users, this slight shift in the meaning of the words *competency* or *competencies* evidently has not appeared to be very significant, much less problematic, as they have employed the terms. Yet, as our writers have pointed out, this shift in meaning has been great enough to permit synonomizing with the word *competency* another word *performance* that has a connotation corresponding to the first (and only to the first) connotation stated for *competency* (a concrete category, in which a person may be judged to be competent). Whether doing multiplication problems, or writing a precis, or teaching the concept of democracy, all these and similar actions or performances have been taken to be *categories of competence* that could be tested and measured for *competence*, for the *quality* of being competent.

This treating of achievements in performance as *qualities* of persons is indeed a semantic shift that is unjustified on any grounds. The consequences of this imprecision in word-usage are many, some of them quite unfortunate, as the analysis of several of our authors demonstrates: performance on tests has been equated with competence; minimal competencies have had to be demonstrated on very particular things without qualitative criteria for "minimal performance" being already articulated or justified; competency lists have been derived empirically and set up as expected performance, though attributes evidencing true competence can only be *ascribed* to someone, not *prescribed*; conformity with accepted definitions and criteria thwarts free, objective inquiry in the rush to meet specific, prescibed expectations in performance; materials are developed that control the learning activities toward some preset outcomes and demonstratable performances; teachers forget the careful thought processes that pupils must engage in as well as the search for relevant information that pupils must undertake if they are to acquire over time the habits and skills that deserve the ascription "competent;" and as disturbing as these sins of commission may be, the omission of a correct grasp of the meaning of competence as a quality or state of being, having a referent in the subjective experience of persons and not in the thingness of their particular acts or performances, may be the worst sin (consequence) of all.

Some of these practices have been followed out to their logical conclusions by the analyses of Professors Fagan, Noddings, Pearson, Johnson, Aoki, Apple, Beittel, Doll, and van Manen, and found faulty. And much of the impetus for these faulty practices seems to have originated in this slippage in terminology from *competence* and *compe-*

tency to *performance* as adopted by both theorists and practitioners in competency-based education (CBE) and competency-based teacher education (CBTE). Some of the implications of attempting to rectify these errors within CBE and CBTE will be touched upon later. It is quite clear from reading our authors that correcting these misconceptions does not mean that the use of the term *competence* needs to be abandoned; only that policies and practices should be reconceived in light of a more complete understanding of the meaning and acquisition of competence.

It should be pointed out that many of the unfortunate educational practices just listed do not result simply from inadvertent or unwitting use of imprecise terms. There have also been deliberate political factors at work. Variously attributed by our writers to "behaviorist psychology or philosophy," "ideological pressures by the powerful connection of free enterprise and the schools," "public demand for accountabiltiy," "the forces for equal educational opportunity for neglected groups," "the back-to-basics movement," "Darwinism," "the scientific management movement in education," "the need to run a tight ship and keep pupils in line," "positivistic science," "the technological world view," etc., these forces have capitalized upon, and perhaps even initiated, the use of the *competency* vocabulary. It served their purposes well, as long as educators and others did not stop to ask whether, as Fagan puts it, the terminology accurately labels the thing being addressed, or as Beittel puts it, the experience that precedes the words is not lost in the manipulation of the language.

In pointing to these political and ideological factors that have influenced both the educational decisions made and the technical vocabulary used by educators and the public, our writers have not sought to analyze the merits of these various influences per se. Only indirectly, through the analysis of the consequences of the practices, have they raised questions about whether there may not be alternative views that have been overlooked or tossed out in the midst of the competency rhetoric but which deserve attention. Insofar as constructive illumination of the meaning of competence and its acquisition can be provided, just so far will arguments among various views be able to focus upon real issues rather than be veiled in the confusions of language or be restricted to those that can be handled by a particular set of vocabulary.

A second domain of clarification attempted in the inquiries brought together in this volume concerns the ancillary question of *teaching competence*. The meaning of competence extends to both teachers and pupils in educational settings. What constitutes pupil competence in school learning will, of course, differ from what constitutes teacher competence, even though the definition of the term competence remains the same in both instances. Our writers, however, did not attempt to specify the elements in which pupils ought to become competent as a result of their educational experience, nor did they attempt to specify those elements in which teachers ought to be competent. They have left these tasks to others and have concentrated upon the more fundamental task of analyzing the meaning of competence in the context of teaching and learning.

Immediately, they were confronted with the fact that competence in teaching involves not only the what and the how of teaching but also the intent and very being of the teacher. In other words, the nature of teaching competence depends upon one's definition of *teaching*. Analysis of the meaning of *teaching*, therefore, has been a part of nearly all of these inquiries.

At least two contrasting sets of definitions of *teaching* were identified in these papers. One set encompasses definitions of teaching that specify fixed, pre-determined skills, actions, and duties, such as imparting knowledge, monitoring discipline, or preparing and giving tests. (There can, of course, be considerable difference of opinion on what the fixed list of teaching performances shall consist of in any given context.) Some of the early CBTE models adopted this sort of definition of teaching as the basis for their approach to teacher education. Johnson's research shows a long history of efforts to establish effective "techniques" for teachers. The other set of definitions of *teaching* admits activities involving both routine performances and other activities on which intelligent judgment must be exercised. *Teaching*, defined in this manner, as Pearson typified it, requires both "habitual skill knowledge" and "intelligent skill knowledge."

Aoki gave examples of these two contrasting types of teaching under differentiating schema associated with "instrumental action" and "praxis," where "technique" is paramount in the former and "reflection and communicative action" is paramount in the latter. Apple identified the phenomenon of "deskilled" and "reskilled" teachers wherein the scope of their activities and expertise is intentionally limited. This definition of teaching falls in the fixed, pre-determined category. Doll quite clearly points to the necessity for the other type of teaching when he demonstrates the diferent decisions a math teacher must make in teaching different children if their cognitive capacities are to be engaged in learning math. Both Beittel and van Manen stipulate definitions of teaching involving the experiential and ethical dimensions of the teacher's life and being, thus putting their definitions into the second major category. A mere technician would not find congenial the "norms of action implicit in qualitative experiencing" (Beittel) nor the compassionate responsiveness of the person-as-pedagogue (van Manen).

The point to be observed from this review is that since teaching has been conceived in a variety of ways, what one means by *teaching competence* depends on which definition of teaching is adopted. Whether one considers teaching to be more in the direction of "techniques routinely applied," or the opposite, "thoughtful adaptations to pupil circumstances" (or something in between or entirely different), *teaching* must be recognized as a normative concept, that is, one which represents a value choice among differing conceptions. So when we deal with the idea of *teacher competence*, we are inevitably dealing with a normative concept also. If we think of *pupil competence*, we must recognize the existence of varying conceptions of the *pupil* and recognize *pupil competence* as a normative concept as well. It will take its meaning from whatever notion of the *pupil* is selected. The same reasoning applies to any other domain of *competence* one might wish to consider—plumber competence, presidential competence, journalistic competence, parent competence, etc. My conclusion, therefore, is that regardless of the modifier used with the term *competence*, *competence* itself has to be understood as a normative concept. Several of our authors have pointed out that much of the confusion and misinterpretation resulting from using the competency vocabulary is a consequence of assuming *competence* to be a descriptive concept rather than a normative concept, and its referent a *thing* or an *activity* rather than a *quality or state of being*.

Let me now review some of the normative conceptualizations of *competence* that have been identified and analyzed throughout this volume.

(1) When competence is conceived to be *a competence* or *a competency* (competencies), the article "a" gives a clue to its being thought of as a *thing*. A *behavior* is one class of *things*; a *performance* (group of integrated behaviors) is another. To be able to demonstrate competence as a particular behavior or performance is necessarily to be able to demonstrate something very specific and limited. To specify behaviors, as is done in behavioral objectives, or to specify performance, as is done in performance testing (recall Fagan's rhetorical analysis), is to designate acts that can be accomplished (satisfactorily) quite independently of any on-going purpose or intent. And yet, the real test of competence occurs in real situations where purpose or intent obligates one to choose the most appropriate behaviors or performances as well as to enact them satisfactorily (recall Pearson's normative analysis). (I'll not ask what one does when one's repertoire of behaviors or performances, competent as they may be, is not sufficient for the situation.) To add an objective that calls for "selecting appropriate and timely teaching techniques," for instance, as Noddings points out, is to specify something very broad and complex, not at all of the same order as other specific behaviors or performances. If in particular cases there is a logical connection (or even an empirical connection) between specific behaviors or performances and some larger unit of competence, Noddings laments, it has yet to be demonstrated. Given these descriptions and limitations to the conception of competence as *behavior* or *performance*, it would be wise not to employ this conception except in circumstances where particular behaviors and/or performances are identical with the largest unit of competence one wishes to judge in a concrete category. This would probably be the case with certain physical skills or in some aspects of practical training in which replicative uses of the learned behaviors or perfor-

mance is entirely appropriate, and little or no cognitive judgment needs to be exercised in doing so. Competence is rightly understood here as the doing of particular *things* (behaviors or performances).

(2) Competence has also been conceived as having command of pertinent *knowledge and/or skills*. Pearson points out that such *knowledge and/or skills* may be either systematic or practical in nature and that persons with competence, in this sense, do not have exhaustive authoritative knowledge and/or skills, only basic or adequate information that is more than merely minimal. Both "habitual skill knowledge" and "intelligent skill knowledge" are usually involved in this sense of competence, as Pearson points out. Conceiving of competence in this way implies something more than the doing of some behavior or performance. It implies choosing and knowing why one does what one chooses to do. A perspective is at work within the activity not just a drive for proficiency of performance. Here we get closer to incorporating within a normative conception of competence the purpose or intent of the activity, an intent external to the activity. Whether that long-range purpose is "control" or "liberation," as Aoki analyzes them, or some other short-range, narrower intention, such as solving a problem, winning an election, or teaching someone to read, knowledge and judgment must be brought to bear on the activity by the person engaging in it. The selection of the particular knowledge and/or skills for use in a given situation, and the choice of when to use them, are governed by the purpose or intent that the person has in that situation. This conception of competence goes far beyond the "skilling" (deskilling or reskilling) of the person for particular activities; it draws the activities themselves into scrutiny, where a variety of knowledge and skills at the person's command are utilized in determining what may be the appropriate activity to do as well as how to do it. Doll has reminded us of the central place of the mind and cognition in mastering and applying knowledge and skills. Competence of this kind truly requires thinking. Johnson reminds us that it has been no easy matter to determine what knowledge and skills teachers require if they are to be competent. Yet this conception of competence as the command of pertinent *knowledge and/or skills* has served as the basis for many educational programs, teacher education programs among them, even prior to recent versions of CBE.

(3) Competence has also been conceived as a *degree or level of capability deemed sufficient* in a particular category of activity. This conception adds a public dimension to the personal behaviors, performances, knowledges, or skills that a person may have at his/her command. This view admits that a judgment of competence has to be made by someone other than the one being judged, using some standard or criteria external to that person's own subjective standard. The problem, of course, is what that public standard shall be. I shall expand on this difficulty a little bit later, but now the focus of concern is on the

fact that competence has been conceived, and the concept employed, as an *indicator or sufficiency* in some realm of activity.

Pearson laid stress on the inevitability of making value judgments when declaring the competence of someone in some particular domain. This value dimension, though quite reasonable on the surface of the matter, has frequently been ignored in favor of specifying the *things* a person can do, or the *knowledge and/or skills* a person has at his/her command, but leaving unspecified how much of these is *enough* or how well they should be accomplished. If one is willing to admit that what it takes to count as competent, as minimally competent, as sufficiently or adequately competent, and as maximally competent are not all the same things, then one has to find a way to distinguish between these various levels or degrees of competence or incompetence. The fact that criteria for sufficiency (under which a person is declared as having the required degree of competence) may fluctuate from time to time, or as a result of changing circumstances, does not exempt us from employing criteria and making judgments; it only makes us recognize the qualitative character of the ascription, "competent."

If educational programs are to utilize this conception of competence, then the prescribed *degree of sufficiency expected* will have to be found (as Noddings recognizes) for each category of activity. The probability of being able to do this is not high when dealing with capabilities more complex than behaviors and performances, and there are dimensions of competence, as I have indicated, more complex than these. Individual connoisseurs would have to make judgments on these qualitative matters in language or symbols especially created to render their judgments communicable, though different connoisseurs could not be expected to have their judgments corroborrated by one another's evaluations.[6]

It is difficult to address the problem of criteria apart from concrete statements that pertain to a specific category of activity. However, a few points can be stated in general terms. It has been recognized explicitly by Pearson and Noddings, and implicitly by Johnson, Fagan, Aoki, Beittel, and van Manen, that criteria cannot be found ready-made, by turning to authorities or to empirical investigations; they represent value judgments (as does the using of them) and therefore they must be constructed, determined, by someone or some group in particular circumstances. Who, therefore, should participate in their creation is a crucial political question to be resolved. There most certainly can be legitimate differences of opinion about what such criteria should cover and what level of sufficiency should be established by them. The effort to create alternative criteria for judging competence in any given realm or category of competence, and to deliberate and to debate their relative merits before adopting and applying a particular standard is indeed a worthy enterprise, in fact a necessary prerequisite to responsible action. Fagan and others have identified several instances in practice where this effort was not made, or not fully accomplished, and the consequences of this too swift acceptance of limited or faulty criteria (later documented, as Fagan reports) have come home to haunt the advocates of some of these criteria, as in MCT or CBTE. The development of criteria is both a political and moral activity, one made no easier by the technical demands to cover appropriate dimensions of competence and to establish and justify a *degree of sufficiency or adequacy* for each in an explicit way, one that will command political acceptance as suitable for use. Is there any way of avoiding dilemmas like these surrounding the need for criteria for competence, when conceiving of competence as a *degree of sufficiency or adequacy*? Perhaps there is, if competence is conceived in still another manner, the fourth normative conception to be identified by our authors and the next to be discussed here.

(4) Competence has been conceived as a *quality* of a person or a *state of being*. Once the nature of a particular quality has been identified and designated as desirable, a person either has it or doesn't have it. Either by inspection or by careful data gathering, a yes or no can be determined regarding whether competence characterizes that person or not. The task imposed by this conception of competence is to define its particular character holisticly. Thus, teaching competence, or mathematical competence, or computer competence must be defined, not by a particular dimension, such as its characteristic behaviors, but by all the conceptual relationships that bear upon the full exercise of that activity. That is, there must be, if not a theory of teaching competence or mathematical competence, at least a systematic conceptual scheme (as Noddings advocates) that interrelates whatever dimensions of the activity are considered integral to it, including behaviors, performances, knowledges, skills, levels of sufficiency, and anything else that may seem relevant, such as intents, or motives, or attitudes, or particular qualities or states of being.

The point is that what this holistic conceptualization sets forth is an understanding of what *quality* it is that is to be identified in the person. It will not be, for example, the particular subfeatures of "teaching competence" (such as particular behaviors or knowledges or degrees of proficiency) but teaching competence understood as a whole that will be characterized by the descriptions of it embedded in the holistic conceptualization of teaching competence. And these descriptors will not be of actions but of characteristic attributes of the person. I hasten to add that this means that there can be multiple "theories" of teaching competence, each defensible in its own ascriptions that make for quality. And we shall again have to choose among these holistic conceptions. Another way of saying this is to say that ascription of competence to someone in teaching depends upon what is construed as good teaching, qualitatively described.

So the task is to create a normative theory of teaching that has identified and justified assumptions, technical and ethical guidelines for practice, and qualitative criteria for judging when examples of teaching come within the norms of the theory. This is, if I am not mistaken, a creative and synthesizing enterprise aimed at fulfilling the inherent implications of a unifying qualitative metaphor, such as van Manen's "caring pedagogue," or Beittel's "dialectic of qualitative experiencing and interpretaton," his "dialogue and organism," or his "whiffs of smoke from dying swamp fires." We have observed many such metaphors in use: teaching as purveyor of knowledge, as facilitator of learning, as disciplinarian; teaching as mutual inquiry, as the art of nourishing the contact of one mind with another, as practical rationality. Teaching as "decision-making" is a metaphor adopted even by some CBTE programs. The question is whether any such metaphors have been fleshed out well enough to form a complete and adequate normative theory of teaching. In any case, these metaphors should not be ones that describe *things, actions, intents,* or even *criteria*; they must be metaphors of *quality* or *value.*[7]

When a normative conception of teaching is built around such a metaphor (a unifying value or quality), it is possible to detect whether a particular teacher consistently exhibits this quality, with its associated norms, ideas, and practices. Explicit guidelines for what to look for in qualitative terms will be found within this normative conception of teaching. I would not insist that a teacher exhibit just a single quality or follow just one normative conception of teaching in all circumstances; the richness of purposes and intent may require the use of several different conceptions from time to time. The application of multiple theories would, of course, require that each be rightly applied in appropriate situations and that they be clearly compatible with one another. If different quality ascriptions for the same person are contradictory, the accuracy of all of them would necessarily come into question.

In this form of evaluation of teaching, whatever quality or qualities (rooted in their corresponding conceptions of teaching) are considered desirable in the circumstance become the basis for a judgment of competence or no competence. And the quality or qualities will not be arbitrary because they take their meaning and justification from the conceptual schemes of which they are a part. When competence is conceived as a *quality*, no evaluation can really take place until the quality being evaluated is clearly understood. This is one advantage of assessing competence conceived as a quality or state of being, as opposed to doing so under other conceptions of competence. It has often seemed easier to accept certain behaviors, performances, knowledges, skills, or degrees of sufficiency as valid bases for evaluating competence, even when it was not entirely clear what justified a particular configuration of behaviors (or of one of the other forms) as constituting competence. There is no temptation to do evaluation under this fourth approach until a particular quality is fully explicated and justified, and once in hand, it is in fact much simpler and less risky to evaluate on the basis of defined qualities than on any other basis.

I have now reviewed and analyzed what came out of our writers' inquiries regarding the meaning of competence. I have formalized this information from the perspective of may own perceptions of what I read and how I understood their work. I know many other important and valuable points were made by them beyond what I have lifted up for review, and these points should not be overlooked by the reader. I think the clarifications that have been detected regarding alternative normative conceptions of competence, however, are seminal and are likely to be quite helpful to those who employ this concept. It is for this reason that I have focused on these clarifications. I will try to draw some implications for practice from this review after making some summary comments about on-going inquiry into the nature of competence.

Lest we forget that these inquiries did not intend to address all of the important questions about the meaning of competence, let me cite some other work that has been reported recently that contributes as well to a fuller understanding of competence. Some of it parallels the work of our writers, and some goes beyond their work.

Heath makes a distinction between *functional* competency and *minimal academic* competency.[8] He recognizes the problem of setting and evaluating *performance levels* of functional competency and introduces the interesting concept of *performance deficit*. Gilbert has asserted that performance alone is not competence. He says, "Competence is a social concept, a comparative judgment about the worth of a performance."[9] Bunda and Sanders distinguish Type A competence from Type B competence. Type A refers to a hypothetical construct, like those in conceptions one and two: skills, objectives, etc. Type B refers to a *standard* of performance, like our third conception.[10] Passmore analyzes *open* and *closed capacities*. Closed capacities allow total mastery while open ones do not. Open capacities are the kind for which no one knows (or has yet achieved) their upper limits.[11] An exploration of competence embedded in a conceptual framework is offered by Chickering and Claxton, in a seminal study published in 1981.[12] They examine four basic principles: 1) that competence is internal and external, situational and personal, 2) that competence is limited by a person's perceptions, neurological system and character, 3) that achieving competence requires diverse learning styles, and 4) that competence itself is a motivational force.

Two tentative implications I would draw from the review and analysis of inquiries reported in this volume. One is that each of the four normative conceptions of competence discussed here has applications corresponding to the scope of its vocabulary. Competence in the form of behaviors or performances has a very narrow range of usefulness and applicability, as several people have noted. Competence in the form of knowledges and skills is much broader but lacks the dimension of what constitutes "enough" for a declaration of competence to be ascribed.

Competence in the form of a judgment of an adequate or sufficient level of capability is still more comprehensively applicable since it incorporates the vocabulary of values and evaluation, a dimension inherent in the notion of competence, and appears to be applicable whether the entities being judged are in the form of behaviors, knowledges, objectives, outcomes, or whatever. Competence in the form of qualities or states of being is the most comprehensive form, dependent as it is upon holistic conceptual schemes that endow particular qualities with precise meanings and that include all dimensions (norms, actions, intentions, etc.) and not just one or two. This makes this fourth conception the most generally applicable. If one is concerned with all forms of competence, this is the conception that should be applied.

The second implication I would draw is that the notion of competence itself is not a very useful conceptual tool for the task for which it has been intended. While it has often been misconstrued and one of its several conceptualizations has been used when another one perhaps was really meant, the clarifications introduced by the inquiries in this volume notwithstanding, there is likely to remain considerable confusion in its meaning and considerable misuse of its various connotations. Political or ideological pressures may account for its being introduced into the vocabulary of curriculum and instruction, but competence is not very central to the enterprise of education. It is of use only in rendering a judgment on the status of what someone can do at a particular point in time and that may be necessary only rather infrequently. To employ the vocabulary of competence on a regular basis has the effect of constricting the rich vocabulary and experience of education to the vocabulary of "status evaluation." It seems prudent not to force this confusing and imprecise vocabulary onto matters beyond "status evaluation" and thereby constrict or muddle thinking in those other areas of education where reasonably useful and worthwhile vocabularies have developed.

The Acquisition of Competence

Perhaps less can be derived from these inquiries about the acquisition of competence than was gleaned about its meaning. This is due in part to the small number of inquiries directly addressing this problem that were brought together in this volume and in part due to the particular disciplinary perspectives taken in these studies. We have no studies directly concerned with examining the processes involved in acquiring competence and establishing descriptive generalizations about how these processes occur or might be aided or abetted. One study (Doll's) approaches aspects of acquiring mathematical competence, but it mainly offers possibilities for larger-scale try-out derived from very limited practical experience—a case study if you will. For the most part, this paper and the other three in the section on acquisition of competence are think-papers, contributing ideas, drawing upon new sources, uncovering problems and possibilities, stimulating awareness of previously unrecognized realities that bear upon the acquisition of competence. Occasional passages in the early part of the book also illuminate aspects of this topic although this was not those writer's primary purpose. In this section, we have inquiries done by critical social analysis, by psychological cognitive analysis, by artistic hermeneutical analysis, and by phenomenological analysis. Consequently, the results of these kinds of analyses are primarily concepts and perspectives on acquiring competence that are seldom given attention in the research on general processes of acquisition or on the pedagogical methods of engaging someone in learning by these processes.

My first observation about these papers is to say how very interesting they are. These unusual approaches have brought many novel ideas to the fore, ones that in conjunction with one another provide considerable insight into what may be done to enhance the acquisition of competence or what may be done to thwart it or to deflect the process. How many of us have known that the very structure of the curriculum and the teaching procedures tied to these forms can teach quite different ideas and practices than the program's outcome statements may have stipulated? Students grasp much from the aesthetic form of their experience and from the norms governing their activities and their interactions with materials and other persons, including both students and teachers, as Apple's work has shown.

One might ask in this connection how one keeps the acquisition of competence in a particular realm focal, when these ancillary influences, sometimes not under the student's or the teacher's full control, seem so prone to deflect what is acquired from its expected target. So many questions, both for research and for practice, are raised by Apple's inquiry. Ones about intentional or unintentional ideological influences; ones about keeping textbooks and materials and methods of instruction centered on educationally sound goals; ones about teacher and student power and resistance; ones about substituting hidden competences for overtly sought competencies; ones about minority rights versus the rights of those exercising legal or de facto power. Is teacher competence to be judged by the degree of conformity to plans and procedures or the degree of teacher-determined adaptations for particular learner's circumstances? Is what gets acquired by students of public and moral import or just a matter of prudent manipulation? Is the "deskilling" of teachers merely a management and efficiency issue or one affecting the long-term outcomes of our children's education? As Noddings says, lists of competencies and the way we organize to learn them are not neutral. Apple has uncovered a number of these value and ethical issues hidden behind the vocabulary of competence and accountability. Much more work needs to be done in this direction.

The concept of *experience* takes a central role in the papers by Beittel, Doll, and van Manen. One implication of the "truths" generated by their inquiries is that anything done in a pedagogical setting that replaces someone's interior life and its authentic expression by that person with someone else's verbalizations or imposed behaviors is doomed as a pedagogical approach. This puts sharply into question whether anyone but the learner can formulate objectives, competencies, or appropriate activities for his/her own learning. On the other hand, it raises profound questions about how to expand someone's interior experience. Should the student be left to himself to create and expand his/her experience? Isn't teacher intervention required, and if so, in what manner? Beittel talks of dialogue, but what of the content of this dialogue? Granted the student must come to his own understandings through qualitative experiencing and interpretation (no one can do that for him/her), but what is the role of the teacher? What conception of teaching respects this pre-verbal subjective experiencing and guides the talk and activity during "sharing of experiences"? How does one formulate educational goals compatible with this conception? One clue Beittel gives us: it requires abstract thought and metaphoric expresssion if wholeness-of-being is to be preserved. Analysis and segmentation are likely to divide experience conceptually and thereby contribute to the loss of being. We should follow up on Beittel's eight pointers to *The Art of Qualitative Thinking*.

Doll's paper reminds us also that competence entails thought, not just behavior. His exploration of the cognitive psychologists takes us far from the behaviorist psychologists to whom many who use the competency vocabulary have turned. The *incompetent* person is virtually defined as one who is incapable of thinking abstractly. Intelligent (and correct) handling of higher order cognitive processes is a hallmark of the competent person. Certainly one has to respect stages of intellectual development of children; motivational theories of competence do provide the impetus for acquiring intellectual competence; and the pupil must construct his/her own understandings of his experience. Doll sees the role of the teacher, however, as that of ascertaining the cognitive structure of the learner at a given point, knowing the structure of the content to be acquired (math was his example), and directing attention to the "organizing elements" that will bring the two into alignment. The mind of the learner has to grasp these abstractions and make the connections. A teacher cannot do it for the learner. Doll does not grapple directly with making judgments of pupil competence, so it is difficult to know whether he takes competence to mean *knowledge and/or skills* or *criteria* or *quality of being* (he does not mean *behavior* or *performance*). Nonetheless, his math teaching example would suggest he is dealing with competence largely in the knowledge realm. Doll seems to believe that we possess much of the required know-how for assisting pupils to acquire thinking processes if we will just use it.

Nowhere in this volume is the sense of competence as a *quality* or *state of being* more clearly exemplified than in van Manen's work. I dare to call it conceivably one of the most beautiful renditions of what it means to be a competent teacher and to qualify for the ascription of "pedagogically competent" that could possibly be written. Granted, he has a very special theory of teaching competence with which not everyone would agree, but how one would "be" (live) in relation to the young is made unmistakably clear. The ramifications of the teacher's "power of presence" do not include mastery of particular behaviors, skills, or even knowledges. They involve rising fromlived experience to understandings about how to be with children. The thinking component of pedagogic competence is given high status in this view. It is a kind of moral thinking. What responsively and responsibly to do in each pedagogic encounter is the question to be thought out. It will be far from a know-nothing, sentimental response, despite the high status also given to fundamental emotions, like caring, empathizing, communicating without words at a very deep level. Have you not seen a teacher (perhaps several) who would qualify as competent under this normative conception of teaching competence? They are authentic and effective, and I would be happy to see their kind multiply.

Once again, a great many questions arise from van Manen's work. Is phenomenological thinking something anyone can learn to do or would it require something like "deprogramming" for many of us before we could be able to begin? Are there teacher education programs operating on this model? Do they screen entrants for just the right perspective and thereby avoid the "conversion" that would undoubtedly be necessary for the run-of-the-mill trainees? Does this "high calling" wear down with years in the profession? How exactly does one evaluate the work of such a teacher? What special skills does one need for this kind of teaching? Don't overlook the fact that there are a great many clues to the answers to these questions in what van Manen has given us. Still, this is a domain of inquiry rich with potential.

I suppose it is only fair to point out that these four rather different illumations of the problems and possibilities related to the acquisition of competence, provocative as they are, do not provide a major quantum leap forward in our understanding of the whole matter. I, for one, am pleased at the contributions that have been made here, however. I know that these four persons, as do I, hope others will take up similar dimensions of inquiry (and some other ones as well) and move this topic forward with multiple disciplinary inquiry of the first rank.

I had hoped to close this final chapter witha list of very specific do's and don't's that stem from what has been presented in this volume. There are too many to enumerate; I leave this task to the careful reader. I'll just note several areas in which I think we will have to change educational policies and practices if we are to act in accordance with the clarifications and challenges presented here.

The technology of competency measurement will clearly have to be rethought to adjust for various conceptions of competence. If we are willing to take "status evaluations" of competence only at extended intervals, we can proceed to employ qualitative assessment processes and obtain quite valid judgments without the use of the cumbersome (and some say, questionable) processes of quantitative testing. We will have to localize the definitions of the expected *qualities* to be sure (within larger conceptual schemes), and much development work will be necessary before actual assessments can begin.

Considerable work for theory builders lies ahead in order for them to offer alternative models of normative conceptions of competence to local competence evaluators and curriculum planners. With such models available, it will be possible to adopt or adapt something appropriate for local circumstances rather than to have to start from scratch. A wide variety of such models is needed which will embody very different philosophical and value positions regarding what constitutes acceptable *quality*, whether in teaching, in car repair, in expository writing, or in other realms.

Some examination of the most viable way to formulate student outcomes from educational programs will be needed. This is a very different question from how to formulate "status evaluation" categories and criteria. If specific competencies cannot serve this role, what can be used instead? Some leads may be derived from suggestions by Peterson to move from outcome-oriented statements to attainment-oriented ones.[13] Monjan and Glassner have proposed a process-oriented curriculum.[14] Passmore offers the concept of a capacities-based curriculum.[11] Gilbert an accomplishment-based curriculum rather than the current acquirement-based one.[9] Chickering and Claxton show how a competency-based program may still be utilized with competencies clearly embraced by a more holistic conception of competence.[12]

We need new designs for CBTE programs that take account of the conceptions and implications of competence reported in this volume, utilizing the notion of holistic competence rather than a series of competencies. We need some fully explicated normative conceptions of teaching developed for which conceptions of holistic competence can be derived. We need more papers like van Manen's and Beittel's that will provide the intellectual resources for the development of such conceptions of teaching.

Finally, we need to undertake a great deal more research on the process of the acquisition of competence and on those teaching methods appropriate thereto. We need to continue to explore also the contextual influences on this process, such as political, social, economic pressures.[15]

FOOTNOTES

[1] Joseph J. Kockelmans (Ed.), *Interdisciplinarity and Higher Education*. University Park, PA: The Pennsylvania State University Press, 1979.

[2] Michael Polanyi & Harry Prosch. *Meaning*. Chicago: University of Chicago Press, 1975, p. 79.

[3] Joseph J. Schwab. In Ian Westbury & Neil J. Wilkof (Eds.), *Science, Curriculum, and Liberal Education*. Chicago: University of Chicago Press, 1978, pp. 342 ff.

[4] Alfred Schutz. *The Problem of Social Reality*, Collected Papers, I. The Hague: Martinus Nijhoff, 1967, pp. 167-168.
[5] Marie E. Wirsing. Educational competence and wire cages. *The Educational Forum*, 1982, *47*, 9-23.
[6] Elliot Eisner. *The Educational Imagination*. New York: Macmillan, 1979, Ch. 11.
[7] Among useful attempts to construct theories of teaching and teaching competence are: Donna H. Kerr & Jonas F. Soltis, Locating teacher competency: An action description of teaching, *Educational Theory*, 1974, *24*, 3-16; Nel Noddings, Teacher competency: An extension of the Kerr-Soltis model, *Educational Theory*, 1974, *24*, 284-290;Nel Noddings, Competence theories and the science of education, *Educational Theory*, 1974, *24*, 356-364; Thomas F. Green, Teacher competence as practical rationality, *Educational Theory*, 1976, *26*, 249-262.
[8] Robert W. Heath. Reactions. In Richard M. Jaegar & Carol K. Tittle (Eds.), *MinimumCompetence Achievement Testing*. Berkeley, CA: McCutchan, 1980, pp.136-141.
[9] Thomas F. Gilbert. *Human Competence: Engineering Worthy Performance*. New York: McGraw-Hill, 1979, p. 29.
[10] Mary Anne Bunda & James R. Sanders (Eds.), *Practices and Problems in Competency-based Education*. Washington, D.C.: National Council on Measurement in Education, 1979, Ch. 2.
[11] John Passmore. *The Philosophy of Teaching*. Cambridge, MA: Harvard University Press, 1980, pp. 40 ff.
[12] Arthur Chickering & Charles Claxton. What is competence. In Ruth Nickse & Larry McClure (Eds.), *Competency-Based Education: Beyond Minimum Competency Testing*. New York: Teachers College Press, 1981, Ch. 1.
[13] Gary W. Peterson. Attainment rather than competence: Legitimate basis for the certification of learning outcomes. 1977. ERIC: ED 145 766.
[14] Susan V. Monjan & Suzanne M. Glassner. *Critical Issues in Competency Based Education*. New York: Pergamon Press, 1979.
[15] Material appearing in Edmund C. Short, Competence revisited, *Educational Theory*, 1984, *34*, Summer Issue, has been drawn upon in preparing this chapter.

Competency Based Education: A Bibliography

A. Expository Writings

Stanley Elam. *Performance-Based Teacher Education: What is the State of the Art?* Washington, D.C.: American Association of Colleges for Teacher Education, 1971.

W. Robert Houston & Robert B. Howsam (Eds.) *Competency-Based Teacher Education: Progress, Problems, and Prospects.* Chicago: Science Research Associates, 1972.

Benjamin Roser. *The Power of Competency-Based Teacher Education.* Boston: Allyn & Bacon, 1972.

Dan W. Anderson, *et al. Competency Based Teacher Education.* Berkeley, CA: McCutchan, 1973.

Martin Haberman & T. M. Stinnett. Competency-based teacher education. In their *Teacher Education and the New Profession of Teaching.* Berkeley, CA: McCutchan, 1973, pp. 93-110.

Margaret Lindsey. Performance-based teacher education: Examination of a slogan. *The Journal of Teacher Education*, 1973, *24*, 180-186.

Allen A. Schmieder. *Competency-Based Education: The State of the Scene.* Washington, D.C.: American Association of Colleges for Teacher Education, 1973.

W. Robert Houston (Ed.) *Exploring Competency Based Education.* Berkeley, CA: McCutchan, 1974.

Herbert F. LaGrone & Sandy A. Wall. A framework for CBTE. In W. Robert Houston (Ed.) *Exploring Competency Based Education.* Berkeley, CA: McCutchan, 1974, pp. 145-153.

AACTE Committee on Performance-Based Teacher Education. *Performance-Based Teacher Education: A 1975 Commentary.* Washington, D.C.: American Association of Colleges for Teacher Education, 1975.

John Aquino (Ed.) *Performance-Based Teacher Education: A Source Book.* Washington, D.C.: American Association of Colleges for Teacher Education, 1976.

Gene E. Hall & Howard L. Jones. *Competency-Based Education: A Process for the Improvement of Education.* Englewood Cliffs, NJ: Prentice-Hall, 1976.

William G. Spady. Competency based education: A bandwagon in search of a definiton. *Educational Researcher*, 1977, *6*, 1, 9-14.

John Raven. On the components of competence and their development in education. *Teachers College Record*, 1977, *78*, 457-475.

James H. Block. The 'C'in CBE. *Educational Researcher*, 1978, *7*, 5, 13-16.

Peter W. Airasian, George F. Madaus, & Joseph J. Padulla. *Minimum Competency Testing.* Englewood Cliffs, NJ: Educational Technology Publications, 1979.

Mary Anne Bunda & James R. Sanders (Eds.) *Practices and Problems in Competency-Based Education.* Washington, D.C.: National Council on Measurement in Education, 1979.

Margaret Lindsey. Defining teaching performance and performance-based teacher education. In Elizabeth Hunter (Ed.), *Margaret Lindsey: A Teacher Educator Speaks.* North Bergen, NJ: P.O. Box 572, 1979, pp. 45-51.

Arthur Chickering & Charles Claxton. What is competence? In Ruth Nickse & Larry McClure (Eds.) *Competency-Based Education: Beyond Minimum Competency Testing*. New York: Teachers College Press, 1981, pp. 5-41.

Thomas F. Greene. Competence. In Arthur W. Chickering & Associates, *The Modern American College*. San Francisco: Jossey-Bass, 1981, pp. 544-546.

B. Status Studies

Donald M. Medley. Closing the gap between research in teacher effectiveness and teacher education curriculum. *Journal of Research and Development in Education*, 1973, *7*, 1, 39-46.

Benjamin Roser & Patricia M. Kay. Will the promise of C/PBTE be fulfilled? *Phi Delta Kappan*, 1974, *55*, 290-295.

Robert W. Heath & Mark A. Nielson. The research basis for performance-based teacher education. *Review of Educational Research*, 1974, *44*, 463-484.

Bruce Joyce. Assessment in teacher education: Notes from the competency orientation. In W. Robert Houston (Ed.) *Exploring Competency Based Education*. Berkeley, CA: McCutchan, 1974, pp. 191-208.

Margaret Lindsey. Competency-based teacher education and certification in New York State: An overview. *Teachers College Record*, 1976, *77*, 505-516.

Hazel Whitman Hertzberg. Competency based teacher education: Does it have a past or a future? *Teachers College Record*, 1976, *78*, 1-21.

J. Galen Saylor. *Antecedent Developments in the Movement to Performance-Based Programs of Teacher Education*. Working Document. Washington D.C.: American Association of Colleges for Teacher Education, 1976.

William G. Spady. Competency based education: A bandwagon in search of a definition. *Educational Researcher*, 1977, *6*, 9-14.

Robert Frahm & Jimmy Covington. *What's Happening in Minimum Competency Testing*. Bloomington, IN: Phi Delta Kappa, 1979.

Beatrice M. Gudridge. *Teacher Competency: Problems and Solutions*. Arlington, VA: American Association of School Administrators, 1980.

Richard M. Jaeger & Carol K. Tittle. *Minimum Competency Achievement Testing: Motives, Models, Measures, and Consequences*. Berkeley, CA: McCutchan, 1980.

David P. Resnick. Minimum competency testing historically considered. In David C. Berliner (Ed.), *Review of Research in Education, 8: 1980*. Washington, D.C.: American Educational Research Association, 1980, pp. 3-29.

Donald M. Medley, *Teacher Competency Testing and the Teacher Educator*. Reston, VA: Association of Teacher Educators, 1982.

C. Critical Analyses

Michael D. Andrew. Developing positive identity as a teacher: Feelings of autonomy, competence, and commitment. *Teachers Should Be Human Too*. Washington, D.C.: Association of Teacher Educators, 1972, pp. 6-12.

Michael Apple. Behaviorism and conservatism: The education views in four of the 'systems' models of teacher education. In Bruce Joyce & Marsha Weil (Eds.), *Perspectives for Reform in Teacher Education*. Englewood Cliffs, NJ: Prentice-Hall, 1972, pp. 237-262.

Harry S. Broudy. *A Critique of Performance-Based Teacher Education*. Washington, D.C.: American Association of Colleges for Teacher Education, 1972.

Harry S. Broudy. Why oppose 'performance based teacher evaluation' and 'competency based teacher evaluation'? Paper presented to the Society of Professors of Education. Chicago, February 22, 1973.

Vincent Gazzetta, Harry S. Broudy, Albert Shanker, & Sheldon Stoff. *Is This What We Want?* Garden City, NY: Adelphi University Press, 1973.

Martin Haberman & T. M. Stinnett. Competency-based teacher education. In their *Teacher Education and the New Profession of Teaching*. Berkeley,CA: McCutchan, 1973, pp. 93-110.

Herbert M. Kliebard. The question in teacher education. In Donald J. McCarty & Associates. *New Perspectives in Teacher Education*. San Francisco: Jossey-Bass, 1973, pp. 8-24.

Margaret Lindsey. Curricular Developments. In Donald J. McCarty & Associates. *New Perspectives in Teacher Education*. San Francisco: Jossey-Bass, 1973, pp. 178-193.

Paul Nash. *A Humanistic Approach to Performance-Based Teacher Education*. Washington, D.C.: American Association of Colleges for Teacher Education, 1973.

Frank H. Blackington, III, & Ann G. Omated. A sociophilosophic perspective on the potential of schooling. In W. Robert Houston (Ed.), *Exploring Competency Based Education*. Berkeley, CA: McCutchan, 1974, pp. 101-112.

C. A. Bowers. The existential nature of teaching. /Conclusion: What can be done? In his *Cultural Literacy for Freedom*. Eugene, OR: Elan Publishers, 1974, pp. 91-113; 172-177.

Arthur W. Combs & Suzanne M. Kinzer. The University of Florida's Childhood Education Program: An alternative approach to CBTE. In W. Robert Houston (Ed.), *Exploring Competency Based Education*. Berkeley, CA: McCutchan, 1974, pp. 173-188.

Margaret Lindsey. Ferment in teacher education: Enhancement of quality. In her *Ferment and Momentum in Teacher Education*. 1974 AACTE Hunt Lecture. Washington, D.C.: American Association of Colleges for Teacher Education, 1974, pp. 8-14.

W. David Maxwell. PBTE: A case of the emperor's new clothes. *Phi Delta Kappan,* 1974, *55*, 306-311.

Robert J. Nash & Edward R. Ducharme. The unversity *can* prepare teachers—An unfashionable view. *The Educational Forum*, 1974, *39*, 99-109.

Elvira R. Tarr. Some philosophical issues. In W. Robert Houston (Ed.), *Exploring Competency Based Education*. Berkeley, CA: McCutchan, 1974, pp. 79-90.

Harry S. Broudy. CBTE/PBTE—Do they mean what they say? In Ralph A. Smith (Ed.), *Regaining Educational Leadership*. New York: John Wiley & Sons, 1975, pp. 24-35.

Henry C. Johnson, Jr. Not one 'unnecessary wriggle': Some questions about the presuppositions of C/PBTE. *Educational Theory*, 1975, *25*, 156-167.

Mauritz Johnson. Conceptual confusion and premature policies. In Ralph A. Smith (Ed.), *Regaining Educational Leadership*. New York: John Wiley & Sons, 1975, pp. 46-63.

Robert J. Nash. Humanistic teacher education: A future look. *Concern (AACTE Bulletin)*, 1975, *27*, August, 1.

Frederick C. Neff. Performance-based teaching: A new orthodoxy? In Ralph A. Smith (Ed.), *Regaining Educational Leadership*. New York: John Wiley & Sons, 1975, pp. 36-45.

Robert M. W. Travers. Empirically based teacher education. *The Educational Forum*, 1975, *39*, 417-433. Responses published by the Society of Professors of Education, in Occasional Paper No. 3, August, 1974, *Teacher Education as Actor Training*; and in Occasional Paper No. 7, January, 1975, *Teacher Education, Role-Playing, and Analogies to Art*, both edited by Ayers Bagley.

Arthur G. Wirth. PBTE: A question of values. In Ralph A. Smith (Ed.), *Regaining Educational Leadership*. New York: John Wiley & Sons, 1975, pp. 212-223.

Romulo F. Magsino. A credible PBTE model: What is it like? In Romulo F. Magsino & James R. Covert (Eds.), *The Modes of Teaching*. Washington, D.C.: University Press of America, 1977, pp. 35-56.

Gary W. Peterson. Attainment rather than competence: A legitimate basis for the certification of learning outcomes. 1977. ERIC: ED 145 766.

Alan R. Tom. Critique of performance based teacher education. *The Edcuational Forum*, 1977, *42*, 77-87.

Romulo F. Magsino. Competencies for teaching: Confronting the real priority in Canadian Education. *Canadian Journal of Education*. 1979, *4*, 4, 66-80.

Gerald Grant, *et al. On Competence: A Critical Analysis of Competency-Based Reforms in Higher Education*. San Francisco: Jossey-Bass, 1979.

Susan V. Monjan & Suzanne M. Gassner. *Critical Issues in Competency Based Education*. New York: Pergamon Press, 1979.

Paul Thurston & Ernest R. House. The NIE adversary hearing on minimum competency testing. *Phi Delta Kappan*, 1981, *63*, 87-88.

Michael W. Apple. Curriculum form and the logic of technical control. *Economic and Industrial Democracy*, 1981, *2*, 293-319. (A revised and expanded version of the paper given at Penn State in May, 1980, and included in this volume. Other expanded versions appear in Len Barton, Roland Meighan, & Stephen Walker (Eds.), *Schooling, Ideology, and the Curriculum*. Sussex, England: Falmer Press, 1980, pp. 11-27; Chapter 8, Michael W. Apple, *Cultural and Economic Reproduction in Education*. Boston: Routledge & Kegan Paul, 1982; and in Chapter 5, Michael W. Apple (Ed.), *Education and Power*. Boston: Routledge & Kegan Paul, 1982.)

Samuel Messick. Evidence and ethics in the evolution of tests. *Educational Researcher*, 1981, *10*, 9, 9-20.

Marie E. Wirsing. Educational competence and wire cages. *The Educational Forum*, 1982, *47*, 9-23.

D. Substantive Analyses

Robert W. White. Motivation reconsidered: The concept of competence. *Psychological Review*, 1959, *66*, 297-333.

Isreal Scheffler. Philosophical models of teaching. *Harvard Educational Review*, 1965, *35*, 131-143. Also in his *Reason and Teaching*. Indianapolis: Bobbs-Merrill, 1973, pp. 67-81.

Harry S. Broudy. Can we define good teaching? *Teachers College Record*, 1969, *70*, 583-592.

Frank E. Nardine. The development of competence. In Gerald S. Lesser (Ed.), *Psychology and Educational Practice*. Glenview, IL: Scott, Foresman, 1971, pp. 336-356.

Gerald M. Reagan & Richard N. Pratte. An understanding of schools: An aspect of teacher competence. *Theory into Practice*, 1973, *12*, 1-4.

Stanley D. Ivie. Teaching as an aesthetic experience. *Kappa Delta Pi Record*, 1974, *10*, 106-109.

Donna H. Kerr & Jonas F. Soltis. Locating teacher competency: An action description of teaching. *Educational Theory*, 1974, *24*, 3-16.

Nel Noddings,. Teacher competency: An extension of the Kerr-Soltis model. *Educational Theory*, 1974, *24*, 284-290.

Nel Noddings. Competence theories and the science of education. *Educational Theory*, 1974, *24*, 356-364.

Kingsley Price. The sense of 'performance' and its point. *Educational Theory*, 1974, *24*, 313-327.

Thomas F. Green. Teacher competence as practical rationality. *Educational Theory*, 1976, *26*, 249-262.

William E. Doll, Jr. The role of contrast in the development of competence. In Alex Molnar & John A. Zahorik (Eds.), *Curriculum Theory*. Washington, D.C.: Association for Supervision and Curriculum Development, 1977, pp. 50-63.

Thomas F. Gilbert. *Human Competence: Engineering Worthy Performance*. New York: McGraw-Hill, 1978.

Robert W. Heath. Reactions to Bruce Eckland's paper: 'Sociodemographic implications of minimum competency testing.' In Richard M. Jaegar & Carol Kehr Tittle (Eds.), *Minimum Competency Achievement Testing*. Berkeley, CA: McCutchan, 1980, pp. 136-141.

John Passmore. Developing capacities. In his *The Philosophy of Teaching*. Cambridge, MA: Harvard University Press, 1980, pp. 37-55.

Allen T. Pearson. The competency concept. *Educational Studies*, 1980, *11*, 145-152. (Reprinted in this volume.)

Edmund C. Short. Competence: Analysis, critique, reassessment—A conference report, 1983. ED 229 337.

Arthur C. Wirth. *Productive Work in Industry and Schools*. Washington, DC: University Press of America, 1983.